Rubberstamping

Rubberstamping

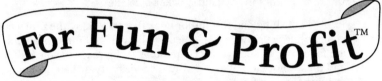

For Fun & Profit™

Maria Given Nerius

PRIMA HOME
An Imprint of Prima Publishing
3000 Lava Ridge Court • Roseville, CA 95661
(800) 632-8676 • www.primalifestyles.com

Grateful acknowledgments to B.B. Daly, DeAnne Ip, Sabrina Lou, Lisa Ruffner, and Jennifer Schlener for creating projects shown in the color insert.

Interior illustrations by Laurie Baker McNeile

Library of Congress Cataloging-in-Publication Data

Nerius, Maria.
    Rubberstamping for fun & profit / Maria Nerius.
        p.   cm.
    Includes index.
    ISBN 0-7615-2039-2
    1. Rubberstamp printing. 2. Handicraft—Marketing. 3. Selling—Handicraft. I. Title.
    TT867.N47 2000
    761—dc21
                                                                00-038549
                                                                   CIP

00 01 02 03 04 ii 10 9 8 7 6 5 4 3 2 1
Printed in the United States of America

How to Order

Single copies may be ordered from Prima Publishing,
P.O. Box 1260BK, Rocklin, CA 95677; telephone (800) 632-8676, ext. 4444.
Quantity discounts are also available. On your letterhead, include
information concerning the intended use of the books and
the number of books you wish to purchase.

Visit us online at www.primalifestyles.com

Contents

The FOR FUN & PROFIT™ SERIES

Introduction

I **HAVE A CONFESSION** to make, and it seems that the introduction to this book is a fine place to share the secret. When I was a child, more than anything else I wanted to grow up to be an artist. I have vivid memories of walking through the woods behind my childhood home in Indiana and being in awe of the masterpieces I saw everywhere in nature. I wanted to paint these remarkable scenes. I wanted to draw and illustrate the joy of colorful birds and the chirping crickets. I wanted to share the excitement I experienced climbing the tall strong trees, and to visually express the wonder of the world I saw from those heights. Those enchanting trees could magically change their leaves from brilliant green in the spring and summer to breathtaking yellows, reds, and oranges in the fall.

I'd laugh with pure joy at the antics of the chipmunks and squirrels who dashed and flew about, chattering away the morning. The smooth surface of the pond that was encircled by the trees would ripple when a dragonfly fluttered above it or a cool breeze gently blew across it. By late afternoon the pond's peaceful surface had turned into a mirror that reflected a mystical land of make-believe. Later, at home, I would triumphantly tell my mom of my wonderful adventures in the woods, but deep down I wanted to pick up a pencil and draw for her the beauty I'd seen.

I would often sit down with a pad of paper and pencil and try my best to draw what I saw before me, but my crude sketches could never quite capture the magic of the woods. It frustrated me to no end. I couldn't draw a straight line with a ruler, and I couldn't draw a circle that didn't look like an egg. I'd crumple the sheets of paper, and as any child would, I declared the world unfair. Then my third-grade art teacher sealed my fate. I've long forgotten her name, but her disappointment with my "art" was obvious each time she picked up my work to show the class how not to do something. From then on, whenever I picked up a pencil it was to write for my mother a description of what I'd seen, since I couldn't seem to be able to draw it. This assessment of my abilities would remain with me, stubbornly, until I discovered rubberstamping.

No matter how unfair I felt my lack of artistic ability to be, I never lost my secret desire to grow up and be an artist. All that hidden joy was still in my heart. As a way to be creative and enjoy the wonder of art, I began collecting. My first rubberstamps were additions to my other collections: I purchased rubberstamps of Winnie the Pooh to add to my Pooh collection and several rhino stamps to add to my rhinoceros collection. I never planned to use my rubberstamps as anything more than items sitting on a curio shelf.

I'm the first to admit that when I was introduced to rubberstamping, I considered it a juvenile recreational activity. I would watch a rubberstamping demonstration at a trade show or retail shop and think, "Boy, that's child's play." The demonstrators made everything look so easy. Most never even got ink on their fingertips. I remember laughing when one demonstrator used her toaster as a heat source for embossing a greeting card. As tempting as the designs were, I just couldn't get excited about a child's craft. Part of me remembered being told as a child that I was no artist. I was an adult now, and I wasn't about to be disappointed twice in my life.

I now realize I was wearing blinders when I considered rubberstamping to be child's play. When I was inspired to make some personalized thank-you cards, I decided that one of my precious Winnie the Pooh stamps would be the perfect artwork for the greeting card. *Just how difficult could it be to tap a rubberstamp to an inkpad and press the stamp to the paper?*

It took several attempts to get a clean image. Even when I got the basic stamping technique perfected, I wasn't satisfied with a plain dye-inked image on card stock. I wanted more. Something was missing in my work. I learned to emboss the image, but found the embossed image still lacked color and excitement. I tried magic markers, crayons, pastel chalks, watercolors, colored pencils, and even acrylics. I might not be an artist, but I surrounded myself with great art supplies. When my experimenting was done, I ended up with a dozen very different images. My cards were small works of art! In a way much different than I had first assumed, rubberstamping *was* child's play. It was fun. It was exciting. It was a joy. It was a delightful way to play. The thank-you cards have long since been mailed, but my love of rubberstamping grows each time I sit down to stamp. I am happily hooked on stamping and want to share with you that joy!

In a roundabout way, rubberstamping gave me back the charm and grace of taking a walk in nature. Most of the stamps I have collected over the years are images of trees, flowers, animals, and even a few quiet images of tranquil ponds. Every time I get a little homesick for my childhood playground of the woods, I take out a few stamps and re-create my memories with a vibrant visual that I can mail to a friend or frame as a gift. I know I'm not the accomplished artist of my childhood dreams, one who can create on a whim without rhyme or reason. However, I do know that rubberstamping lets me express all my artistic passions. I have a hunch that you will feel that same thrill as you sit down to stamp.

There is a bit of magic in rubberstamping. With a stamp, some ink, and paper, within seconds you can create a masterpiece. Add some color, a dab of glitter, and a smidgen of creativity and you have before you something special—something you created with your own hands and heart. Anyone, even a person who couldn't color within the lines of the worksheets used in elementary school, can become an artist. And that's what this book is all about!

How to Use This Book

In the first part of this book you'll be guided through the different techniques of rubberstamping. To help you understand the lingo of the stamper, you'll find a mini-glossary in chapter 1. In later chapters, you'll learn about the wonderful tools and supplies that bring your stamped images to life. You'll find tips and hints for setting up the perfect work area. There are plenty of projects in chapters 4 and 5 to keep you busy and creating.

The second part of this book will provide you with valuable information about how you can profit from your love of stamping. You'll learn about the options of rubberstamping as a business, from demonstrating rubberstamping to selling your work at a gallery or craft show. Guidelines are given for pricing and packaging your work. The copyright policies of rubberstamps are explained, and you'll learn what an angel company is!

This book is intended to give you all the information you'll need to enjoy rubberstamping as a recreation or a vocation! With each chapter you will learn more about stamping and how you can apply what you learn to exciting designs that you can use throughout your home. Get ready to have some fun! You'll make unique greeting cards. You'll make personalized picture frames. And you'll make keepsakes for yourself and those you care about. I hope you too become the artist walking through the woods enjoying the magic of your creativity.

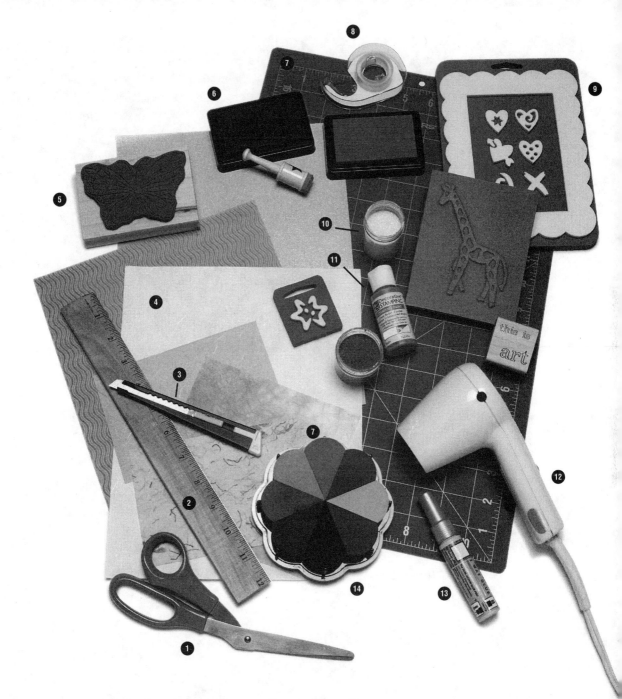

Basic Tools for Rubberstamping

1 Scissors
2 Ruler or straightedge
3 Utility knife or blade
4 Decorative paper
5 Rubberstamp
6 Ink pad
7 Self-healing cutting mat

8 Double-stick tape
9 Foam stamps
10 Embossing powder
11 Acrylic stamp paint
12 Heat source
13 Paper glue or tacky craft glue
14 Pigment-ink rainbow pad

Part One

For Fun

The Joy of Rubberstamping

▼▼

RUBBERSTAMPING VARIABLES GO FAR beyond a stamp, some ink, and a white piece of paper. There are hundreds of images to select from, and thousands of ways to combine these images into exciting creations. There is a rubberstamp to meet every creative need and satisfy every artistic taste, and the choices of ink and colors to mix and blend are endless. Paper isn't just white anymore, nor does it consist of just your standard sheet of copier stock. Simple white paper has expanded to include vellum, rice, handmade, coated, and so much more. And there's a wide variety of types and sizes of inkpads available. You can create anything your mind visualizes! You are now the magician, the artist.

Rubberstamping is a great outlet through which all age groups, backgrounds, and genders can express their creativity. There are no boundaries to what can be stamped and how each surface can be decorated with stamped images. (You'll learn more about surfaces in chapters 2, 4, and 5.) But no matter what technique you use— from simple ink images to the sophisticated look of embossing—the more you practice and experiment with new creations, the better you become. Experience will let you learn the feel of each rubberstamp you use; the right amount of ink needed to reproduce a

3

LORI'S STORY

I started rubberstamping as a quiet activity I could sit down and enjoy at the end of a long day of work and taking care of my home and family. I started slowly and began to really enjoy each new technique I learned. I made greeting cards and gifts my son could give his teachers. Nothing too big or extravagant, just fun stuff my son, Christopher, and I could do together," said proud mom and stamper, Lori Gosslin.

"As Christopher got older and went to school, he got very involved in school and community sports. I began to spend more time driving to different events, taking pictures, and being a typical mom! I really missed the relaxing evenings when I rubberstamped. Then the memory album craze became a big subject of conversation with the other moms. Since I already loved rubberstamping and paper crafts, I volunteered to make pages for the different teams and events. It was a big success. Everyone loved the pages!

clean, sharp image; and how different papers absorb ink and what colors give the best results on paper. The one common thread to rubberstamping is that the more you do it, the better you get at it. Read on and discover the endless possibilities.

What Can You Do with a Rubberstamp and Ink?

When you think of rubberstamping, you probably think of making handmade greeting cards. But there is much more to rubberstamping than just cards. Here are just a few of the many ideas of items to stamp or projects to create.

The kids have wonderful keepsakes of their sporting teams and events and feel very special that I take the time and effort to create pages just for each one of them. Yes, it's a lot of work and a lot of time, but it is a labor of love.

"I think learning the basics of design while I was learning rubberstamping really helped me stretch creatively," says Lori. "It's wonderful that rubberstamping encompasses so many wonderful projects and creations. Plus, I just love the fact that my son likes to help me. It's a great family activity."

Address labels
Announcements
Awards
Book covers
Bookmarks
Bookplates
Boxes
Business cards
Calendars
Ceramics
Clothing
Curtains
Eggs
Envelopes
Flash cards

Gift certificates
Gift tags
Hats
Jewelry
Journals
Lunch bags
Memos
Name tags
Napkins
Newsletters
Paper bags, cups, and plates
Photo albums
Placemats or cards

Playing cards
Postcards
Recipe cards
Rugs
Scrapbooks
Stationery
Stickers
Tablecloths
Terra cotta pots
Tile
Tissue paper
Valentines
Wrapping paper

Rubber Gets a Name

An important event in the history of rubberstamping was the discovery of a gooey substance that for many years went ignored. Spanish explorers observed South American Indian tribes playing with a substance that bounced and was sticky. Charles Marie de la Condamine, a French scientist who explored the Amazon River, sent a sample of a gummy material to the Institute de France in 1737, but little or nothing was done with it. Some 34 years later, in England, Sir Joseph Priestley noted a substance that could wipe or *rub* out black lead pencil from paper. Rubber was given a name.

Rubberstamping— an Art or a Craft?

Rubberstamping offers the best of two creative worlds—the inspiring world of art and the stimulating world of craft—and during the past few decades, rubberstamping as a technique or medium has always maintained a delicate balance between art and craft.

Many professionals and hobbyists refer to rubberstamping as an art, because many of the images are truly fine examples of art and because the images created with rubberstamps are often beautifully enhanced by pencil, paint, and pastel. Others view rubberstamping as a craft because, though it may look easy, creating a perfect stamped image requires skill (or crafting talent).

Whether rubberstamping is an art or a craft is a timeless debate with no real compromise, nor is there really a hope of solving the dilemma. The key is for *you* to enjoy the wonder and joy of working with rubberstamps. My goal is to clearly communicate to you the possibilities for creating impressive finished pieces of work.

Learning the Lingo

Even before you start to make a list of the supplies you need and before you gather the supplies you may already have, you'll want to learn a few of the terms used in rubberstamping. Take the time now rather than later to learn stamping jargon, and you won't have to look up the meaning of basic terms when you're in the middle of a project. Get this out of the way now and you'll have more fun stamping later!

Handy Hint

To keep track of your stamps, create a small journal where you'll keep a running list of all your stamps (and supplies too!). Once that list grows, break your stamps down into the categories of your choice.

The Basics

Angel company: Company that will let you use their images to make a product that you intend to sell. The company will partially waive their copyright to the image on an individual basis. Most angel companies will allow you to hand-stamp their images with limitations and sell the stamped work for resale.

Bone: Tool made from various materials that has a pointed end to help you score a card. The side of the bone is used to press down the paper to form a neat, crisp, clean crease or fold.

Brayer: Stamping tool that looks like a small rubber rolling pin with a handle, or a roller paintbrush. Often used with a linoleum block print, brayers are used by stampers with unblocked stamps, smoothing paper, and large stamps to get an even print. (See sidebar, What to Do with a Brayer, on page 8.)

Water-based brush markers: Marking pens with a long broad base and narrow tip that can be used like a paintbrush to color in stamped areas in a design. Can also be used directly on a stamp.

Burnish: To smooth and raise a design by rubbing paper with an embossing tool, stylus, or burnisher; also called *dry embossing*.

What to Do with a Brayer

A brayer is most commonly used to create backgrounds. Brayers come in various densities: foam, soft rubber, and hard rubber. Most rubberstampers find that the soft-density brayer is best suited to their needs. They come in various lengths; choose a size that most closely matches the size of your project.

The simplest way to create a background is to roll the brayer over an inkpad until the brayer is evenly coated, and then roll it over a sheet of paper. You can do this over a single-color pad or a multicolored pad and create all the background colors you could ever need. You can also create multicolored backgrounds using more than one inkpad. Roll the brayer over the first pad, and then roll it over only a portion of your background paper. Clean the brayer and roll it over the second inkpad. Roll the second color over the remaining section of the paper. You can separate the paper into two distinct colors or blend them at the line where they meet for a gradual change in color.

Cushion: Piece of foam rubber between the die and the mount of a stamp.

Die: Rubber area of a stamp that holds the image, pattern, or design.

Dye ink: Water-based, washable ink; but permanent once stamped onto paper. Stamps well, dries quickly, but fades over time.

Embossing: Technique of using stamp, slow-drying ink, embossing powder, and heat source to create a raised surface and stamp design on paper, ribbon, terra cotta, wood, and other stampable surfaces. Also called *wet embossing*. Dry embossing produces a raised image by pushing the paper up from the back of a stamped image. Also called

You can use markers to color directly on the brayer and then roll it over your paper. If your brayer has a detachable roller, wrap rubber bands around the brayer, ink the brayer, and then roll it over your project to create wavy lines.

A small stamp can be put into reverse with a brayer. First ink the stamp, then roll the brayer over it, turn the brayer over so the image is now facing the opposite way, and then roll the brayer with the stamped image over your project. Use a brayer to spread Liquid Appliqué on a surface and you'll create a suede-like look when the liquid is heated. Brayers are great for smoothing surfaces and helping spread glue on the back of stamped images. Let your brayer become an essential tool in your rubberstamping toolbox!

blind embossing. Dry embossing can also be done with brass stencils.

Embossing ink: Very wet, slow-drying clear or tinted ink or fluid used as the medium that holds the stamped image while embossing powder is applied to the surface.

Embossing powder: Fine-grained substance that will melt when heat is applied to it; when melted the powder leaves a raised design.

Embossing tool: A tool used to raise the surface of paper. Most embossing tools are metal with a ball-shaped tip.

Explosion card: Series of folds in a piece of paper creating a card that when opened can make confetti "explode" upon the recipient.

First generation stamping: First impression made with a stamp after inking.

Heat gun: Also referred to as a *heat tool*; device that looks much like a blow drier, but has a much hotter heating element.

Heat source: Device used to melt embossing powders; and be at least 250 degrees. Stampers use high-watt light bulbs, stove-top burners, ovens, and heat guns. A heat gun may be referred to as an *embossing gun* or *tool*. (Do not confuse a heat gun with an embossing tool, which is used in dry embossing.)

Huffing: Placing a stamp close to your mouth and breathing on it to re-wet the ink.

Juicy image: Using too much ink on a stamp so that image has too much ink on lines.

Laminate: To bond plastic film to paper, or to glue paper to chipboard or corrugated cardboard.

Liquid laminate: Plastic applied to paper as a liquid, then bonded and cured into a hard, glossy finish.

Mounted stamp: Dye adhered to a wood or other block of material, which acts as a handle of the stamp.

Opaque: Not transparent; light cannot be seen through the material.

Overstamping: To stamp wholly or in part over another stamped image.

Permanent ink: Either water-soluble or solvent-soluble ink that will not fade with time or light. Solvent-based inks dry by evaporation rather than absorption.

Pigment ink: Thicker, richer, and highly fade-resistant type of ink as compared to dye inks. Slow-drying, so works as a perfect embossing ink.

Pop-up cards: Cards that feature a raised or pop-up image when the card is opened. These pop-up or pop-out cards can be created in a variety of ways: by cutting slits in the paper, by cutting and folding, and then gluing on stamped images.

There are even pop-out template stamps that create the pop-out for you.

Positioner: Acrylic or wood tool used to place a stamped image in a particular position on your project. Most often a T-shaped, clear acrylic instrument used for achieving precise placement of images and borders.

Rainbow or multicolor inkpad: Pad with three or more colors on the same inkpad; more recently the pads have been made in separate, removable sections.

Score: To compress paper along a line so that paper will fold more easily.

Second generation, third generation: Succeeding stamped images after the first generation stamped image is completed. Gives unique effects to stamped work.

Single-color inkpad: Only one color in a box with a pad that may or may not be detachable from the pad box.

Stylus: Small hand tool with metal balled tips in varying sizes, used for making perfect dots. Also used as a burnisher.

Translucent: Semitransparent; light can be seen through material.

Transparent: Clear or see-through.

Unmounted stamp: Dye with no mount or cushion.

Warning: Rubber Is Addicting!

Rubberstamping doesn't have to be an expensive hobby. However, I must warn you, it is very easy to get carried away with purchasing new stamps and supplies. I rarely get out of a rubberstamp store without handing over 25 to 50 bucks! It's easy to lose track of time as you wander around a store that sells rubberstamps. Each stamp has the capacity, when nestled in your hands, to be a thousand different finished images. There are so many wonderful surfaces to stamp, and new surfaces pop up on shelves each week. Keep your

▼▼▼▼▼▼▼▼▼▼▼▼▼▼▼▼▼▼▼▼▼▼▼

Did you know???

From its early beginnings,
the rubberstamp was considered
a marking device: a tool to help
a person—rather than a
machine—add identification or
instruction to a work or product.

head and keep a budget for your stamping plea-sures, and you won't feel that the hobby has taken over your personal checking account (although my husband has mumbled under his breath more than a few times that our pay-checks should be direct deposited to my favorite rubberstamp stores!)

Keeping the Spending to a Minimum

Besides keeping yourself on a strict budget, there are better and more exciting ways to avoid spending a fortune on your stamping hobby.

Swap or Exchange Supplies

I often exchange rubberstamps with friends who are also stamp en-thusiasts. We each pick three to six stamps from our collections and exchange the stamps every few months. This helps keep the costs of this craft to a minimum, while the inspiration of "new stamps" keeps fresh design ideas coming. This habit led me to throw rubber-stamping parties to expand my fun.

Rubberstamp Exchange and Swap Guidelines

You can conduct exchanges and swaps through the mail or in person. These guidelines are foolproof for a successful swap or exchange.

1. One person, who acts as the chair of the exchange, keeps track of all the members of the exchange. The chair is some-times referred to as the "exchange or swap mom." Informa-tion to track includes member name, address, and phone number.

2. Select a theme for the exchange. You can exchange rubber-stamps, papers, notions, and more. Or you may decide on a holiday theme like Easter or Valentine's Day. Or you may decide to exchange finished greeting cards or candles. Set a dollar amount limit, like $5 to $7 or $7 to $10. An exchange doesn't work if one member gives a $10 item and receives an item of lesser value.

3. Select a time frame for the exchange. Keep the dates marked on the calendar.

4. Send out invitations to join the exchange. Make sure the invitation includes the information listed in steps 2 and 3.

5. Gather the names and addresses of members and randomly match names of people who will swap items or round-robin the exchange. To round-robin you pick names and number them. Number 1 member gives an item to member number 2, member number 2 gives to member number 3, and so on. The last member gives an item to member number 1. Make sure every member knows who he or she will be sending the item to.

6. Set a 2-week time frame for all exchanges to be completed, whether in person or by mail.

7. Upon receipt of the exchange item, each member should contact the chair and the member who sent him or her the item. Thank-you notes (hand-stamped, of course) are a wonderful policy for any exchange.

8. Check out other exchanges and swaps. Every group has its own way and system of conducting an exchange.

Fun Things to Exchange and Swap (Permanent Exchanges)

- Cards and surfaces
- Decorative acid-free papers with a theme

- Envelope of punched paper designs
- Envelope templates
- Favorite card instructions
- Glitter
- Handmade envelopes
- Handmade papers
- Magazines and books
- Specialty embossing powders
- Stickers
- A variety of stamped and embossed images

Fun Round-Robins (Temporary Exchanges)

- Brass stencils
- Decorative rotary blades
- Decorative scissors
- Magazines and books
- Punches
- Stamps
- Templates

Parties and Soirees

For my rubberstamping get-togethers, I ask each person invited to bring something for the party, from paper to ink to rubberstamps to embellishments. We spend the afternoon using the communal supplies to create projects that each person may take home. Often each attendee will create enough designs to hand out to the other partygoers. It's a fun way to learn and share ideas—and save money on supplies.

Party Guidelines

1. Pick a theme or surface; the hostess of the party can supply the surface on which the group will stamp. Greeting cards are the easiest for your first party.

2. Pick a date and a time. Allow at least 3 hours of stamping fun at the party.

3. Make a list of attendees. Send invitations, and make sure to give partygoers a few options of what they can bring.

4. Confirm what each attendee will bring. If some important supplies are missing, either supply them yourself or ask guests to bring them. For example, you can ask each guest to bring a pair of scissors for the party.

5. Ask everyone to bring a refreshment (this can be optional—it's fun to have refreshments, but not necessary).

6. Organize some work areas for the party and provide seating for each guest.

7. Ask each guest to create a specific number of cards. If they make more, that's great, but the specific number of cards will be handed out to other guests. You may decide to put the cards in plain brown shopping bags and make a grab bag. Or get creative and play a trivia game; each right answer gets the guest a chance to pick a card of choice.

Handy Hint

Have your party or swap members send you a "wish list" of supplies, motifs, themes, and techniques they want to explore and learn. Keep and update the wish lists and refer to them when you need inspiration for a stamping party or a rubber swap.

Fun Things to Bring to the Party

- Stamps (This is the key; this way the guests can get the widest variety.)
- Charms, buttons, and other notions
- Creativity and imagination
- Decorative scissors and punches
- Heat guns
- Markers and pencils
- Paper cutter

- Papers
- Pearl or specialty embossing powders
- Rotary cutter with decorative blades
- Scented embossing powders
- Watercolors

Fun Themes for Parties

- Animals or pets
- Art and collage
- Baby
- Birthdays
- Boxes
- Bridal and wedding
- Calendars
- Camping
- Cards for a local nursing home
- Childhood daydreams
- Christmas
- Fairy tales
- Family
- Flower pots
- Frames
- Friendship cards
- Fun jewelry
- Garden
- Halloween
- High tea
- Inspirational
- Mail art
- Memory pages

- Metallic and jewels
- Mother's Day
- Oriental
- Pretty in pink
- Rainbow (color, color, color!)
- Rainy days and Mondays
- Recipe cards
- Refrigerator madness
- Save the _____ (planet, whales, rubber trees!)
- Sports
- Teacher cards
- Thanksgiving

Rubberstamping Plusses

Rubberstamping can be a lone activity or a group activity, depending on one's needs and mood. From a morning of stamping and embossing while looking out my studio window to an afternoon party with my friends—in any setting—rubberstamping is a rewarding hobby. Whether you're just beginning or are experienced, there are so many things that make rubberstamping easy and fun. I discuss some of them in the sections following.

Instant Gratification

If, like me, you have a short attention span and like instant reward for your efforts, stamping is the perfect art and craft. You can complete simple projects in minutes, and as you become more skilled you'll also gain more patience and curiosity. Soon you'll find yourself wondering about more complex and intricate designs, and less about getting your simple projects finished quickly.

Just For Fun

Major holidays celebrated in the United States are perfect excuses to make more stamped greeting cards for your family and friends!

- **New Year's Day**, January 1
- **Martin Luther King Jr.'s Birthday**, third Monday in January
- **Groundhog Day**, February 2
- **Lincoln's Birthday**, February 12
- **Valentine's Day**, February 14
- **Presidents' Day**, third Monday in February
- **Washington's Birthday**, February 22
- **St. Patrick's Day**, March 17
- **April Fools' Day**, April 1
- **Mother's Day**, second Sunday in May
- **Armed Forces Day**, third Saturday in May

Sharing with Others

The opportunity to share the results of your creativity with others is a very rewarding aspect of stamping. I often make cards for my local hospice and hospital. You might want to make cards for the children's ward of a local hospital, or even do a demonstration!

A Minimum of Clutter

Rubberstamping doesn't take up a lot of space. You can dedicate an area for your stamping supplies (to keep them out in the open ready to stamp at a moment's notice) or store your supplies away until

- **Memorial Day**, last Monday in May
- **Flag Day**, June 14
- **Father's Day**, third Sunday in June
- **Parents' Day,** fourth Sunday in July
- **Independence Day**, July 4
- **Labor Day**, first Monday in September
- **Columbus Day** (traditional), October 12
- **Columbus Day**, second Monday in October
- **Halloween**, October 31
- **Election Day**, Tuesday on or after November 2
- **Veterans Day**, November 11
- **Thanksgiving Day**, fourth Thursday in November
- **Christmas Day**, December 25

you have time to sit down and stamp. Rubberstamps are attractive enough that, rather than storing them in a closet, you can display them in old printer's boxes or shadow boxes. My "stored" stamps became part of my studio décor—much more attractive than my other décor theme of dust!

Lots of Flexibility for Busy Schedules

Another convenience of stamping is that you can do it in stages. You don't have to finish a project in one sitting. You may decide to spend an hour just stamping images and leave them until a few days later when you can sit down and use the images on a greeting card or other design. You may devote 1 day to embossing dozens of images that you can store for future use. With time as a rare treasure in most hectic lives, rubberstamping is your own perfect gift: time used effectively and creatively.

An artist must devote time and energy to developing the skills needed to draw or paint, and many spend years learning the tricks of the trade. Rubberstamping provides a quick route to a similar end. I am in no way discounting the vocation of an artist, but you may not have, or wish to devote, the time needed to such a singular focus. Rubberstamping is an easy way to make a large number of designs without a lot of effort, time, or expense. However, if you choose to, you *can* spend more time detailing, enhancing, embellishing, and crafting the rubberstamped image rather than studying color theory and the proper brush to use for highlighting a landscape. Rubberstamping is an art and craft flexible enough to fit into anyone's lifestyle and schedule.

As I mentioned in the introduction, rubberstamping techniques build on each other. It's important to understand this at the very beginning of your stamping adventures, so that you don't become frustrated and give up.

This chapter may seem like a hodgepodge of rubberstamping information and random thoughts from a compulsive stamper, but that's sort of what rubberstamping is. It's a little of this and a little of that. Some color here and some color there. It's an image and ink and paper and more. Get ready to fulfill your creative wants and needs. Your passion for rubberstamping has just begun!

Did you know???

Stencil makers were the first manufacturers in the marking-device industry. Soon these dedicated stencil makers branched out and created some of the earliest rubberstamps.

chapter 2

Getting Started

▼▼▼

TAKE A DEEP BREATH AND get ready to make an impression! Here you'll find the fundamentals of all the rubberstamping techniques with a primer on the rubberstamp, inks, inkpads, papers, and more. In fact, you may want to refer back to this chapter every once in a while as you develop your rubberstamping skills. As you read through and learn more about rubberstamping, you'll find that each component of stamping basics builds on the next component. Don't rush or glance over the basics. The more you know about rubberstamps and all of the elements, the better your finished results of any project will be.

The Bare Essentials

The following supplies are needed to learn the basics of rubberstamping:

The Rubberstamp

Your rubberstamp may be purchased as a mounted or an unmounted stamp. A rubberstamp should have three distinct parts:

The *die* is the rubber that takes the ink and creates an impression; the *mount* has traditionally been a wooden handle, which now can be made of many different types of materials including clear Lycra; the *cushion* is the padded foam part between the die and mount. Some unmounted stamps come as just the die, while others come as the die with cushion. Temporary adhesive can be used to mount the stamp, or you may choose to permanently mount the die. Some unmounted stamps can be used with great ease if the unmounted stamp has a cushion. It's your preference whether to use mounted or unmounted stamps. It is less expensive to purchase unmounted stamps, which can often be purchased in sets of multiple images.

Rubberstamps traditionally come in categories of design and image. I've changed and added to these mainstream categories to help clarify and help you know what to look for when shopping for rubberstamps.

- Word stamps are any stamps that feature *only* a word or words. Word stamps are the best type of stamp to use when you are first learning to emboss. The stamps are simple, and the line work gives you instant results, so you can see how well you are embossing.

- Outline stamps are merely an outline of an image with little or no additional detail like shading or fine detailing. Outline stamps are excellent for coloring and learning to highlight and shade with color. The openness of the image allows you to control color, whether the color is from pencil, pastels, watercolor paints, watercolor pencils, or markers.

- Detail stamps have very detailed images, leaving little for the stamper to add except small amounts of color or embellishment. Detail stamps are beautiful because of the fine detailing and work as interesting backgrounds or stand-alone designs. Avoid this type of stamp when you are first learning to emboss because the intricate detailing of the stamp makes it difficult to control the embossing process.

- Action stamps can be either outline or detail stamps. Use them with other stamps, or stamp, cut out, and glue several images to the original image to create dimension or action. The variety of things you can do with this stamp is one of the things that make rubberstamping so exciting. You can learn to make a rose pop out of the page or add motion to an image. You can take a rubberstamp image of a balloon and stamp it to a teddy bear, creating the effect that the teddy bear is holding the balloon. You can take an image of a rosebud and stamp a second image. Cut out a few rosebud petals and arrange them so the petals look like they are falling off the bud.

- Foam or sponge stamps (made of foam or sometimes a sponge) have no mount or cushion. For years, stampers would simply cut out a shape from a kitchen sponge and use it to stamp backgrounds. The craft industry soon created product lines to meet the needs of these creative stampers. Decorative painters often use this type of stamp when painting large pieces. They stamp the image and then paint in the details. Usually a foam or sponge stamp is used for stamping images onto walls or large surfaces, but smaller images have come onto the market and are often used to stamp on fabric or clothing.

Ink and Inkpads

The two types of ink used for most rubberstamping projects are dye ink and pigment ink. The main difference between the two inks has to do with each one's drying time, thickness or body, and over-all color and colorfastness. Dye inks dry very quickly and are thin-bodied. Under normal conditions a dye ink will fade over time.

Pigment inks dry slowly, are thick-bodied, and are the most fade-resistant. For an ink to last and not fade, the ink should be out of direct sunlight and under glass to prevent damage from temperature and humidity. Since you probably won't go to these extremes, it's impor-tant to understand that dye inks will fade quickly, and because of their quick-dry nature it's not easy to emboss an image stamped with such ink. (In chapter 4 I discuss a method that can help you emboss an image created with dye inks.)

There are some other "inks" used in rubberstamping, which I discuss below (see sidebar, Inks at a Glance, for a brief description of each).

An acrylic paint (labeled as "stamp paint") is formulated for large foam or sponge stamps and can be found at art and craft sup-ply stores. Paint glazes can also be used for these stamps.

The colors available are incredible. You may have to shop around several art, craft, or rubberstamp stores to get a feel for the spectrum. The most popular colors of inks for rubberstamping are black, gold, red, blue, and green. You can purchase a variety of inks at art supply stores, craft retailers, print shops, office goods retailers, and the Internet.

Make sure you understand what kind of ink you're buying. Some permanent inks will damage rubber over time, so only buy permanent inks designed for rubberstamping. Water-based inks will be labeled as permanent or washable. A washable ink (usually de-signed for children) is not permanent and will wash or bleed when water is applied.

Handy Hint

When using a rubber-stamp on fabric, you need to use a fabric ink, so that the fabric can be washed with-out fading the color of the image.

Inks at a Glance

Dye ink: Water-based, washable ink (use mild soap and water to wash from stamps and hands), permanent once dried on papers. Dye ink dries quickly, thus is not good for embossing. Works well on coated papers, but tends to run or bleed on highly absorbent papers. Dye inks will fade.

Pigment ink: Water-based, washable ink (use mild soap and water to wash from stamps and hands), permanent once dried on paper. This ink is thicker than regular dye ink. Pigment ink is very slow to dry, so avoid smudging. It's excellent for embossing images. Works best on uncoated papers and must be embossed on coated papers. Highly fade-resistant and does not fade once embossed. Rarely bleeds. Colors tend to be richer, more brilliant than regular dye inks.

Fabric ink: Ink that's specifically designed to help create a permanent image on fabrics. Some fading may be experienced.

Disappearing ink: Ink used by quilters, painters, needle artists, and people who sew. This ink is tinted with a pink or blue hue. The image is stamped on fabric or paper, and is then stitched or painted. The ink will "disappear" when water is used to dampen the fabric; some disappearing inks fade out over time as the ink evaporates. The most common usage is on fabrics.

Permanent ink: Water-soluble or solvent-based ink. Not as easy as other inks to wash from stamps or hands. This ink dries by evaporation, not by absorption like dye or pigment ink. Little fading occurs. Stamps must be cleaned immediately with solvent when using solvent-based permanent inks. These inks are handy for stamping on surfaces other than paper, including tile, wood, plastics, metals, and other nonporous surfaces.

Ink is used with an inkpad. It is very rare that you would ink a stamp directly from an ink bottle. Inkpads come in two styles: flat and raised. Most dye inks come in flat cloth pads, but don't be surprised to see dye ink in a raised pad. Pigment inks come in raised foam

A Few Words about
Acid-Free and Archival Needs

Clearsnap is a company that has been developing art supplies for rubber-stamping since 1996, when the company created the Rollagraph rollerstamp system. One of the company's contributions to stamping was the concept of "Option Pads," which allowed the rubberstamp artist to select one color plate (detachable from the whole pad) out of a palette of colors. The company had this to say about dye and pigment inks on their Web site, www .clearsnap. com:

> Dye inks are a more recent invention. They are designed to penetrate and stain the paper surface rather than adhere or bond to it as pigment inks do. While this approach produces bright, vivid colors, it is inherently unstable and produces a "light fugitive" effect, meaning that colors fade and shift rapidly when exposed to normal environmental factors such as light, heat, and moisture.
>
> Some dye inks are *acid-free*, but even those, like all dye inks, are light sensitive and are best used for stamping on glossy paper and where archival quality is not a great concern.
>
> Pigment inks have been used for thousands of years to create long-lasting imagery found in caves, monasteries, museums, and other protected environments. The coloring agents are solid particles that are relatively stable, insoluble, and non-reactive with other materials sitting on the stamping surface. pH balanced pigment inks are recommended for archival applications. In other words, "acid-free" is just one component of "archival quality." With inks,

pads. Raised-surface inkpads are available in a variety of sizes and forms. The larger pie-shaped or long rectangular multicolor pads have removable sections so that you can select a color and remove it to ink your stamp. This type of pad is also called a "rainbow pad." Rainbow pads for dye inks do not have these detachable sections. All inkpads can be reused for many years by applying new ink to the pad.

what is sought is "pH balance," which means this media will be less reactive with other materials in your archival project. Papers typically contain many additives to achieve an acid-free status. The buffers, fillers, and pigments added to paper create an interesting environment for inks.

Try this simple test: Take a typical piece of heavy "chrome coat" or glossy paper, which normally has a heavily alkaline surface. Stamp the dye inks you are wondering about and observe the stamped image periodically during a 2-hour period. If you notice substantial color shifting or fading, you are witnessing the acidic elements in the ink reacting to the alkaline elements in the paper. This is called "reactivity" and is the chief concern of most archival enthusiasts.

The truth is, if you protect your scrapbook from heat, light, and moisture, most dye ink stampings will last a very long time and should not be reactive with your scrapbook elements. Color photographic prints themselves are inherently unstable and will shift or fade noticeably within 20 to 40 years. Given these realities, most concerns about dye inks are somewhat misplaced and overemphasized. If your scrapbook project is intended for frequent use
or if you live in a hot and humid environment, then you should find a way to work with quality pigment inks if at all possible. On the other hand, if you intend for your scrapbook to be in good condition 200 years from now, you should be using only black-and-white photography, 100% certified archival quality materials, and no glue or adhesives of any kind.

The type of pad you use is a personal preference. When you are just beginning you might purchase pads that come pre-inked. However, many professionals and seasoned hobbyists prefer to buy blank or un-inked pads and add the ink themselves. I recommend that you try several types of pads and experiment with the different shapes and sizes.

Paper

There's more to paper than meets the eye and the rubber of your stamps! Following is a list of some of the words used to define specific qualities of different types of papers. Copier paper, unlined index cards, newsprint, and other inexpensive papers are best to use when you first learn to rubber stamp. But as you gain confidence and experience, you'll want to experiment with all kinds of papers. With the increase in popularity of memory crafts and scrapbooks, acidity, archival, and acid-free qualities have become more relevant, so I've included these terms in the list.

Terms Used in Paper and Papermaking

Acidity: State of a substance that contains acid. Paper becomes acidic from the ingredients used in its manufacture, from the environment, or both.

Alum: Astringent crystalline substance used in rosin sizing to hold paper fibers together; responsible for introducing acid into the paper.

Basis size: Standard size of each grade of paper, used to calculate basis weight.

Basis weight: Weight in pounds of a ream of paper cut to the basis size for its grade.

Bast fibers: Refers to a group of fibers commonly used in Japanese papermaking, including flax, gampi, hemp, jute, kozo, and mitsumata.

Brightness: Characteristic of paper referring to how much light it reflects.

Buffering: Process that gradually neutralizes a paper's acidity by adding an alkaline substance, like calcium carbonate, at the pulp stage. Buffering helps reduce the acidity of paper over time.

Coated paper: Papers with a finish, glossy or matte. Accepts most inks, markers, and colored pencil, but pigment ink must be embossed.

Cold pressed: Mildly textured surfaces produced by pressing the paper through unheated rollers. Generally categorized as falling between rough and hot pressed.

Cut stock: Paper distributor term for paper 11 × 17 or smaller.

Deckle: Wood frame resting on or hinged to the edges of the mold that defines the edges of the sheet in handmade papermaking. Also, on the wet end of a paper machine, strap or board that determines the width of the paper web.

Deckle edge: Natural, fuzzy edges of handmade papers, simulated in mold-made and machine-made papers by injecting a jet stream of water while the paper is still wet. Handmade papers have four deckle edges, while mold-made and machine-made papers usually have two.

Dull finish: Characteristic of paper that reflects relatively little light.

Durability: Degree to which paper retains its original qualities with use.

Fibers: Slender, thread-like cellulose structures that cohere to form a sheet of paper.

Filler: Generic term to describe the non-oxidizing clays or minerals added to the pulp at the beater stage to improve paper density.

Finishing: Term used to describe the cutting, sorting, trimming, and packing of paper.

Gampi: Blast fiber from the gampi tree; used in Japanese papermaking to yield a translucent, strong sheet.

Gm/m^2: Grams per square meter; metric measure of weight for artist papers. It compares the weights (in grams) of different papers, each occupying 1 square meter of space, irrespective of individual sheet dimensions. Another way of comparing paper weights is pounds per ream. A 140-pound paper indicates that a ream (500 sheets) of that paper weighs 140 pounds.

Gloss: Characteristic of paper, ink, or varnish that reflects relatively large amounts of light.

Grade: One of seven major categories of paper: bond, uncoated book, coated book, text, cover, board, and specialty.

Grain: The direction in which fibers are aligned.

Grain direction: Direction in which the fibers of machine-made paper lie, due to the motion of the machine. When machine-made paper is moistened, the fibers swell more across their width than along their length, so the paper tends to expand at right angles to the machine direction. Handmade and mold-made papers have indistinguishable grain directions.

Grain long or grain short: Paper whose fibers parallel the long or short dimension of the sheet.

High alpha: Nearly pure form of wood pulp that has the same potential longevity in paper as cotton, linen, or other natural fiber.

Hot pressed: Smooth, glazed surfaces produced by pressing the paper through hot rollers after formation of the sheet.

Kozo: Most common fiber used in Japanese papermaking, it comes from the mulberry tree. This is a long, tough fiber that produces strong absorbent sheets.

Linters: General term for preprocessed pulp, cotton or wood, purchased in sheet form. Cotton linters are fibers left on the seed after the long fibers have been removed for textile use. They are too short to be spun into cloth but can be cooked and made into paper. Stiffer and more brittle than long-fibered cotton, linters produce a low-shrinkage pulp good for paper casting. They cannot produce a paper with the strength of cotton rag. Wood linters are called hardwood or softwood depending on grade.

Mitsumata: Used in Japanese papermaking, bast fiber that yields a soft, absorbent, and lustrous quality.

Mold: Tool for hand-papermaking, a flat screen that filters an even layer of fibers through it to form the sheet. In Western papermaking, it is accompanied with a wooden frame called a *deckle.*

Opacity: Characteristic of paper that helps prevent printing on one side of the paper from showing through to the other.

Permanence: Degree to which paper resists deterioration over time.

pH: Measure of the hydrogen ion concentration of water solution and substance, denoting acid or alkaline. A paper's pH is measured on a scale from 1 to 14. Seven is neutral. Numbers higher than 7 are alkaline and numbers lower than 7 are acidic. Papers with a pH of 6.5 to 7.5 are generally considered neutral.

Plate finish: Smooth surface found on paper that has been run under a calender machine one or more times.

Ply: Single web of paper, used by itself or laminated onto one or more additional webs as it is run through the paper machine.

Did you know???

Cotton paper is made from left-over scraps of cotton clothing.

Pulp: General term describing the beaten, wet mixture of stock used in making paper, whether its contents are wood, cotton, or other fibers.

Rags: Processed clippings of new cotton remnants from the garment industry for use in high-quality papers.

Rough: Heavily textured surfaces produced by minimal pressing after sheet formation.

Size: Material, such as rosin, glue, gelatin, starch, or modified cellulose, added to the paper stock at the pulp stage, or applied to the surface of the paper when dry, to provide resistance to liquid penetration.

Sulfite: Term for pulp made from wood. Depending on how it is processed for papermaking, it can either be acidic or neutral pH.

Surface-sized: Term applied to a paper whose surface has been treated with a sizing material after the sheet is dry or semi-dry.

Uncoated paper: Papers with a higher absorbency rate than coated paper; easier to use with most inks, markers, watercolors, and colored pencils.

Watermark: Design applied to the surface of the paper mold, which causes less pulp to be distributed in that area and results in the transfer of the design to the finished sheet.

Web: Continuous ribbon of paper, in its full width, during any stage of its progress through the paper machine.

Wet strength: Strength of a sheet of paper after it is saturated with water.

Choosing a Paper

You can use any of a multitude of papers in your rubberstamping projects. Some are relatively inexpensive, while handmade or imported papers can get costly. You can find a variety of papers at art supply stores, craft retailers, party supply outlets, office goods retailers, print shops, and the Internet. Don't think of paper as just 8½ × 11 sheets. Paper comes in all different sizes. You can find great paper used for napkins, placemats, paper tablecloths, magazines, old books, paper bags, plain or printed gift wrap, origami papers, foils and Mylars, cardboard, recycled greeting cards, and more.

There is no right or wrong paper to use. When choosing a paper, determine whether it's a coated or uncoated surface. A coated paper has a protective coat or a finish that allows it to repel, or not absorb, liquids. On coated paper, pigment ink must be embossed to retain the image. Even dye ink doesn't dry as quickly on coated

Surfaces to Stamp

Stamping is not just for paper! If it's not moving, stamp it! Here are some great surfaces to stamp.

Candles	Plastics
Ceramic	Shrink plastic
Copper	Terra cotta
Fabric	Tile
Foil	Tin
Glass	Tissue paper
Paper	Wood

paper, so you must be careful to allow the dye ink to dry completely before handling or coloring the image. Coated paper usually has a gloss or glossy look to it. Also take note whether the coated paper is coated on one side or both sides.

Papers also vary in weight or body. You can see this demonstrated when you compare a piece typing paper with card stock or card stock with watercolor paper. Typing paper can't hold up its own weight, while card stock and watercolor paper stand rigid.

Papers come in a variety of colors ranging from neon brights to matte earthtones. If the number of different types of papers doesn't overwhelm you, the palette of available colors just might! Consider purchasing paper in an assortment package. That way, the color you select for the paper for a project can coordinate with the stamp image, the color of ink, or the embossing powder, or the color might be just what is needed for a card. Although the color of the paper doesn't directly affect the color of the ink used, different colors mixed together do affect the end result.

In chapter 4 I explain how to create your own color chart of paper, inks, and embossing powders. As you advance into rubber-stamping you may want to keep such a color chart handy, so you can use it to mix and match your colors before you start a project.

Types of Paper

Following are descriptions of some key types of paper you can look for when you go on your paper searches.

Acetate: Thin, flexible sheet of transparent plastic used to make overlays. Not a paper per se, but often used as a surface.

Acid-free paper: Paper that has no free acid, or a pH of at least 6.5. The use of a synthetic sizing material allows the paper to be manufactured with a neutral or alkaline pH.

Acid-sized paper: Paper manufactured under acid conditions; has no surface buffering capacity.

Board paper: Grade of paper commonly used for file folders, displays, and postcards.

Bond paper: Grade of paper commonly used for writing, printing, and photocopying.

Book paper: Grade of paper suitable for books, magazines, and general printing needs.

Bristol paper: Type of board paper used for postcards, business cards, and other heavy-use products. Some types of bristol are referred to as vellum bristol, but are not true translucent vellum.

Buffered paper: Paper made in an acid environment and then buffered on the surface to obtain a required pH.

C1S: Paper coated on one side.

C2S: Paper coated on both sides.

Cardboard paper: General term for stiff, bulky paper such as index, tag, or bristol.

Corrugated paper: Fluted paper between sheets of paper or cardboard, or the fluted paper by itself.

Cotton content paper: Paper made from cotton fibers rather than wood pulp.

Dry gum paper: Label paper, or sheet of paper with glue that can be activated by water.

Enamel paper: Another term for coated paper with gloss finish.

Handmade paper: Sheet of paper made individually by hand using a mold and deckle.

Index paper: Light-weight board paper for writing and easy erasure.

Laid paper: Paper with a prominent pattern of ribbed lines in the finished sheet. Laid is accomplished in handmade paper using a screenlike mold of closely set parallel horizontal wires, crossed at right angles by vertical wires spaced somewhat further apart.

Linen paper: Refers to the finish of a paper that resembles a linen cloth with faint, but distinct, horizontal and vertical lines.

Machine-made paper: Sheet of paper produced on a rapidly moving machine called the Fourdrinier, which forms, dries, sizes, and smoothes the sheet. Uniformity of size and surface texture marks the machine-made sheet.

Manila paper: Strong, buff-colored paper used to make envelopes and file folders.

Mold-made paper: Sheet of paper that simulates a handmade sheet in look, but is made by a slowly rotating machine called a cylinder-mold. The machine was introduced in England in 1895.

Parchment: Paper that simulates writing surfaces made from animal skins.

Rag paper: Paper made from fibers of non-wood origin, including actual cotton rags, cotton linters, cotton or linen pulp. Rag papers contain 25%–100% cotton fiber pulp.

Rice paper: Common misnomer applied to lightweight Oriental papers. Rice alone cannot produce a sheet of paper. Rice-straw is only occasionally mixed with other fibers in papermaking. The name may be derived from the rice size once used in Japanese papermaking.

Shrink medium: Sheet of thin clear or opaque plastic that once heated shrinks in size. Not a paper per se. Best known is called Shrink-It.

Specialty paper: Term for carbonless, pressure-sensitive, synthetic, and other papers made for special applications.

Synthetic paper: Plastic or other petroleum-based paper.

Tissue paper: Thin, translucent, lightweight papers available in many colors.

Waterleaf paper: Paper with little or no sizing, making it very absorbent. If dampening is desired, this paper can be sprayed with an atomizer.

Wove paper: Paper with a uniform unlined surface and smooth finish, generally made on a European-style mold with a woven wire surface. Most papers produced are of this type.

Vellum: Stiff, translucent paper available as clear, white, marbled, colored, or embossed.

Velveteen paper: Also called plush or suede paper; paper with velvet feel.

Every paper reacts differently to ink. Some quickly absorb ink while others may cause ink to bleed. What may be a negative to one stamper is a to-die-for quality to another stamper. You may find it exciting and interesting to stamp onto paper that already is printed with a design or motif. And paper isn't just for stamping. You may wish to use a specialty paper as your card stock or background paper, or as ripped confetti in a collage. If possible make a friendly contact with a local printer. Printers get paper samples from paper mills; ask your local printer to give you a call when he or she is ready to throw out those paper samples. It's a great way to recycle and will add variety to your paper collection.

Embossing Supplies

Most novice rubberstampers can't wait to try embossing. It adds that extra touch to rubberstamping projects. Embossing is really two different techniques with the same name. One style of embossing is "wet embossing." Rubberstampers use this technique when they use a pigment or embossing ink with embossing powder and heat. The powder melts under the heat and raises the image. Another style of embossing (also very popular with stampers) is referred to as "dry embossing." This technique uses a stencil or brass template, a light source, a stylus or burnisher, and paper. (Wet and dry embossing are covered step-by-step in chapter 4.)

You will need the following for embossing:

Rubberstamp Beginners should use a word stamp or outline stamp to practice embossing.

Pigment ink or embossing ink and pad Use your choice of color.

Embossing powder Don't confuse embossing powder with glitter, flocking, or other powders. Embossing powder may contain glitter or foil, but it's more than just those additives. Embossing powder appears dull or without gloss before heating, but after heating, many embossing powders take on a gloss or shine. Not all embossing powders will melt glossy; some of the blended colors or faux finish blends remain matted.

Heat source You can use many different sources for the heat of at least 200 degrees needed to melt the embossing powder. Consider: 75+-watt light bulb, stovetop burner, toaster, toaster oven, heat plate, electric skillet, or oven. If you are serious or enjoy embossing, invest in a heat tool or embossing tool. Only a heat tool can heat the item from the front; all other heat sources heat from the back of the surface, and are limited to heating only images on paper or other very thin surfaces. Of the several models of heat guns, I prefer the quieter wide-mouth, but many like the louder narrow-mouth heater. The narrower the mouth of the heat gun, the more powerful the flow of hot air.

Exciting Extras and Additions to Your Basics

I warned you in chapter 1 that you'd go crazy once you started rubberstamping. I know you are excited and can't wait to go crazy at your local art, craft, or rubberstamp store. I know because I'm hooked myself! The following lists are sorted into three categories. Must-Haves are needed to complete most basic projects. Nice-to-Haves add sparkle and color to your stamped images. The As-Long-As-I'm-Being-Greedy list is a stamper's wish list, because it includes some of the expensive supplies that aren't necessary to have fun stamping, but really do make up a complete, well-rounded collection of cool materials and tools.

Must-Have Supplies

These are the practical supplies needed to complete most rubberstamping projects. Keep these supplies close at hand during your stamping sessions.

Double-stick tape
Paper glue or tacky craft glue

Ruler or straightedge

Scissors (plain for cutting)

Self-healing cutting mat

Utility knife or blade

Nice-to-Have Supplies

As your skills improve, you'll want to expand your supplies with some of these fun tools that add dimension and color to your work.

Blending pen

Brush tip markers

Calligraphy markers

Colored pencils

Embossing pen

Fine tip markers

Tape with tape gun (hand-held, rolling dispenser)

As-Long-as-I'm-Being-Greedy Supplies and Special Touches

These supplies and tools are for any skill level, and add the decorative finishing touches to rubberstamp designs.

Changeable decorative-blade paper trimmer

Circular or oval cutters

Deckle-edge ruler

Decorative-edge scissors

Glitter glues or paints

Hot- or low-temperature glue sticks and glue gun

Laminating machine

Paper decorative-corner scissors or punches

Paper punches

Paper trimmer

Fun Stuff to Gather Near When Stamping

Your designs will really come to life and pop off the page when you add a personal touch with embellishments. You don't always have to go out and buy those extra touches; you can often find many in your home or craft box. Many of the following odds and ends aren't absolutely necessary to add spark and spunk to your work.

Acrylic paint	Excelsior
Beads	Fibers and ribbons
Buttons	Flat miniatures
Calendars	Flocking
Canceled postage stamps	Foreign newspapers
Charms	Gel pens
Colored pencils	Glitter
Computer fonts	Glitter glues
Confetti	Leaves and grasses
Crayons	Markers
Dimensional paints	Milky pens
Dried flowers	Music sheets

Pastels and chalks
Personal trimmer
Rotary cutter (with decorative blades)
Stamp positioner
Ultra-fine glitters

Mylar

Old greeting cards

Old magazines

Old maps

Pastels and chalks

Powder blushes

Powder eye makeup

Raffia

Ribbon roses and
flowers

Scraps of fabrics like
cotton, flannel, silk

Scraps of lace

Scraps of leather and
suede

Scraps of paper

ScratchArt sheets

Sealing wax

Sequins

Silk dyes and tints

Small gemstones

Snow texture

Threads, yarns, and
floss

Tinsel

Wallpaper scraps

Watercolors and
watercolor pencils

Woodies or flat wood
cut-outs

Watercolor pencils
Watercolors

In the Resources section of this book you'll find a listing of sources
that sell rubberstamp supplies, from the basics to the special

touches. Once you have the supplies you want, you can begin to set up your rubberstamping area. Chapter 3 offers lots of ideas for your perfect stamping area, and covers organization from A to Z. It's never too early to start organizing your supplies. If you already have a work area set up and your supplies organized, you may want to go directly to chapter 4 for techniques and tips. Either way, you are well on your way to creating with rubber!

Setting Up Your Personal Workspace

▼▼▼

NOT EVERYONE FINDS THIS PROCESS exciting, but I love to set up a work area for any craft. And a work area for rubberstamping is one of the most exciting to create! For me, the most important aspect of a work place is that I can relax, get inspired, and create in it. For years I worked and crafted in my home in a confining, cramped extra bedroom that was the dumping ground for household items that needed storing, from Christmas decorations to old radios that no longer worked. The one saving grace in these tight quarters was that my worktable was set up in front of a window. Even when I felt like I couldn't move without knocking something over, I could look out to a garden in my yard. The view of my garden inspired me and made me feel like my microscopic creative space was huge and lit by sunshine. No matter what it takes, create your own personal world in which you can loosen up and get creative. Close out the noise and enjoy the quiet of creativity.

If you are lucky enough to have a dedicated workspace for your stamping pleasures, that's a blessing, but don't be discouraged if you need to use the kitchen table or set up in the basement or garage. Any place will work with some efficient planning and smart use of available space. After a few years in that extra bedroom, I decided that I'd convert our home's living room into a studio. The living room was seldom used, since we really "lived" in our family room, which contained the TV and stereo system. During the past 15 years my studio has become my masterpiece, but trust me, I didn't start out with the perfect work area. Every once in a while I still have bad dreams about Christmas ornaments with big teeth and old radios that play opera endlessly. I wake up and run into my studio just to make sure it's still there, waiting patiently for me to come and play with my rubberstamps. You will find that your work area grows and changes as you grow and change as an artist.

Your Space: A Safe Place to Create

Few of us stop to think about our work area as we craft, but it is important to set up an inviting and cozy place to create in (even if the work area is just temporary). An uncomfortable environment is the last thing you want while enjoying a leisure activity. Plus, if you plan on spending a lot of time in your work area (which I'm sure you will), ergonomics are important. Long-term effects from uncomfortable surroundings can be miserable. Though you may get excited about starting your project, it is very important to take some extra time to make your working environment safe and comfortable. Besides, the more relaxed and at ease you feel while rubberstamping, the more creative you'll be.

Worktable

Chances are, you will use the rubberstamping techniques discussed in this book while sitting at a worktable. It should be sturdy and be able to hold the weight of your supplies. You should not have to hunch your shoulders or slouch over your work while rubberstamping. The height of your table should be no lower than your stomach (use your belly button as a placement guide) when you are sitting. It's natural to want to get closer to your images and materials, but excessive slouching will strain your back and neck muscles. Be aware of your posture while stamping: Sit straight, and use a small pillow or cushion to support the lumbar region of your back. If you must stand while stamping, place a high stool behind you so you can sit, lean on, or stand and sit on the stool if your legs get tired. Make sure you take breaks if standing, and to avoid slipping, remove any rugs from the floor beneath you.

Chair

I recommend an adjustable chair if you stamp or craft more than 20 hours per week. The best investment you can make if you partake in an art or craft for several hours at a time is an ergonomically correct chair. The chair should be padded and support your back and legs. Your feet should rest comfortably on the floor and not dangle or curl under. Swivel chairs are a bonus and allow you more access to all your workspace. Office supply stores that carry furniture usually have several models of chairs to try out.

Tools

Many tools are now designed for extra comfort. Look for tools that are spring-loaded and have cushioned handles. Grips and handles come in three basic sizes (small, medium, and large); make sure to match your hand size to the grip on a tool. Try using the tool before purchasing it. If you suffer from arthritis, tendonitis, carpal tunnel syndrome, or fibromyalgia, I recommend trying Handeze Therapeutic Gloves and/or Wristeze Wrist Gloves made by Berroco. The gloves and wristband relieve muscle stress, cramping, and fatigue. Made of Med-A-Likra, unlike many other gloves or braces on the market the gloves allow full hand and wrist movement. They are sized to hand size and make a big difference to those who suffer pain with hand motion and movement. Fiskars, a company that carries an extensive line of scissors, punches, and cutting tools, has designed an ergonomically correct line called Softouch. This company also has scissors designed for left-handed artists and craftspeople. Get the right tools and enjoy your creativity more.

▼▼▼▼▼▼▼▼▼▼▼▼▼▼▼▼▼

Handy Hint

To prevent an aching back, stand and stretch your muscles every 30 minutes.

▲▲▲▲▲▲▲▲▲▲▲▲▲▲▲▲▲

It's important that you watch for repetitive motions you may make while you're stamping. Repetitive motions cause fatigue and overstressed muscles that can lead to permanent problems like carpal tunnel syndrome. Don't stamp, cut, or color your images without taking breaks. Rubberstamping is a leisure activity that shouldn't lead to a pain in the back or numbness in the hand! Be aware of your body and the messages it might be sending you. If you experience pain or numbness, reevaluate your work area.

Lighting

Good lighting is essential to successful rubberstamping. Every technique and medium uses color, and poor lighting can lead to errors in color judgment. Work near a window during the day for natural lighting, or make sure your area lighting is full spectrum. Details are clearer in full-spectrum light, and you avoid eyestrain. Home improvement centers have full-spectrum lamps available, but this type of lighting is generally more expensive than regular light systems. To approximate full-spectrum lighting without spending much, my husband mixed two different tubes in one overhead fluorescent lighting unit for my studio at half the cost of a full-spectrum lamp.

When designing a work area, consider fluorescent bulbs and tubes. Fluorescent lighting offers the full spectrum of color and gives off a soft light with little glare or reflection. Lighting should be overhead or off to the side. Take a minute to check that your lighting reaches the entire work area. Many artists and crafters use halogen lights, but keep in mind that this strong, bright lighting tends to heat up the work area.

Often when rubberstamping you will find yourself working with small intricate lines and images. Ott-Lite has designed and developed some wonderful lighting tools to help make detail work less eye straining. The lighting systems are portable and incorporate a magnifying glass to enlarge the work enough that you can color even the tiniest image with no mistakes.

General Care, Caution, and Safety in Rubberstamping

Supplies

Most rubberstamp supplies are nontoxic, but especially when stamping or crafting with children, it never hurts to double-check the ingredients that are listed on package labels. Never assume you can use a product in a way that is not recommended by a manufacturer. When in doubt, call or write the manufacturer's consumer department. Most manufacturers will list their toll-free number on packaging.

Make sure your stamping area is well ventilated. Keep the floor clear of materials and supplies. One thing most hobbyists and even professionals don't think about, but is a leading cause of accidents, is working while you're tired or preoccupied. Our responses and reactions can slow down when we're tired, so make an attempt to

Handy Hint

An inexpensive way to get full-spectrum lighting is to use different colored bulbs or tubes in the same light fixture.

be well rested while stamping. Concentrate on your craft rather than letting your mind worry about what else you should be doing or what chores need to get done. To stamp safely in your work area, keep in mind the following:

- Look for expiration dates on products and don't use after the date recommended.

- Do not eat, drink, or smoke while stamping.

- Don't forget to wash your hands before and after you work. Make sure all your supplies are cleaned up and tops and lids are secured.

- Keep all supplies out of children's reach, or supervise all activities with children.

- When cleaning up, vacuum or wet mop; avoid sweeping with a broom, which can send particles airborne.

- Don't put any materials in your mouth, and don't rub your face or eyes until you've washed your hands.

- Read how to store each supply. In general you should not store or use supplies near heat, sparks, or an open flame. Some supplies may need to be sealed in an airtight container. Some supplies can't be exposed to high temperatures or direct sunlight while in use. When in doubt, contact the manufacturer.

- Protect wounds or cuts on skin with gloves or adhesive bandages.

- Some waste or leftover materials need to be disposed of in a special manner. For example, never pour paint or glue down your drain.

- Materials or supplies that may be hazardous are required to have the following labeling: a signal word such as *Caution* or

Warning, a listing of all ingredients in the product that are hazardous, a listing of how the product may harm you if not used properly, instructions on how to use the product properly, telephone number of the manufacturer or importer, and a statement that the product is inappropriate for use by children.

■ Heat sources are used in embossing. Be very careful when working with any heat source. Never touch any metal on a heat tool or gun. Allow your heat tool or gun to cool before storing.

Other Important Considerations in Your Work Area

Any work area should be clean and clutter-free. Dust and other impurities from the air can smudge or discolor your rubberstamping projects and supplies. Wipe down your work area frequently with a household cleaner and paper towel. Don't forget that hands are often the culprits behind dirt and oil on a project. Wash your hands before and during a rubberstamping session. It's always a good idea to cover the work area or worktable with newspapers or an old plastic tablecloth if the worktable is not solely dedicated to rubberstamping. Most supplies clean up with soap, water, and a little elbow grease, but why worry about the clean-up when it can be as easy as tossing the newspaper into the recycle bin? You may not need to cover a desk that is only used for rubberstamping, but you probably do want to cover and protect your dining room table. Paints, glues, embossing powders, heat guns, and other liquid supplies can damage the varnish used to seal most wood tables.

Did you know???

The temperature needed to emboss is high enough to burn and blister skin.

Your tools and supplies should be within easy reach while you're sitting or standing. Ideally, you should not have to stretch over supplies when reaching for a tool or material. You should have enough room to move your arm freely over the work area without knocking over or tipping a bottle of glue or jar of embossing powder.

Your work area should contain a waste can. It doesn't matter if it's a brown paper grocery bag or a heavy-duty garbage can on wheels. Having a place to put waste keeps your work area clean and clutter-free. One of the best ideas I ever saw was in a quilter's sewing room. This quilter was very clever and taped a small paper bag to the side of her sewing machine table and another one to her cutting table. With little effort she could toss into the trash threads and fabric scraps that were too small to save. I incorporated such a bag on my stamping table.

Feel free to use your own judgment in arranging your work area. The main idea is to create a space you are comfortable working and creating in. You'll want to be able to relax and enjoy your projects.

Embossing: It's a Messy Situation

Stamping enthusiasts and rubberstamp artists highly recommend that you set up a separate area or table for embossing. Even the most careful stamper can easily scatter embossing powder over a work area. And if the powder ends up on your other work or your table surface, it can end up melting in the wrong places! I got so frustrated with embossing powder escaping from my jar that I decided to use a small fold-up TV tray table for embossing. Using a separate table allows me to keep my main work area clean and particle-free for coloring and adding details to my stamping projects.

I also use old catalogs and magazines when embossing. I rip a sheet out of the catalog and place it on my embossing table. I stamp and emboss the image and throw out this sheet of paper. Then I rip a new sheet and place my powdered image on it, and apply the heat to emboss the image. It's a few extra steps, but I never have a messy work area. I've never been the neatest of people, but this system has helped me considerably because it is simple and inexpensive to keep up.

Organizing All Your Cool Rubberstamping Stuff

This section should be called, "I'm sorry but I can't make any sense of your organization logic." There are times when the thought of being organized can seem baffling and overwhelming to even the most structured creative soul. It is almost as if the act of organizing is too staggering to undertake, yet, being organized is an effective way to get more work and play done in a given day! A recent consumer magazine stated that by simply having "a place for everything and everything in its place" a person can save 3 days in a year. Imagine having an extra 72 hours in your schedule because you haven't spent precious minutes hunting for the scissors, locating the gold and silver embossing powder, or running around aimlessly for the scrap of paper on which you wrote the address of a new Web site for rubberstampers. I'm not a stickler for time management, but I do love having more time to stamp.

You'll probably find that the best way to handle any overwhelming job (yes, organization can seem like work) is to break the job down into smaller tasks. The first step is to become a list maker. Memory is an interesting (yet mysterious) concept for most creative individuals. It is wisest not to rely on your memory to get organized. Most creative people have great memories for things they enjoy, like embossing or coloring. But memory gets very selective

Five Ways to Be Organized in Your Studio or Manufacturing Area

1. Schedule 6 months out, and post all deadlines, due dates, and deliveries.

2. Try to spend at least 30 minutes of each workday playing or experimenting with your stamp supplies. Keep your interest up and your creative passions fueled.

3. Break down a product or design into as many steps as possible. Work each step to the maximum, then move on to the next step.

4. Keep a current list of supplies or materials that are low or need to be ordered within the next month so you don't run out without notice.

5. Take breaks. Every 30 to 60 minutes, stand up, stretch, or take a short walk. Refreshing your body and mind leads to clearer thoughts and more effective use of time. Use an answering machine when in production; interruptions break your rhythm.

when the "boring things"—like finding that butterfly stamp you used last month or the new punch you just purchased—surface and need to be tackled. A notebook or journal will help keep you on track. As you become more organized, you'll fill your notebook with categories and subcategories. But if you are a beginner just starting your journey into becoming organized, take it slowly. Take pride in the fact that you can locate your list journal. Then move on to the next step, which involves the formation of your list.

Your first list should be a list of questions: What do you need more time to do? (Stamp, of course.) What needs organizing within your rubberstamping area? The stamps? The notions? The papers? What items or tasks would help you accomplish, schedule, and coordinate rather than confuse your efforts? A storage cabinet? A file cabinet on wheels? A tacklebox? What activities give you the most frustration? Finding paper? Locating glitters? The real key to organization is to know what you want to organize. Breaking down what you want to accomplish will allow you to focus on the individual goals you want to achieve. Putting your thoughts into writing is simply a way to organize your thoughts. Seeing the tasks on paper, in black and white, makes them just a little less overwhelming, unless of course, your list gets lengthy! If the list is giving you heart palpitations, break the list up into smaller lists. This is actually a good thing. Dividing a list up means you have just taken a giant step toward organizing the chaos.

> **Handy Hint**
>
> Make a notebook or journal the permanent location for all your lists.

Like all new adventures or any attempt at change, the road to organization has ups and downs, bumps and curves, and even a few icy patches that can raise the hair on your neck! Work with your natural thought patterns and processes rather than fight old habits. Creative people seldom recognize that their creativity is really a process. Creativity doesn't just *happen*. Ideas don't have any value unless someone notices and approves of the idea. The first person to "notice" the idea must be the idea creator: you!

Pay close attention to how you come up with and utilize your creative thoughts, ideas, and designs. Find your own patterns, processes, steps, and organizational thinking. I organize my rubberstamps of butterflies with my rubberstamps of animals. According to the dictionary, butterflies are insects, not animals. But I know if I had a box of insect stamps I'd avoid opening that box! Don't feel that you need to follow the suggestions in this book or in a magazine article on how to organize your life in 12 easy steps. Get organized *by* yourself and *with* yourself. It's the only way in the long run that you will stay organized.

There are many components and supplies for rubberstamping. When you first start stamping it will be easy to keep your supplies organized, but as your collection of stamps, inks, papers, surfaces,

Five Ways to Be Organized in a Blink

1. Keep one calendar or schedule. Write everything down on the calendar as it happens. Start the day with a quick look at the current day and the next 3 days.

2. Use an answering machine. Return calls at a set time each day. Use voicemail and leave messages for friends, clients, suppliers, and customers.

3. Don't allow your work area to become crowded or stacked. Try to clear your work area each time you leave it. Every 6 months, remove all items, papers, catalogs, magazines, newsletters, and supplies that you have not found useful.

4. If possible, computerize. Computers are amazing! Computer programs on the market today take half the work out of organizing billing, invoices, correspondence, and many everyday office tasks.

5. Get enough rest. Fatigue and frustration go hand in hand! Don't rubberstamp when you are tired or overwhelmed. Take a nap. Go to bed early. Take a nice warm bath. Drink some hot chocolate.

and other supplies starts to grow, your stuff can quickly get out of control. If you can't find your embossing powders, glues, or glitters, you can't use them, or worse, you will buy duplicates of supplies you already have. In any type of organizing scheme, you need to do it in a way that is natural and easy for you to remember. There are dozens of books and hundreds of magazine articles on organization, but if a system doesn't work for you, that system is useless. Because as a professional I am used to dealing by name with manufacturers and companies, I often keep all the supplies of one company together, but this might be confusing for a hobbyist who would feel more comfortable organizing by category or by project.

There are a few common needs to consider when organizing your work area and your rubberstamping supplies. Most rubberstamps and supplies should be kept out of prolonged exposure to sunlight, excessive temperatures, and high humidity. There are dozens of organizers on the market, from plastic shoe boxes to cardboard drawer systems to elaborate totes. Spend some time researching all the makes and models of organizers at your local craft store, rubberstamp store, fabric shop, office supply retailer, and on the Internet. Organizers range from cardboard to plastic to wood. Find the ones that meet your needs. Don't overlook fun containers like decorative tins, old printer's drawers, or glass curio cabinets. My one rule is that my containers must be see-through. Out of sight means out of mind for me. Any container that you can't easily see into should be clearly labeled with its contents!

Organization Tips

I researched many books, magazine articles, and Web site pages to find tried and true organization tips for this book. I was already familiar with many of the tips from personal use, but wanted to make sure other rubberstampers had the same concerns and same formulas for solving organizational problems. Here's a list of great ways to organize your supplies.

Stamps

Keep a written log of all the stamps in your collection or inventory. Include if possible: manufacturer, place of purchase, date of purchase, price, and a title with a descriptive tag. Note whether the stamp is mounted or unmounted.

Categorize this log. You may categorize by theme, motif, size, or any other way you feel comfortable with. Note where you are storing each category. For example, if using the plastic shoe boxes, number or letter the shoe

Handy Hint

Unmounted stamps and dies store well in plastic pocket sleeves used for baseball cards, computer disks, or other flat items.

boxes. Note that the flower stamps are located in boxes number 1 and number 2. As your collection grows you may wish to note that a specific stamp is located in box number 1.

It's helpful to keep the image of each stamp on an index card. Organize the index cards exactly the same way as your log. Then when you need Christmas images you can first go the index cards, then the log to find the selected stamps.

Paper

Keep a running list of the types of papers you have on hand. Keep a log of each paper with the name, manufacturer, place of purchase, price, and your personal comments about the paper.

You can store paper flat in sturdy cardboard or plastic stackable shelves that hold up to a ream of most papers. Paper can also be stored in file folders or hanging folders. These items are usually found at office supply stores.

Other Supplies

Keep a running list of all your supplies, and keep it updated. Note on this list where the items are stored. Label storage units and organizers clearly and concisely.

The kinds of storage available for supplies are almost as endless as one's imagination, but consider: drawers and containers on wheels, carousel or upright storage bins, stacking containers, storage units with drawers, airtight containers with lids, and pantry units with drawers.

Let the Stamping Begin!

Envision this: You have your supplies. Your supplies and your life are organized so well that your mom and Dear Abby are smiling!

And you have a place to stamp. Once you reach this point, there's nothing left to do but STAMP! The real joy is just around the corner or the flip of a page. There is always something new cooking with stampers and rubberstamp artists, but chapter 4 will give you a solid foundation of knowledge, making it a breeze to try what's new in stamping. Surfaces, in addition to paper, are explained, so you'll never be limited in your imagination. And if you don't feel like reading chapter 4 from start to finish before trying out the techniques, don't feel guilty. That's part of the excitement of stamping! Put the book down as you need to and try the techniques with your own hands and heart! Chapter 5 will complete your body of knowledge with some wonderful hands-on projects that build your skill and confidence.

Creative How-To's

▼▼▼

I REMEMBER, AS A CHILD, standing at the window, watching the first winter rainfall as the drops hit the glass and slowly rolled down. After a while it became boring and I would wander my way into the other room where my mom was indulging in some sort of cozy winter activity—baking cookies, making homemade soup, or simply curling up on the couch with that novel reserved just for rainy days. "I'm bored." I would say, waiting for my mom to snap her fingers and create a circus in the middle of our living room. She always offered the same remedy; in fact, it seems I would have learned on my own to find my way to the toy chest for the coloring books and crayons, but it was always better when Mom did it. I knew once she had them in her hands, her winter activity would go to the back burner and suddenly we would be coloring together.

"Stay in the lines," she would tell me, patiently. "I'm trying . . . I keep messing up," I would respond with frustration. She taught me to color a dark border on the outside of the lines for a textured wall. "When you color it in, your crayon will feel the heavy outline and stick. That's how you know where to stop." It would work for me—as it did every other winter—and by the end of the day I would have a masterpiece, beautifully restricted within the lines. When I was finished I found the sharpest crayon in the box (usually the ugliest color) and autographed the picture to my mom. "Look, Mom!" I would hold it up. "It's for you." "Oh, it's beautiful," she would say, as if I just handed her a Picasso, and place it on the fridge for the rest of the winter.

There was something magical about those days—all the color crayons to choose from, finding the perfect picture to draw, and planning exactly how I wanted to color it before I even started. This same magic is found in rubberstamping, but it also requires the same kind of practice. You can't expect to stamp a perfect image the first time—or even the second—just like I could never get a perfect first picture on the first rainy day. But once you get all those pretty colors and stamps spread out in your workspace, it won't feel like practice!

Stamping an Image

In rubberstamping, the most basic and key skill is to stamp a clean image. Once you master this, you can master any of the techniques that follow it in this chapter. Spend some time practicing the techniques presented here, and then spend some time just fooling around with what you learn. There are three basic ways to stamp a simple image. The first two use only a rubberstamp and an inkpad; the third involves water-based colored markers. Unless otherwise noted, all techniques described in this chapter use paper as the surface, though most can be used on a multitude of surfaces. Practice stamping with both dye and pigment inks. Practice on different kinds of paper too. You'll build your skill level by repeating and practicing each technique. I urge you to practice all of the basic methods before skipping ahead to harder projects. (See the sidebar, Coloring Images, on page 98 for a variety of coloring options to use in stamping.)

Practice Makes Perfect

Set aside time to practice stamping different images. Some stamps need only slight pressure, while others may need more pressure to stamp an entire image. Usually the larger the stamp image surface, the more pressure it takes to complete the entire image. To apply more pressure for larger stamps, hold the stamp down with one hand and apply pressure with your other hand. Beginners should not stamp the intended design surface (such as a card or box) until they have practiced stamping the image several times on a piece of scrap paper.

Note: When stamping an image, do not rock or wiggle the stamp on the paper. This will cause bleeding or blurring of the image.

Stamp and Inkpad: Method 1

This is the most basic way to stamp an image. It's as easy as 1, 2, 3 . . . 4.

Materials

Rubberstamp, inkpad, and surface to stamp

Instructions

1. Tap the image side of the rubberstamp on the surface of the inkpad several times. Don't pound the stamp into the inkpad; this can cause damage to the pad and over-ink your image. Light tapping until the surface is inked works best.

2. Check the rubberstamp image to make sure the entire image is inked.

3. Image side down, press the rubberstamp to the surface.

4. Lift the rubberstamp cleanly from the surface. You have a stamped image.

Stamp and Inkpad: Method 2

To really control your inking, or to use different colors, you may prefer this method.

Materials

Rubberstamp, inkpad, and surface to stamp

Instructions

1. Bring the inkpad to the image side of the rubberstamp. Lightly tap the inkpad on the image until the entire surface is well inked. Don't pound the stamp into the inkpad; this can cause damage to the pad and over-ink your image. Light tapping until the surface is inked works best.

2. Image side down, press the rubberstamp to the surface.

3. Lift the rubberstamp cleanly from the surface. You have a stamped image.

Stamp and Water-Based Markers

In this method, you can create a beautifully detailed image without stamping it. Water-based markers give you more control over colors and prevent permanent staining of the stamp.

Materials

Rubberstamp, water-based markers or brush markers, and surface to stamp

Instructions

1. Hold the rubberstamp so the image faces up.

2. Using water-based or brush markers, color directly on the rubber of the stamp image. Start with light colors first and then go to dark colors (this way you can go over the light colors if you over-color a certain area).

3. When finished coloring the stamp, breathe or huff on the image to make sure all the ink is wet. (Never use permanent markers; the ink will damage the rubberstamp.)

4. Image side down, press the rubberstamp to the surface.

5. Lift the rubberstamp cleanly from the surface. You have a stamped image.

Using a Heat Source

As we get into embossing in the following section you'll see that a heat source is required. The goal of heat sources is to heat the embossing powder enough to melt it for a successful embossed image, but not to burn the powder. Many of these heat sources are in your home and special heating tools are also available, but all heat sources can be dangerous if not used properly.

See the sidebar, Cool Tools, on page 68, for a tool that helps you keep from burning your fingers when you're embossing. The heat sources that work best for embossing are as follows:

- **Heat gun.** A heat gun is similar to a hair dryer, but gets much, much hotter so be careful when using it. Hold the heat gun several inches away from the stamped image and move it in a back-and-forth motion over all areas of the image until all the powder is melted.

- **75-watt light bulb.** Place the back of your stamped surface about an inch above the bulb. Move the surface around in front of the bulb to distribute the heat evenly until all the powder is melted. It will take a few minutes for the embossing to occur.

- **Stovetop element.** Heat your stovetop to low heat and hold the back of the stamped surface above the stovetop, at a distance that heats the image but keeps the surface from burning. Keep moving the image around above the heat until all the powder is melted.

- **Electric skillet.** Heat the electric skillet to just under 200 degrees. Hold the back of the stamped surface above the skillet, at a distance that heats the image but keeps the surface from burning. Keep moving the image around above the heat until all the powder is melted.

- **Iron.** Heat the iron to warm (delicate) temperature. Hold the back of the stamped surface away from the iron, at a distance that heats the image but keeps the surface from burning. Keep moving the image around in front of the heat until all the powder is melted.

- **Oven (conventional or toaster).** Place the powdered image, face up, on a cookie sheet or sheet of aluminum foil. Turn oven to warm temperature or 200 degrees. Watch the image until all the powder is melted and promptly remove the image from the oven. Never leave the surface unattended.

Embossing an Image

Embossing adds elegance to a stamped image. It's a creative and simple way to change a regular stamped image into a textured or shiny—or even scented—image before your very eyes, using only a few simple tools. Embossing powder comes in a rainbow of colors and with a variety of characteristics. Once you have learned to stamp a clean image, you'll find that embossing is easy and fun.

There are many fun ways to emboss your stamped creations. Don't be afraid to experiment with and layer the powders. Have fun and explore this dynamic technique in stamping. (See chapter 5 for recipes for mixing different colors of embossing powder.)

Standard Embossing

This is also referred to as Wet Embossing and is the most popular method of embossing used. This is simply wetting the image with pigment or embossing ink so the embossing powder sticks to the image until the heat is applied. There are several how-to instructions in this chapter that require embossing in addition to other creative methods. Please use this standard embossing method when an instruction calls for embossing.

> ### Did you know???
>
> You can find embossing powders that are scented, that puff when heated, and that glisten and sparkle.

Materials

Pigment inkpad, rubberstamp, surface to stamp, embossing powder, and heat source

Instructions

1. Bring the inkpad to the image side of the rubberstamp. Tap the inkpad on the image until the entire surface is well inked. (You can also use Stamp and Inkpad: Method 1 instead of Method 2.)

2. Image side down, press the rubberstamp to the surface. Do not rock or wiggle the stamp.

3. Lift the rubberstamp cleanly from the surface. You have a stamped image.

4. Sprinkle embossing powder on the stamped image, enough to cover it.

5. Tap excess embossing powder from the image onto a paper plate or piece of scrap paper and return the excess powder to the container. (Blow hard to remove excess powder.)

6. Lay the powdered image flat on your worktable.

7. Apply heat source until the dull powder melts into a glossy or textured raised image. Don't overheat or burn the embossing powder by heating for too long. (It's been overheated if the embossing is cracked or brittle and flaking off the stamped surface.)

8. Allow 5 to 10 minutes to cool before touching the embossed image. Fingerprints or smudges can appear if the embossed image is not allowed to cool.

Double Embossing

Double emboss your image with a double layer of embossing powder, giving your design a look and feel of enamel or stained glass. This method uses embossing enamel, a large-grain, clear embossing powder. The enamel embossing granules spread out as they are heated, creating an extra-thick surface.

Materials

Rubberstamp, pigment inkpad, surface to stamp, embossing powder, heat source, coloring options (markers, colored pencils, or chalks), sponge or brush (makeup brush or watercolor brush works well), clear embossing ink, and clear or enamel embossing powder

Instructions

1. Stamp and emboss your image.

2. Color in your design.

3. Brush or sponge clear embossing ink on the colored areas of the design.

4. Pour or sprinkle on clear or enamel embossing powder and heat. You have now double embossed the stamped image.

Overembossing

Overembossing is a way to add depth and texture to a rubberstamp design. This method also uses embossing enamel. A single layer of embossing enamel gives a bumpy texture, like water drops on glass. A second coat will build more texture and dimension. A third coat will smooth out the surface.

Materials

Rubberstamp, pigment inkpad, surface to stamp, clear or enamel embossing powder, heat source

Instructions

1. Stamp your image to the surface.

2. Sprinkle clear or enamel embossing powder over your image.

3. Apply heat source until the powder has completely melted.

4. Immediately repeat steps 1 and 2 (before the embossing enamel is hardened) until you have a glossy smooth surface that resembles lacquer.

Cool Tools

Here are some clever tools you can use to enhance your rubberstamping designs and make stamping even more fun! See the Resources section for information on where to find these.

The Art Institute Glitter System

This ultra fine glitter, with a huge selection of color choices, adds sparkle and glitz to any stamped image.

Radiant Pearls

Apply this liquid color for a metallic sheen that adds glamour and elegance to an image. A little color goes a long way.

Cool Fingers Heat Embossing Tool Aid

This tool holds your card or paper while you apply heat to melt the embossing powder, letting you turn the paper without getting your fingertips burned.

Scratch Art Paper

This paper has a thin coat of black wax over a solid color or rainbow of color. Scratching with a pin or scratch tool creates patterns and designs on the paper. There is also a line of paper that gives the effect of stained glass when stamped and hung in a window.

Amazing Shardz

This is a line of ceramic shapes that can be stamped and embossed. Stampers use the shapes to create jewelry and interesting pieces to add to collage work.

VersaMark Inkpad

This nontoxic, acid-free ink creates a delicate image resembling a watermark effect.

Water Embossing

Who would have guessed that water could be a wonderful tool in stamping? Water embossing can add interest and dimension to the simplest of images. Water is inexpensive, so have some fun with it.

Hot Foil Pen

This amazing pen, slightly larger than most fountain pens, operates with two AA batteries. The tip heats up and lays down foil in the pattern or design you draw on a surface.

Pictorico Ink Jet Media

This line of papers is for those who love to combine print art (using a computer to create graphics and design) and rubberstamping. The line includes a beautiful silk paper that lets you use your stamped design as an appliqué.

RollaGraph

This stamp line features a roller handle and wheel stamp. With it, you can roll the stamp across a page to repeat a design.

ColorToolBox and Stylus

This gives you everything you ever needed for coloring with pigment inks, including an interchangeable ink tray with several color palettes.

Staedtler Marscarve Artist Carving Block with Marsgraphic 3000 Art Markers

This stamp-carving material cuts just like butter! The large block can be cut into smaller pieces to make several stamps. All you do is trace a pattern or design on the top of the eraser-like block and cut away the unwanted areas of the image with a wood carving tool or craft knife.

Artisan's Choice Create Your Own Rubber Stamps Kit

This kit comes complete with everything needed to make your own rubberstamp designs. Just draw the image on the transfer paper included and you are on your way to making your own stamp in about four steps.

Materials

Rubberstamp, inkpad, paper or paper-like surface to stamp, embossing powder, heat source, coloring options (markers, colored pencils, or chalks), water, sponge, light box or magazine or other soft work surface, and embossing stylus. Optional: Light box and paper towels

Instructions

1. Stamp, emboss, and color your image.

2. Using water, lightly moisten the back of your design surface with a sponge. Only use enough water to make the paper flexible; avoid using excess water or water dripping from the surface.

3. Place the image face down on a magazine or other soft surface. (Don't use a hard surface or the paper won't protrude.)

4. With an embossing stylus, gently push out or burnish the design areas. (For example, if the image is a flower, you can push out the petals and leaves to give depth.)

5. If you have difficulty seeing what areas to push out with your embossing stylus, use a light box, placing a folded paper towel between the light box and the paper you are water embossing. This will light up the embossed lines of your image and you can burnish the image against the paper towel.

Dry Embossing

This is one of my favorite techniques. Dry embossing employs a template or stencil to raise an image on the surface of the paper. Although it's not pure stamping per se, it's elegant and stylish and can add a lovely design element to rubberstamping.

Materials

Brass stencil or thick template, light box or light source, drafting tape, paper, and stylus or embossing or burnishing tool

Instructions

1. Place the brass stencil or template on the light source. If using a window as your light source, you may wish to tape

the stencil to the glass to keep the stencil still while you're embossing.

2. Place the paper on top of the stencil and tape the paper to secure. You should be able to clearly see the outline of the stencil design through the paper.

3. With a stylus or embossing or burnishing tool (the pointed end of a knitting needle or the handle end of a paintbrush can be used too), apply slight pressure to the paper and follow the outline (outer edge) of the stencil pattern. You don't need to rub the entire design, just the outline. The thicker the paper, the higher the raised surface of the design will be. If you rip or tear the paper, you are applying too much pressure as you outline.

4. Remove the paper from the light source and turn it over. You should see the raised design. If you've missed any lines or spaces, just line up the paper with the stencil again and fix the overlooked areas.

Stencil Embossing

This is another way to use your templates and stencils to create a beautiful image that adds sophistication to the basic stenciled design.

Materials

Brass stencil or template, card or paper, drafting tape, pigment ink or embossing ink, embossing powder, and heat source. Optional: sponges for dabbing ink from large pigment inkpad

Instructions

1. Position the stencil or template in the desired place on the card or paper (use drafting tape to hold it down if you wish).

2. Dab pigment or embossing ink into the open areas of the stencil.

3. Gently and carefully lift the stencil from the card or paper.

4. Sprinkle embossing powder on the stamped image.

5. Tap excess embossing powder from the image onto a paper plate or piece of scrap paper and return the powder to the container.

6. Lay the powdered image flat on your worktable.

7. Apply heat source until the dull powder melts into a glossy raised image. Don't overheat or burn the embossing powder by heating for too long. (It's been overheated if the embossing is cracked or brittle and flaking off the stamped surface.)

8. Allow 5 to 10 minutes of cooling time before touching the embossed image. Fingerprints or smudges can appear if the embossed image is not allowed to cool.

Handy Hint

Weave or add strips of paper behind your stamped image for background interest. The strips can vary in size and you can weave them loosely, tightly, or in a random pattern.

Stamping Surfaces Other Than Paper

I love to stamp on everything! Stamping is very creative and you'll enjoy discovering the perfect way to create personal touches around your home by using your stamps. This section is filled with fool-proof techniques and methods shared by many wonderful stampers at craft and art stores, in my classes, and in Internet newsgroups, bulletin boards, and chat rooms. Enjoy!

Stamping on a Bar of Soap

You can personalize a bar of soap with your rubberstamps. It may look too pretty to use, but the image will hold up even when you use the soap. This makes a great gift.

Materials

Rubberstamp, inkpad, embossing powder, heat source, coloring options (markers, colored pencils, or chalks), tissue paper, scissors, clear spray acrylic sealer or spray fixative, paraffin wax (enough to brush coat the entire bar of soap), double boiler, flat brush, and bar soap of your choice

Instructions

1. Stamp, emboss, and color your image on tissue paper.

2. Cut out the design.

3. Spray a light coat of clear spray acrylic sealer on the front and back of the design. You can also use spray fixative to seal the design.

4. Melt a small amount of paraffin wax in the double boiler.

5. Brush a layer of wax on the top of the soap.

6. Place the design on top of the layer of wax.

7. Top with another thin layer of paraffin wax.

Stamping on Aluminum Foil

As I said earlier, rubberstampers will stamp *anything!* Well, aluminum foil is a fun, shiny surface that makes a great background for greeting cards and stationery!

Materials

Heavy-duty aluminum foil, glue or glue adhesive spray, magazine or other soft work surface, rubberstamp, fast-drying dye ink, embossing stylus, and coloring options (markers, colored pencils, or chalks)

Instructions

1. Fold a piece of aluminum foil in half, making it slightly larger than your stamped image, and glue the insides together with glue or glue adhesive.

2. Place the foil on a magazine or other soft work surface and smooth it out as much as possible.

3. Ink a bold outline stamp using fast-drying dye ink.

4. Stamp the image on the aluminum foil. (You are stamping the backside of the design, so you will not see the ink when the project is complete.)

5. Using an embossing stylus, go over all the lines with slight pressure. (Too much pressure can tear or rip the aluminum foil.)

6. Turn the aluminum foil over to check how the design is coming. Continue using the stylus until you're happy with the design.

7. Color your image.

8. Cut out the image and add to a background of your project.

Stamping on Wood

Stamping on wood is just as easy as stamping on paper, but you get a different effect and a sturdy surface.

Materials

Fine-grain sanding paper or brown paper (grocery) bag, wood surface, tack cloth, clear acrylic spray sealer, rubberstamp, inkpad, and coloring options (markers, colored pencils, or chalks). Optional: embossing ink, embossing powder, and heat source

Instructions

1. With fine-grain sandpaper or a piece of a brown paper bag, lightly sand wood surface until smooth. Wipe down with a tack cloth to remove any dust.

2. Apply a thin coat of clear acrylic spray sealer and lightly sand again after the sealer dries. (This is only if you want your project to have a long life. Sealing the wood prevents sap from coming through the wood and damaging the design.)

3. Stamp, emboss (optional), and color your image directly onto the wood. You don't need to emboss if you don't desire that effect for your project.

4. Apply a top coat of clear acrylic spray sealer.

Stamping on Terra Cotta Pots or Other Curved Surfaces

Terra cotta is a very popular medium for home décor. And minimal surface prepping creates less work for you.

Materials

Clear acrylic spray sealer, terra cotta pot, rubberstamp, inkpad, and coloring options (markers, colored pencils, or chalks). Optional: embossing ink, embossing powder, and heat source

Instructions

1. Spray a light coat of clear acrylic spray sealer on the terra cotta pot inside and out.

2. Ink your rubberstamp image.

3. Gently hold one side of the image against the curved surface of the pot and slowly move your wrist in one direction so that the stamp image is laid down along the curve. You may allow the stamped image to dry, or you may want to emboss the stamped image immediately.

4. Color and emboss (optional) your image.

5. Finish with a coat of clear acrylic spray sealer.

Stamping on Fabric

Fabric stamping lets you make everything from unique clothing to decorative table coverings.

Materials

Fabric or garment, wax paper or cardboard (for garment), rubberstamp, fabric inkpad or fabric stamping paint, and coloring options (fabric markers, fabric paint, fabric dye, or a permanent black marker)

Instructions

1. Pre-wash and iron the garment or piece of fabric. Do not use any type of fabric softener during the wash or dry cycles.

2. Place fabric or garment flat on a protected, covered work surface.

3. Place wax paper or cardboard between layers of fabric to prevent unwanted ink or color from leaking or spreading to another part of the garment.

4. Ink your stamps with fabric ink or fabric paint designed for stamping (read labeling).

Handy Hint

When you emboss an image and cut it out, sometimes the embossing powder chips off, exposing the paper beneath. When this happens, simply take a marker the same color as the embossing powder and color in the exposed area.

5. Stamp images on the fabric.

6. Color with fabric markers, fabric paint, or fabric dye. Detailing can be done with a permanent black marker.

7. Allow fabric to dry for 78 hours, then heat-set the fabric. You can heat-set by ironing the design on the proper heat setting—cotton setting for cotton fabric, for example—or by placing the fabric in a clothes dryer for 20 minutes.

8. Do not wash the fabric for at least a week. When you do wash it, observe these instructions: Avoid fabric softeners when washing, hand wash when possible, air dry, and turn garments inside out when machine washing or drying.

Stamping on Velvet Fabric

Velvet is perfect for a soft, romantic look. The image that results from this process is permanent and will hold up to cleaning.

Materials

Velvet fabric, spray bottle, rubberstamp, ironing board or other heat-resistant work surface, and iron. Optional: pressing cloth

Instructions

1. Lightly mist the back of the entire piece of velvet fabric with a spray bottle.

2. Place the clean, non-inked stamp, image side up, on your ironing board or other heat-resistant work surface.

3. Lay the dry side of the fabric on the stamp image.

4. Press the iron (set on the velvet or delicate materials setting) to the fabric and hold it there for 10 to 20 seconds without moving or wiggling it.

5. Gently and carefully lift the iron off the fabric. The image is now "stamped" into the velvet. If you find that 20 seconds is not long enough to stamp the image, repeat the previous step, pausing between 10 and 20 seconds.

6. If you have a problem with steam holes showing up on the stamped image, use a pressing cloth between the iron and the velvet.

Stamping on Velvet Paper

Also called *velveteen* or *plush paper,* velvet paper has a slight nap and feels soft to the touch. Stamping on velvet paper is similar to stamping on velvet fabric. There are some slight changes in the process, however, so read the instructions carefully before trying this technique. The resulting image is permanent.

Materials

Rubberstamp, ironing board or other heat-resistant surface, velvet paper, iron, and pressing cloth (optional)

Instructions

1. Place the stamp, image side up, on your ironing board or work surface.

2. Lay the paper right side down, with the nap side on the rubberstamp.

3. Press the iron to the back of the paper for 10 seconds. Don't move or rock the iron.

4. Lift the iron gently and carefully.

5. If you have a problem with steam holes showing up on the stamped image, use a pressing cloth between the iron and the velvet.

Variation: Ink your stamp and then follow steps 1–4, or stamp on velveteen paper, skipping the iron process altogether.

Stamping on Candles

Enhance a plain candle by stamping an image on it. This candle is burnable.

Materials

Candle (size/type of your choice), scissors, tissue paper, rubber-stamp, inkpad, embossing ink, embossing powder, heat gun, coloring options (any), sponge, water, and embossing tool

Instructions

1. Consider and plan out your candle design.

2. Cut tissue paper slightly larger than the size(s) of the image(s) you want to stamp on the candle.

3. Stamp, emboss, and color the image on the tissue paper.

4. Carefully cut out the image, leaving as little as possible of the excess tissue.

5. Sponge just enough water on the back of the tissue paper to enable it to stick smoothly on the surface of the candle (or sponge the candle with water and smooth on the tissue-paper image). Do not over-wet.

6. Preheat your heat gun for a few seconds, then apply heat from the heat gun to the surface of the tissue-covered area. Move the gun uniformly around the area for even heating. The tissue paper will dry and then disappear as the heat melts the surface of the candle, and the wax absorbs the tissue. Only your heat-embossed design will remain.

Stamping on Leather

Leather is great for stamping—find leather blanks at most craft stores.

Materials

Rubberstamp, dye inkpad, leather, and clear acrylic spray sealer

Instructions

1. Consider and plan out your design.
2. Stamp your image on the leather. (Only dye ink can be used on leather.)
3. Spray several light coats of clear acrylic spray sealer over the image.

Stamping on Craft or Fun Foam

This technique produces what is referred to as faux leather because of the soft feel of the foam once it's heated. Many stampers color the finished stamped images in natural shades of real leather.

Materials

Scissors, craft or fun foam, rubberstamp, inkpad, heat-resistant work surface, and heat gun.

Instructions

1. Consider and plan out your design.
2. Cut the foam to the exact size you need or just slightly larger than your stamped image, or cut foam into a shape (square, rectangle, oval, etc.).
3. Ink your stamp. Set to the side within easy reach.

4. Lay the foam on a heat-resistant surface such as ceramic tile.

5. Heat the foam with your heat gun for 15 to 20 seconds on each side. The foam will be hot, so use care when you turn it over. The foam might curl at the edges slightly.

6. Once you have heated the foam properly, firmly press the stamp into the foam. Allow it to cool for 30 seconds before removing the foam from the stamp. Use your hands to smooth and press down the foam.

Stamping on Shrink Plastic

Shrink plastic is a plastic that shrinks down to 50% of its original size when heated, shrinking the image too (but the image keeps its shape). It's good for making shapes, jewelry, buttons, or to just have fun watching the design shrink. The two most widely available kinds of shrink plastic are clear and opaque. Shrink plastic has a grain, so to get your images to look the same you must stamp all images in the same direction. Color the image before or after you shrink the plastic, but remember that it will shrink dramatically and the color intensifies when shrunk. Use pigment ink for best results. If you plan to add any holes for stringing a necklace or jump rings for a bracelet, you must add them *before* you shrink the plastic.

Materials

Fine-grain sandpaper, shrink plastic, rubberstamp, inkpad, scissors, baby or other talcum powder, cardboard (sized to your oven or toaster oven rack), and heat source (oven, toaster oven, or heat gun). Optional: clear acrylic spray sealer or lacquer

Instructions

1. Consider and plan out your design.

2. Sand the plastic with a fine-grain sandpaper in all directions.

3. Ink your stamp and stamp the image to the plastic.

4. Cut out the image.

5. Powder the cardboard with baby or other talcum powder, just covering the entire piece of cardboard.

6. Place the plastic on the cardboard and put it in the oven or toaster oven at the temperature recommended on the shrink plastic package label. The plastic might curl or even flip during heating, but will lay flat when it is done.

7. Once the plastic flattens, remove the plastic from the oven or stop heating with the heat gun. Use care and caution when removing the plastic from the oven, and allow the plastic to cool before touching it.

8. Finish with several light coats of acrylic spray sealer or a coat of lacquer if you wish to protect your coloring.

Stamping Glass

You'll like the elegant look you'll get from stamping on glass with a permanent image.

Materials

Glass surface, etching crème or dip, rubberstamp, pigment inkpad, embossing ink, embossing powder, heat gun, and coloring options (enamel, glass, ceramic, or porcelain paint)

Instructions

1. Consider and plan out your design.

2. Read my instructions for terra cotta pots (see page 75) if you are working on a curved glass surface.

How Did My Potato Become a Stamp?

1. Cut a raw potato in half with a kitchen knife.

2. Draw your design or pattern on the cut potato with a permanent black marker. An easy way to draw a design is to place a stencil on the potato and trace around the inside.

3. Use a sharp kitchen paring knife or craft utility knife to carefully cut away the parts of the potato that are not needed. (I blacken all the areas that I don't want.) Always take care with a sharp knife; cut away from body, hands, fingers, design, and anything else you value!

4. Pour paint on a plastic or glass plate. Use a large flat brush or foam brush to apply a healthy coat of paint to your carved image. If you want to just dip your potato stamp into the paint, remember to tap the potato stamp on a paper towel after you dip it to remove excess paint.

5. Stamp away on your surface. Reapply paint for each stamping. If stamping on a garment or fabric, please review the section called Stamping on Fabric for preparing and heat-setting of the material.

3. Using an etching crème or dip, etch the surface of the glass to give it "teeth." Teeth means that the surface has been roughened up so that ink or paint can adhere to the non-porous surface.

4. Ink the stamp with pigment ink, stamp the image, and emboss. Color the image, if desired.

5. Allow the glass 24 hours to dry before use. Hand wash only.

Stamping Porcelain or Ceramic Tile

Add some character to your porcelain or ceramic tile. Put accentuating images on your bathroom walls or in your kitchen.

Materials

Porcelain or ceramic surface, rubberstamp, inkpad, and spray sealer

Instructions

1. Consider and plan out your design.

2. Read my instructions for terra cotta pots (see page 75) if you are working on a curved surface.

3. Stamp the surface with permanent ink. Allow it to dry.

4. Apply a light coat of spray acrylic sealer to the surface.

Variations

1. Emboss the outside lines of your image.

2. Apply enamel, glass, ceramic, or porcelain paints directly to the stamp with a paintbrush, stamp the image, and then let it dry. If you do this, clean your stamps immediately with the method recommended by the paint manufacturer.

Stamping on Polymer Clay

Polymer clay is a very versatile surface that holds almost any image.

Materials

Polymer clay, rolling pin, wax paper, tape, rubberstamp, scissors or sharp knife, cookie sheet, aluminum foil, and oven or toaster oven

Instructions

1. Consider and plan out your design.

2. Place a sheet of clay on a piece of wax paper on your work surface.

3. Condition the clay by kneading it in your hands until it becomes warm and pliable.

4. Flatten the clay as much as you can with your hands and fingers.

5. Cover a rolling pin with wax paper and tape the wax paper.

6. Using the wax paper-covered rolling pin, flatten the clay to about ⅛-inch thickness.

7. Cut the clay, with scissors or a sharp knife, into the shape you wish to stamp. Smooth any rough edges with your fingers.

8. Using steady, even pressure, stamp the image into the clay. Do not rock or wiggle the stamp. Lift the stamp straight up to remove.

9. Read your clay package label carefully before baking the clay. Polymer clays manufactured by different companies vary slightly in the baking temperature and time required. Never bake polymer clay at a temperature higher than 260 degrees; it is better to heat at a lower temperature for a longer time. If polymer clay burns, it releases toxic fumes.

10. Place your stamped clay on a cookie sheet covered with aluminum foil and bake in an oven or toaster oven.

11. Remove from the oven after the allotted cooking time and allow to cool.

Stamping on Paper Clay

It's easy to stamp on paper clay, and it's hassle-free because it air dries. Perfect stamping surface for children.

Materials

Paper or air-dry clay, rolling pin, wax paper, rubberstamp, scissors or sharp knife, bowl of water, and coloring options (ink, markers, and paint)

Instructions

1. Consider and plan out your design.

2. Flatten clay to about ¼-inch thick with your hands or a rolling pin. Work on a hard level surface covered with wax paper.

3. When paper clay surface is even and level, press the stamp into the clay with a firm even pressure. Do not rock or wiggle stamp.

4. If desired, cut out the stamped images from the flattened clay, using scissors or a sharp knife. You can smooth rough edges with your finger and a drop of water.

Note: If you want to have any holes for stringing this piece, make them before drying. It is possible to create a hole with an awl or drill bit after the clay is dried, but there is always the chance of damaging the piece.

5. Allow the clay to air dry for 24 hours. Turn the piece over at least twice for even drying.

6. Once the clay is dried, use ink, markers, or any kind of paint to color the image.

Other Great Stamping Techniques

Here's a hodgepodge of other fun stamping techniques. It's never ending!

Resist Stamping

Sometimes resist stamping is referred to as *ghosting.* In resist stamping, you creatively use stamping supplies to produce polished and artistic designs. It takes some practice to become perfect, but your creativity will make the practice time fly by.

Materials

Rubberstamp, card or paper, clear embossing inkpad, clear embossing powder, heat gun, dye inkpad or markers, and brayer

Instructions

1. Consider and plan out your design.
2. Stamp an image on a card or paper using clear embossing
   ink.
3. Emboss the image with clear embossing powder.
4. Ink a brayer with dye inkpad or markers. Roll the brayer
   over the embossed image, and the clear embossed image
   will pop out.

Bleach Stamping

You read right! Regular old household bleach! This technique has
the coolest effect on colored paper and tissue paper. On blue paper,
the image reminds me of bleached denim jeans.

Materials

Bleach (less than 1 teaspoon), small glass bowl or custard cup, small
round paintbrush, rubberstamp, paper towels, and card or paper

Instructions

1. Consider and plan out your design.
2. Pour the bleach into a glass bowl or custard cup.
3. Using a small paintbrush, apply bleach to a bold outline
   stamp. Tap the brush onto a paper towel to remove excess
   bleach, and brush up any excess bleach that might spill over
   on the stamp image.

Troubleshooting

Most of the problems you'll run into while stamping have simple solutions. So you'll know what to expect, here are the most common problems for novice stampers.

Blotchy Image

A blotchy image is caused by too much ink. It's a common problem with solid stamps. To correct it, gently tap the stamp on scrap paper before stamping on the final surface. This will help eliminate too much ink on your stamp.

Incomplete Image

This happens when there is not enough ink on the rubber or you have not applied enough pressure to your stamp. To correct, re-ink your stamp or press firmly over the entire image.

Extra Line Near the Edge of an Image

If you ink areas of your stamp that are not part of the desired image, or if you rock your stamp, a line may appear near the edge of your image. Practice not rocking

4. Carefully stamp the image on a card or paper.

5. Lift your stamp smoothly and immediately. Watch as the bleach image pops out of the paper.

Basic Masking

This technique allows you more freedom to create realistic scenes, because more than one rubberstamp image is used in a design. For example, you can have grass and flowers growing around a tree or fence, or you might want clouds and the sun behind an image of an angel. The mask is used to protect the foreground image.

Materials

Rubberstamp, inkpad, card or paper, self-sticking note for making the mask, scissors or craft utility knife, and coloring options

your stamp when you make an imprint. If this does not solve the problem, wipe the rubber's edge to remove excess ink from areas that are not part of the image. If all else fails, carefully trim the problem rubber area from your stamp with a utility knife.

Blurred Image

Usually caused by movement of the stamp once it is placed on paper. Be sure to remove your stamp immediately and carefully once you have made your image.

Embossing Powder Brushes Off

The image was not heated long enough to melt all the embossing powder. You may be able to save the image by reapplying the heat gun.

Embossed Image Is Brittle and Breaks Off

You've overheated the embossing powder and as a result burned the melted embossing. Try again. Heat only long enough for the dull powder to melt and turn glossy.

Instructions

1. Consider and plan out your design.

2. Pick out the image to appear in the foreground and stamp the foreground image on your card or paper (see step BM-1).

3. Stamp the same image on an index card or self-sticking note (see step BM-2). If using a posting note pad, stamp close to the top so that the sticky part can be used to adhere to the surface as a mask.

4. Cut out the image from the card or self-sticking note, staying just inside the stamped outline (see step BM-3). This cut-out is your mask.

Handy Hint

Save your mask pieces. They can be used again and again.

5. Place the mask over your original stamped image on the paper, lining it up exactly (see step BM-4). Only the outline of your stamped image should show from behind. Making the mask slightly smaller than the original image will prevent a white halo effect from forming where the ink doesn't print.

6. Stamp a different (background) image, overlapping the first image (see step BM-5).

7. Lift the mask off the card or paper (see step BM-6). When the mask is lifted, your new image will disappear behind the first one (see figure 1).

Step BM-1. Stamp the foreground image on your card or paper.

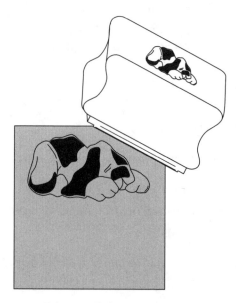

Step BM-2. Stamp the same image on an index card or self-sticking note.

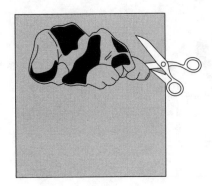

Step BM-3. Cut out the image from the card or self-sticking note, staying just inside the stamped outline.

Step BM-4. Place the mask over your original stamped image on the paper, lining it up exactly.

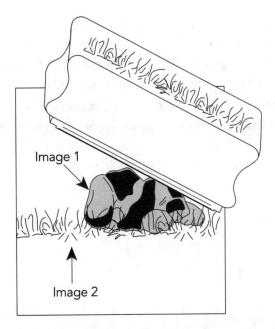

Image 1

Image 2

Step BM-5. Stamp a different (background) image, overlapping the first image.

Step BM-6. Lift the mask off the card or paper.

Figure 1. Example of Basic Masking.

Mortise Masking

With this technique you can also create realistic scenes by using more than one rubberstamp image in a design. For example, you can fill a stamped image of a Mason jar with a stamped image of a frog, or you can put fruit images into a basket image. It takes some practice, but the results are worth it! This mask protects your background image.

Materials

Rubberstamp, inkpad, card or paper, self-sticking note pad for making the mask, and scissors or craft utility knife

Instructions

1. Consider and plan out your design.

2. Pick out the image to appear in the foreground and stamp the foreground image on your card or paper (see step MM-1).

3. Stamp the same image on an index card or self-sticking note (see step MM-2). If using a posting note pad, stamp close to the top so that the sticky part can be used to adhere to the surface as a mask.

4. Cut out the inside of the image, staying just inside the stamped outline of the card or self-sticking note (see step MM-3). This is your mask.

5. Place the mask on your card or paper over your original stamped image, lining it up exactly (see step MM-4).

6. Stamp your other desired image(s) in the open or exposed area of the mask (see step MM-5).

7. Allow the ink to dry, then lift the mask off the card or paper (see step MM-6). The new images will appear inside the first stamped image (see figure 2).

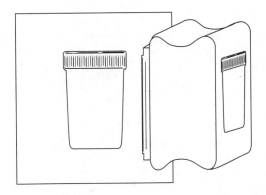

Step MM-1. Stamp the foreground image on your card or paper.

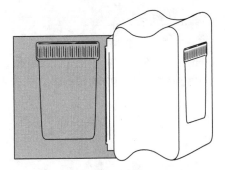

Step MM-2. Stamp the same image on an index card or self-sticking note.

Step MM-3. Cut out the inside of the image of the card or self-sticking note, staying just inside the stamped outline.

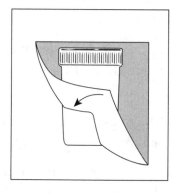

Step MM-4. Place the mask on your card or paper over your original stamped image, lining it up exactly.

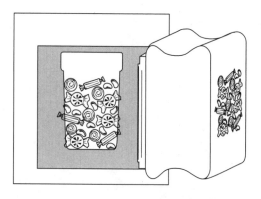

Step MM-5. Stamp your other desired image(s) in the open or exposed area of the mask.

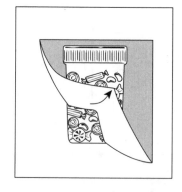

Step MM-6. Lift the mask off the card or paper.

Figure 2. Example of Mortise
Masking.

Direct to Paper

A fairly new technique, direct to paper has stampers chatting and
sharing up a storm as they explore and develop the craft. The great
thing about stamping is there is rarely a right or wrong way to experiment with a technique.

You can use this technique to make backgrounds (discussed in
chapter 5), or color an embossed image by using pigment ink as the
color instead of markers or other color options. I love to use the di-
rect-to-paper method to create several sheets of background paper
and then use decorative scissors and paper punches to punch out a
variety of shapes—from circles to hearts to diamonds—to use as
confetti or borders of cards.

Materials

Pigment inkpad, card or paper, clear embossing powder, and heat
source

Tips for Masking

■ Always work from the front of the scene to the back of the scene, so that the images or subjects closest to the viewer are at the edge of the front of the scene. This is the exact opposite of the technique used to create backgrounds in painting, in which you complete the background first. For rubberstamping, mask the front images and work your way back.

■ It takes time and patience to cut a mask. It's worth it for the stunning results and professional appearance of your finished work.

■ Save your masks in an envelope and stamp the image on the outside for future reference, or place your masks in clear pocket sleeves in a binder or file folder.

Instructions

1. Consider and plan out your design.

2. Stamp your card or paper directly with the inkpad. This works best with the smaller eye-shaped pigment inkpads or the pigment inkpads with removable rectangular or pie-slice pads.

3. Make random designs, layer colors, and just have fun playing. You don't need to press the pads into the paper. Just create a light coat of color by tapping the pad on the paper.

4. Sprinkle clear embossing powder on the stamped image. Tap excess embossing powder from the image onto a paper plate or piece of scrap paper and return the powder to the container. Lay the powdered card or paper flat on your worktable.

5. Apply heat source.

6. Heat only until all the powder is melted. You can overheat or burn the embossing powder if you heat it for too long. (It's been overheated if the embossing is cracked or brittle and flaking off the stamped surface.)

7. Allow 30 to 60 minutes of cooling time before touching the embossed image. Fingerprints or smudges can appear if the embossed image is not allowed to cool.

Rubbings

This is a great technique for a background or a collage. Choose a flat object that has some detail to it. You might select a leaf, an embossed business card, or even a tombstone! Place a piece of letter-weight paper over the top of the object, and color over the object with a colored pencil or crayon. Make sure you hold both your paper and your object in place. You will see the outline of the object as you rub.

Moving on

Did you ever think there was so much involved in rubberstamping? I've covered so many different techniques and how-to's that you may feel as though your mind is spinning. The best way to deal with all of this information and continue learning is to start using all these wonderful techniques in some fun projects! Chapter 5 is just brimming with simple, whimsical designs to enjoy making.

Coloring Images

Color is one of the favorite parts of designing and stamping for many artists. Almost every coloring medium has been used, from paints to pastels to markers. Practice and play with any new medium before you attempt to apply the color directly to your designs. Colors can be blended and mixed with each other. Don't be afraid to explore and try new techniques and methods. Just as rainbows make the world a brighter place, so do colors added to stamped images. Here are several types along with hints for using them.

Colored Pencils

- Keep your strokes soft and even. It's better to add more color by applying more soft strokes than to try to remove a harsh stroke.

- After sharpening your pencil, dull the sharp-pointed color on a scrap piece of paper to avoid tearing papers.

- Practice your strokes on scraps of different types of papers. Learn how your pencils react to each kind of paper. Learn what the color results will be from soft to hard strokes.

Gel and Milky Ink Pens

- These are available in a multitude of colors, including metallics.
- Milky pens are wonderful on dark papers.
- The flow of ink is so smooth that these pens are a breeze to control.
- Keep pen tips clean by wiping away built-up dried ink.
- Store all ink pens in a horizontal position.
- Always replace the cap of pens when you're done using them.

Paint Pens

- These are available in a multitude of colors, including metallics.
- Metallic pens are wonderful on dark papers.
- Shake very well before using.

- Keep pen tips clean by wiping away built-up dried paint.
- Store all ink pens in a horizontal position.
- Always replace the cap of pens when done using them.

Pigment Inks

- Use small paintbrushes or sponges to apply to image.
- Use care when coloring, as ink will smear and smudge.
- Pigment ink takes a long time to dry and will not dry on glossy papers.
- Best result is when pigment ink is embossed.

Metallic Crèmes and Stencil Crèmes

- Use small paintbrushes or sponges to apply to image.
- Use care when coloring, as crèmes will smear and smudge.
- Crèmes take a long time to dry.
- Best result is when crèmes are sprayed with a light coat of clear acrylic sealer.

Lacquers and Liquid Colors

- Purchase these in tube-like bottles with a medium flow tip.
- Best to invest in a fine tip, which is packaged separately.
- Tap bottle tip down several times to remove air bubbles.
- Remove the cap and start the liquid flow to remove excess air bubbles.
- Best results are when the image is first colored with markers or pencils, then colored lacquers are added on top.
- Keep the flow even and steady while filling in image areas.
- Take care to keep fingers out of wet lacquer.
- Allow 24 hours to dry.

(continues)

(continued from page 99)

Markers

- So many are available that you'll want to try one or two of a brand before investing in a set.
- There are many different sizes and styles of tips. Keep a variety of brush, fine, and extra-fine tips in your marker collection.
- Practice with each different style of marker on scrap paper before trying them on a stamped image.
- Keep strokes even and don't apply heavy pressure to tips of markers.
- Allow colors to dry before introducing a new color.
- Work from your lightest color to darkest color on an impression.
- Always cap a marker not in use.
- Store markers in a horizontal position to keep tips from drying out.

Pastels and Chalks

- Keep on hand a supply of cotton swabs, eye makeup sponges, and cosmetic sponges.
- You can also use small round and flat paintbrushes to apply color to image.
- Load up swab or brush with the powder from the pastel or chalk, then apply that powder in a gentle circular motion to area.
- Pastels are also available in pencil form.
- Pastels and chalks can be blended easily in powder or on your image.

■ Add pastel or chalk powder to your embossing powder for extra color and a more interesting effect.

■ A fixative must be used to make the pastel or chalk color permanent. A fixative can be anything from aerosol hairspray or clear acrylic spray sealer. If not sealed, the pastel and chalk will fade and brush off.

■ Powdered makeup for cheeks and eyes make wonderful colorants too!

PearlEx Powders

■ These powders are much like chalks in applications, but are metallic-looking and shimmer.

■ Use small paintbrushes or sponges to apply to image.

■ Best results are when crèmes are sprayed with a light coat of clear acrylic sealer.

Watercolors

■ Watercolor pencils are applied just like any colored pencil. However, adding a light touch of water will soften the color so it will look just like watercolor paint.

■ As a concentrate, watercolor paint comes in liquid form. The color is brushed onto the image. You can use the color straight from the bottle or water the color down in a mixing tray.

■ As a tablet or solid form, watercolor will be picked up with a wet brush or in a mixing tray. Add water until you're happy with the color.

■ Make more than you think you'll need. It's almost impossible to duplicate the color from one batch to another.

■ Watercolors can be misted for a softer effect.

Creating Your Rubberstamping Projects

▼▼

SITTING DOWN TO STAMP is one of my favorite activities. Often I use my rubberstamping time to reward myself when I have finished all the "have to do" chores on my list. Even as a professional stamper, I enjoy just stamping for the fun of it! I experience such pleasure when projects begin to take shape as I stamp images, emboss them, and add a touch of color to each piece. Here are some wonderful projects, starting with a few easier ones so you can get the feel of this delightful art, then more advanced projects for when you get ready to really have some fun. Enjoy!

Stationery and Greeting Cards

What could be more fun than going all out, getting wild and crazy with your stamps? Mail Art offers a blast of color, creativity, and the individual uniqueness of each stamp artist. There are many Mail Art mailing lists on the Internet, or you could start your own mailing list with your friends. Being part of such a mailing list is exciting because Mail Art from all over the world will arrive in your mailbox.

But, you don't need a mailing list to create Mail Art. You can have fun just creating unique postcards, stationery, envelopes, and greeting cards to send a happy thought or season's greeting to family and friends.

Pretty Paper Stationery with Matching Envelopes

Make your own stationery by following these easy instructions. Using the stamp patterns of your choice, you can create beautiful stationery sets to fit your tastes. Try whatever patterns you like, leave your stamped creations plain, or emboss them using the embossing methods you learned in chapter 4. Turn to the color insert in the center of the book to see a few examples of the endless possibilities of patterned stationery you can create with stamping techniques.

Materials

Pigment ink
Rubberstamps of your choice
Envelopes
8½ × 11-inch paper
Optional: Embossing powder, paper plate or scrap paper, and heat source

Instructions

1. Ink the stamp.
2. Stamp the image onto envelope and paper.
3. Sprinkle image with embossing powder and remove excess powder (optional).
4. Heat and emboss the image (optional).

"Sending All My Love" Greeting Card

The color insert in the center of the book displays this creation.
This card design shows four popular ways to color a stamped image:

- Gel and Milky Pens
- Pastels and Chalks
- Markers
- Watercolors

Materials

Black pigment inkpad with clear or black embossing powder

Rubberstamp (country mailbox with flowers)

Clear vellum paper plus scraps

Paper plate or scrap paper

Heat source

Gel and milky pens or pastels /chalks, markers, or watercolor
paints

Scissors and craft utility knife

Scraps of decorative or handmade paper

Scrap of cardstock cut into a long 2 × ½-inch rectangle

Permanent black fine-tipped marker

Blank card or cardstock

Optional: Butterfly paper punch, paper glue or 2-Way Glue or
Tombow Adhesive or double-stick tape

Instructions

1. Ink the stamp and stamp the image onto vellum paper.

2. Sprinkle image with embossing powder and remove excess
   powder.

3. Heat and emboss the image. Allow to cool.

4. Color the image as you wish.

5. Trim image on vellum into a square or rectangular shape (see step GC-1).

6. Using a craft utility knife make a vertical slit along the opening of the mailbox (see step GC-2).

7. Double mat the vellum image onto scrap pieces of decorative paper, trimming excess to leave a clean border around vellum (see step GC-3). (Remember vellum is translucent and you'll see the color of the decorative paper through the vellum.)

8. Slide the rectangular scrap of cardstock into the mailbox slit to see if it fits smoothly (see step GC-4); trim accordingly if it's too big. It should look like an envelope peeking out of the open mailbox.

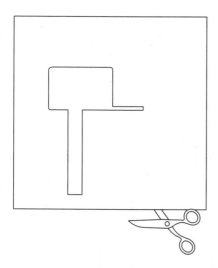

Step GC-1. Trim image on vellum into a square or rectangular shape.

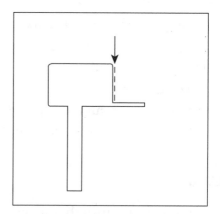

Step GC-2. Using a craft utility knife make a vertical slit along the opening of the mailbox.

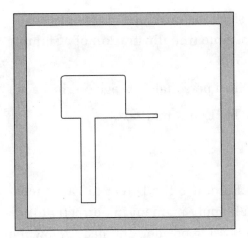

Step GC-3. Double mat the vellum image onto scrap pieces of decorative paper, trimming excess to leave a clean border around vellum.

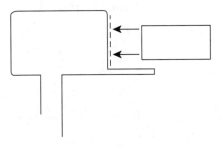

Step GC-4. Slide the rectangular scrap of cardstock into the mailbox slit to see if it fits smoothly.

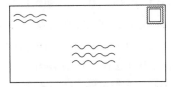

Step GC-5. Use your fine-tipped marker to draw a simple line illustration of a stamp and address.

9. Once you get the correct size faux envelope, use your fine-tipped marker to draw a simple line illustration of a stamp and address (see step GC-5).

10. Flip faux envelope and write a personal message on the back.

11. Place miniature envelope back into mailbox.

Variation

With the leftover scraps of vellum, use the Direct to Paper technique found in chapter 4. You'll apply pigment ink directly to the vellum, sprinkle with clear embossing powder, and heat. Allow the paper to cool, then punch out the butterflies with a butterfly paper punch. Apply a butterfly here and there on the front of the card with paper glue. This technique is a wonderful way to use scraps of paper. The embossed paper can be used in collage or layering techniques. You can also punch out shapes using paper punches. (One of the first rules of rubberstamping is never throw out scraps of paper! The scraps come in handy for smaller projects.)

 # "Christmas Trees Sparkle" Greeting Cards

Guess what? Both the trees on this card—tall and short—are made from the same stamp! This design illustrates how creative you can get by using your stamp images in whole or in part. These cards could have been done by creating a mask and stamping all images directly to the cardstock, but I chose to stamp the images on un-ruled index cards and then cut and trim the trees to different sizes. This allowed me to layer the trees to give more depth to the card front. (See an example of one finished card on the color insert in the center of the book.)

Materials

Black pigment or clear embossing ink inkpad

Rubberstamp: evergreen or other pine tree with snow (pick a stamp
  that has sections or layers that create the tree—as shown in the
  color insert example)

Unruled index cards

Gold, silver, or patina embossing powder (or three colors of
  embossing powder of your choice)

Paper plate or scrap paper

Heat source

Coloring of your choice (markers, pastels/chalks, color pencils,
  or watercolors)

Scissors

Red cardstock and matching envelope

Paper glue or 2-Way Glue or Tombow Adhesive or double-stick
  tape

Instructions

1. Ink the stamp with embossing ink or pigment ink.

2. Stamp the image onto unlined/unruled index card.

3. Sprinkle image with embossing powder and remove excess
    powder.

4. Heat and emboss the image. Allow to cool.

5. Repeat steps 1 through 4 until you create the number of
    trees you want on your card (the color photo shows a card
    with two trees, but feel free to do this step several times
    for more trees), using all the different colors of embossing
    powders.

6. Color the tree(s) you made from step 5.

7. Cut the trees from index cards. One or more of the trees can be shortened by cutting away the widest bottom section of the tree. If you have more than two trees, cut away an additional bottom section, and you have the smallest tree.

8. Start to play with different arrangements of the trees on the front and on the inside of the greeting card. You are free to duplicate my arrangements or have fun creating your own.

9. When you are happy with your arrangement, glue the images to the front and inside of the card with glue or adhesive of your choice.

"Star Gazing" Greeting Cards

Tea-bag folding (see figure 3) is very popular with stampers. (Anything with paper is popular with stampers!) Tea-bag folding is a form of origami using very small pieces of paper squares and triangles. The name came from the fact that the art of folding was originally done with the papers used to package tea bags. Beginners should consider using origami paper to practice folding the simple star used in this card design. Origami paper is designed to crease without damaging the paper and the paper's design or pattern. Once you get the hang of this basic tea-bag folding pattern, experiment with other papers. This finished card is featured in the color insert in the center of the book.

Materials

Origami paper
Scissors

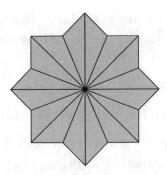

Figure 3. An example of tea-bag folding.

Paper glue or 2-Way Glue or Tombow Adhesive or double-stick
tape

Foil gift-wrap paper or vellum paper

Green cardstock (or color of your choice) and matching envelope

Black pigment or clear embossing inkpad with black, gold, and
patina embossing powder (or colors of your choice)

Rubberstamp: "This is not art" word stamp (or other expression)

Paper plate or scrap paper

Heat source

Instructions

1. Using the origami paper, cut four 5-centimeter squares.

2. Cut each square in half diagonally, making two triangles (see
step SG-1).

3. Fold each triangle in half, then unfold (see step SG-2). This
makes a center line.

4. Fold each corner of the wide end to the top of the triangle,
making crease lines (see step SG-3).

5. On each side of the triangle, fold the crease lines from step SG-3 to the center, folding the point to the outside (see step SG-4).

6. Turn the triangle over (see step SG-5).

7. Repeat steps 2 through 6 with the other three squares.

8. Slide the visible corner point of one folded square behind the folded center of another folded square, gluing them together; connect all the folded squares until you form the star (see step SG-6).

9. Place the star on a square of vellum paper and trim around the star, leaving a slight border (see step SG-7).

10. Glue vellum star to top center of card.

11. Repeat steps 9 and 10 using the gift-wrap foil, except make the foil star the exact same size as the origami star (it should be smaller than the gold star).

12. Adhere the gift-wrap foil star to the gold vellum star cut-out, allowing all star points to show.

13. Adhere the origami star to the top center of card front, again letting all points show.

14. Ink the word stamp with embossing ink or pigment ink. Stamp "This is not art" (or other phrase) directly to the card, below the star.

15. Sprinkle image with embossing powder and remove excess powder.

16. Heat. Allow to cool.

17. Repeat steps 1 and 2 several times, using all the different colors of embossing powders.

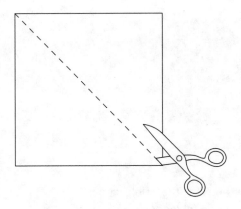

Step SG-1. Cut each square in half diagonally, making two triangles.

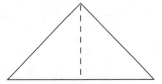

Step SG-2. Fold each triangle in half, then unfold.

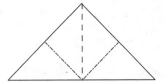

Step SG-3. Fold each corner of the wide end to the top of the triangle, making crease lines.

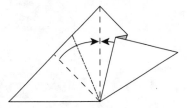

Step SG-4. On each side of the triangle, fold the crease lines from step SG-3 to the center, folding the point to the outside.

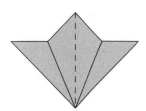

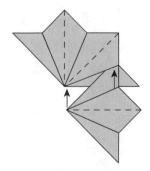

Step SG-5. Turn the triangle over.

Step SG-6. Slide the visible corner point of one folded square behind the folded center of another folded square, gluing them together; connect all the folded squares until you form the star.

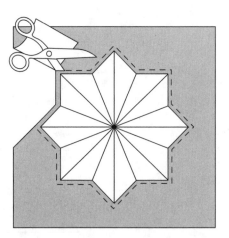

Step SG-7. Place the star on a square of vellum paper and trim around the star, leaving a slight border.

Don't Stop at the Rainbow

Can't find the perfect color embossing powder? Make your own! You'll have fun experimenting with combining colors. Here are some great recipes to start you off.

Antique Gold

3 teaspoons gold embossing powder

1 teaspoon black embossing powder

Beach

½ teaspoon sterilized sand

½ teaspoon clear embossing powder

¼ teaspoon gold ultra-fine glitter

Celestial

2 teaspoons clear embossing powder

1 teaspoon metallic blue ultra-fine glitter

1 teaspoon gold ultra-fine glitter

Glimmering Gold

1 teaspoon pearl gold embossing powder

1 teaspoon gold embossing powder

¼ teaspoon gold ultra-fine glitter

Gold Galore

1 teaspoon copper embossing powder

1 teaspoon gold embossing powder

½ teaspoon gold ultra-fine glitter

Granite

½ teaspoon black embossing powder

½ teaspoon white embossing powder

½ teaspoon silver embossing powder

(continues)

(continued from page 115)

Magic Crystal

2 teaspoons stone gray embossing powder

1 teaspoon silver embossing powder

1 teaspoon crystal embossing powder

½ teaspoon halo ultra-fine glitter

½ teaspoon lavender ultra-fine glitter

Midnight Magic

1 teaspoon black embossing powder

1 teaspoon iridescent embossing powder

⅛ teaspoon lavender ultra-fine glitter

⅛ teaspoon pink ultra-fine glitter

Patriot's Favorite

1 teaspoon aurora blue embossing powder

¼ teaspoon Christmas red embossing powder

1 teaspoon crystal embossing powder

1 teaspoon clear embossing powder

½ teaspoon halo ultra-fine glitter

Precious Metals

1 teaspoon gold embossing powder

1 teaspoon silver embossing powder

1 teaspoon copper embossing powder

1 teaspoon iridescent embossing powder

¼ teaspoon halo ultra-fine glitter

Robin's Egg Blue

1½ teaspoons metallic blue embossing powder

1 teaspoon silver embossing powder

½ teaspoon gold ultra-fine glitter

½ teaspoon blue-violet glitter

Royal Violet

1 teaspoon metallic violet embossing powder

½ teaspoon crystal embossing powder

¼ teaspoon blue-violet ultra-fine glitter

Seascape

¼ teaspoon metallic blue embossing powder

½ teaspoon crystal embossing powder

¼ teaspoon bright blue glitter

½ teaspoon fluorescent green embossing powder

½ teaspoon turquoise embossing powder

Shimmering Sky

1 teaspoon turquoise embossing powder

½ heaping teaspoon clear embossing powder

¼ teaspoon lavender ultra-fine glitter

⅛ teaspoon mint ultra-fine glitter

¼ teaspoon pink ultra-fine glitter

Snowburst

1 teaspoon white embossing powder

½ teaspoon iridescent embossing powder

¼ teaspoon blue-violet ultra-fine glitter

Sparkling Blue

1 teaspoon metallic blue embossing powder

1 teaspoon turquoise embossing powder

1 teaspoon crystal embossing powder

½ teaspoon blue-violet ultra-fine glitter

(continues)

(continued from page 117)

Sparkling Shamrocks

1 teaspoon Christmas green embossing powder

1 teaspoon clear embossing powder

1 teaspoon iridescent embossing powder

½ teaspoon mint ultra-fine glitter

Spring Sparkles

1 teaspoon iridescent embossing powder

½ teaspoon pink ultra-fine glitter

½ teaspoon lavender ultra-fine glitter

½ teaspoon mint ultra-fine glitter

Sunburst

1 teaspoon fluorescent orange embossing powder

1 teaspoon yellow embossing powder

1 teaspoon iridescent embossing powder

¼ teaspoon gold ultra-fine glitter

Thistle

½ teaspoon clear embossing powder

½ teaspoon magenta embossing powder

½ teaspoon pink fluorescent embossing powder

½ teaspoon magenta glitter

White Gold

½ teaspoon gold embossing powder

½ teaspoon silver embossing powder

½ teaspoon copper embossing powder

Wood Frames

Enhance your photos with these delightful rubberstamped wood frames. Stamping on wood is a great way to display creative designs. The wood makes these frames unique, and with the right stamping, they're the perfect fit for any photo! See the color insert in the center of the book for pictures of these completed projects.

"Ivy Leaves" Frame

Simple and basic—perfect for any photo. To see this finished project, turn to the color insert in the center of the book.

Materials

Wood frame
Acrylic paint (color of your choice)
Paintbrush
Green ink stamp pad
Ivy leaves foam stamp (or leaf stamp of your choice—regular or foam)
Green embossing powder (or color of your choice)
Heat gun

Instructions

1. Plan out your design (see color insert for example).

2. Paint frame with acrylic paint and let dry for 24 hours.

3. Ink the stamp, then stamp your first image on the left side of the frame.

4. Sprinkle embossing powder on the image.

5. Heat the embossing powder.

6. Repeat steps 3 through 5, stamping each leaf image from left to right across the frame.

7. Allow finished frame to air dry for 24 hours.

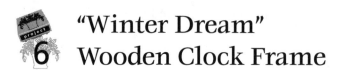

"Winter Dream" Wooden Clock Frame

This frame really captures the moment. It works well with any wintry photos. See the color insert in the center of the book for a glance at this finished project.

Materials

Wood frame with clock insert (Walnut Hollow)
Acrylic color of your choice
Tree stamp
Clear embossing ink
Black, white, and Bridal embossing powder (Ranger brand)
Heat gun
Spray sealer

Instructions

1. Plan out your design (see color insert for example).

2. Paint frame with acrylic paint and let dry for 24 hours.

3. Ink the stamp.

4. Stamp your first image on the left side of the frame. (Note that you will actually see full trees only on the sides.)

5. Sprinkle embossing powder on the image.

6. Heat the embossing powder.

7. Allow to cool.

8. Repeat steps 3 through 8, stamping each tree image from left to right across the frame.

9. Tap embossing ink along the bottom of frame.

10. Sprinkle with white glossy embossing powder.

11. Heat the white glossy embossing powder.

12. After the white glossy embossing powder is completely embossed, slowly heat around entire frame with heat gun.

13. Quickly and lightly sprinkle with the Bridal embossing powder and continue to heat and melt the powder on the frame. All you want is a very light coating of the Bridal embossing powder, which is more translucent and glittery than plain and solid white.

14. Allow frame to cool.

15. Spray several light coats of sealer, and allow to dry completely.

16. Insert clock.

Ceramic Tile and Glass

At one time these non-porous surfaces were simply not practical for stamping. But rubberstampers, being a persistent lot, have now found methods to make these easy to stamp with images that will last a long time. The new glossy/enamel paints have removed the fuss of stamping these surfaces. Imagine all the possibilities for your home and all the ideas that can turn into gift-giving projects. Try your hand at this clever design. See examples of this set in the color insert in the center of the book.

Glass Plate with Matching Tile Trivet

Materials

Plain glass plate

PermEnamel Conditioner

PermEnamel paint in color(s) of your choice (or other glass paint, but read label for directions if not using PermEnamel since you will have to heat-set other brands of paint)

Foam or large flat brush

Craft stamp of your choice (this is not a rubberstamp, but one created with foam for stamping walls, fabric, and other surfaces with stamp paint or acrylic glazes)

Several paper plates and paper towels

Acrylic paint (light and medium shades of green)

Tile square(s).

Optional: Spray sealer

Instructions

1. Plan out your design (see color insert for example).

2. Prepare glass plate by applying conditioner to back of plate (you will be decorating the back of the plate).

3. Allow to dry completely.

4. Brush a thin coat of PermEnamel to the stamp (if you use more than one color on your plate, start with the lightest color first).

5. Stamp the image two or three times to the back of the plate. Don't re-ink (re-apply paint). Because you didn't apply more paint, the second and third prints will add depth to the overall design.

6. Clean the stamp by pressing it several times onto the paper towel.

7. If using more than one color, repeat step 5 with each color, using the lightest colors first. Clean the stamp between colors.

8. Leave plate backside up to dry for 24 hours. You may wish to apply a top coat of sealer after the 24 hours for longer life. Do not machine-wash plate for 7 days to allow paint to completely cure.

To Stamp Tile

1. Apply a thin coat of conditioner to the front of your tile. Allow to dry.

2. Brush a thin coat of a PermEnamel to the stamp (if you're using more than one color on your tile, start with the lightest color).

3. Stamp one to two images to the tile. Don't re-ink (re-apply paint). Because you didn't apply more paint, the second- and third-generation images will add depth to the overall design.

4. Allow to dry 24 hours and apply top sealer, if desired.

5. Do not machine-wash tile for 7 days.

Memo Cubes and Bookmarks

An office is better with creative decoration—and clever bookmarks make reading even more fun. See some examples of these creative designs in the color insert in the center of the book.

"Don't Forget!" Memo Cubes

How will you miss an appointment with this decorative reminder? A perfect gift for your favorite office mate!

Materials

Memo cube
Brush or lint-free towel
Dye inkpad
Stamps of your choice

Instructions

Note: Do not use pigment ink and don't try to emboss the design for this project. I experimented with various techniques and discovered that this project must use a dye ink and inkpad.

1. Check the sides of your memo cube for a clean, smooth surface before stamping it. Brush (with a brush or lint-free towel, not with your fingers) any lint, dust, or particles.

2. Ink your stamp. In one hand hold the cube firmly, and tap the side you will stamp to a hard surface. It's important that all the leaves of paper are aligned and smooth. If the cube of paper is not aligned, there may be areas that your rubber image will skip or not ink!

3. Stamp one side of the cube.

4. Allow the ink to dry for about 2 to 3 minutes.

5. Repeat steps 2 to 4 for the remaining sides. One of the sides will have a rubbery surface that binds and holds the pad together. You can stamp this side, but stamp it last since it may take longer for the ink to dry on this less-porous surface.

Note: Use one big image or many smaller images for this project or even mix and match sides!

Variation: Gift-wrap it! Allow the ink to dry completely. Using a length of plastic wrap, place the cube at the center and bring plastic wrap up the sides. You may tie off with a length of ribbon or use a wrap strip.

"Fall Leaf" Bookmark

What a clever treat for kids heading back to school in the fall! This simple bookmark will mark their place and let them know you were thinking of them. See the color insert in the center of the book for an example of this bookmark.

Materials

Large leaf foam or rubberstamp
Colorbox Pigment Inkpad
White cardstock
Clear embossing powder
Heat source
Scissors
Plain bookmark
Milky gel pen
Paper glue

Instructions

1. Ink your stamp across several colors of the Colorbox.

2. Stamp the image onto cardstock.

3. Sprinkle with clear embossing powder.

4. Heat.

5. Allow to cool.

6. Cut out the leaf.

7. Place the leaf down onto the bookmark at front (the sample shown used a dark color paper for the bookmark).

8. Write your verse using the milky gel pen.

9. Allow to dry.

10. Adhere leaf to bookmark with paper glue.

"Leaping Frog" Bookmark

Show some motion with this leaping frog! It's fun and will bring a smile to anyone who receives it. This bookmark is featured in the color insert in the center of the book.

Materials

Large foam or rubberstamp frog (Duncan's Small Frog Foam Stamp was used in the color insert)
Colorbox Pigment Inkpad
White cardstock
Clear embossing powder
Heat source
Scissors
Bookmark
Milky gel pen
Paper glue

Instructions

1. Ink your stamp across several colors of the Colorbox.

2. Stamp the image onto cardstock.

3. Sprinkle with clear embossing powder.

4. Heat.

5. Allow to cool and cut out the frog.

6. Place the frog down onto the bookmark at front (the sample shown used a dark color paper for the bookmark).

7. Write your verse, using the milky gel pen.

8. Allow to dry.

9. Adhere frog to bookmark.

"Remembrance" Bookmark

The pansy symbolizes remembrance, which is a beautiful way to say "I am thinking of you."

Materials

Black pigment inkpad
Small rubberstamp pansy
White cardstock
Clear embossing powder
Heat source
Scissors
Paper glue
Bookmark
Milky gel pen (optional)

Instructions

1. Ink your stamp.

2. Stamp two images for each flower you want on your book-mark onto white cardstock.

3. Sprinkle with clear embossing powder.

4. Heat.

5. Allow to cool.

6. Color your pansies with milky gel pen or other coloring tool.

7. Cut out each flower (see step RB-1). One pansy will be complete (image 1), while the other will have everything cut away but the inner part of the pansy (image 2).

8. Glue (image 2) to the whole flower from image 1 (see step RB-2). This gives the pansies a three-dimensional look and feel.

9. Repeat steps 1 through 5 (using different colors) to make two more flowers.

10. Place the flowers down onto the bookmark at front (the sample shown used a dark color paper for the bookmark).

11. Write your verse using the milky gel pen.

12. Allow to dry.

13. Glue pansies to bookmark.

"Coffee Anyone?" Bookmark

Give this bookmark to someone who likes to study in a coffee shop! See the color insert in the center of the book for a finished look at this project.

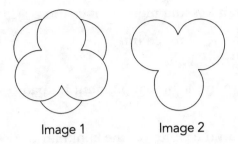 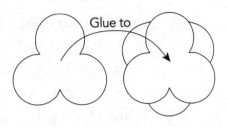

Image 1   Image 2

Step RB-1. Cut out each flower. One pansy will be complete, while the other will have everything cut away but the inner part of the pansy.

Step RB-2. Glue the inner flower you cut from image 2 to the whole flower from image 1.

Materials

Pink, brown, blue, and silver pigment inkpads (or colors of your choice)
Foam stamps: Coffee or teapot, coffee beans, coffee mug with steam
Bookmark
Clear enamel embossing powder
Heat source

Instructions

1. Ink your coffee pot or teapot stamp in the pink pigment inkpad (or other color).

2. Stamp your image, centered, directly on the top portion of the bookmark.

3. Remove stamp.

4. Sprinkle with clear enamel embossing powder.

5. Heat.

6. Immediately apply another coat of clear enamel embossing powder.

7. Heat again (using the overembossing method in chapter 4).

8. Repeat steps 6 and 7 until your stamped image is completely smooth and shiny.

9. Ink your coffee beans stamp in the brown pigment inkpad (or other color).

10. Stamp your image directly in the center of the bookmark.

11. Repeat steps 3 through 8.

12. Bring your blue (or other color) pigment inkpad to the foam stamp, coating only the coffee mug (not the steam).

13. Bring your silver (or color of your choice, other than blue) pigment inkpad to the foam stamp, coating only the steam (not the coffee mug).

14. Stamp your image, centered, directly on the bottom of the bookmark.

15. Repeat steps 3 through 8.

Creating Backgrounds

Backgrounds are vital in the artistry of cards and other stamping creations. There are dozens and dozens of ways to create clever backgrounds, as you can discover by experimenting every time you sit down to stamp.

I prefer to use a full sheet of paper when playing with background ideas and then to cut the size I need from the full sheet. The scraps are great for small matting needs and for collage work. Here are some of my favorite background techniques.

Bubble Fun

Materials

Large glass bowl, water, dishwashing liquid, concentrated watercolor or acrylic paint, drinking straw, watercolor paper or other
heavyweight paper

Instructions

1. In a large glass bowl, combine 1 cup of water, 2 tablespoons
   of dishwashing liquid and several drops of concentrated watercolor or 2 tablespoons of acrylic paint. Mix well.

2. With drinking straw, blow air into the mixture to create bubbles. Bubbles must rise above top of bowl.

3. Tap paper to the bubbles. As bubbles explode, so do the colors
   onto the watercolor paper, creating a lovely bubble effect.

4. Add more colors and experiment with the mixtures.

Direct-to-Paper Flair

Materials

Rainbow Pigment Inkpad, paper, sponges, clear embossing powder,
and heat gun

Instructions

1. Apply pigment color(s) directly to paper. Use the whole
   inkpad or sponge color to paper.

2. Sprinkle clear embossing powder to entire inked area.
   Remove excess powder.

3. Heat.

Wild Webbing

Materials

Paper, spray can of webbing (different colors are available)

Instructions

1. In a well-ventilated indoor area or outside, lay your paper down on an old newspaper or other protective covering of the work area.

2. Shake can of webbing.

3. From different heights above the paper, spray webbing onto paper. The closer the can is to the paper, the thicker the webbing; the farther away from the paper, the finer the webbing.

4. Allow to dry completely.

   Variation: Experiment with different colors of webbing (black with touches of gold is fabulous!).

Textured Treasures

Materials

Paper, spray can of texture paint (lots of colors are available)

Instructions

1. In a well-ventilated indoor area or outside, lay your paper down on an old newspaper or other protective covering of the work area.

2. Shake can of spray paint.

3. From different heights above the paper, spray texture paint onto paper. The closer the can to the paper, the thicker the

texture; the farther away from the paper, the finer the texture. Several light coats of paint are better than one thick coat.

4. Allow to dry completely.

   Variation: Experiment with different colors. White with just a touch of granite or green looks perfect for nature and garden scenes.

A Wash of Watercolor

Materials

Wide flat brush, watercolor paints, paper or watercolor paper, and
   spritz water bottle

Instructions

Note: You can work on dry paper or moistened paper. Each will have a different end result.

1. Brush watercolor(s) onto paper, spritzing several times with mister before the paint dries.

2. Allow to dry before using.

   Variation: While the paper is still wet, sprinkle table salt onto it. This creates a starburst effect within the colors. Allow to dry, then brush off the salt.

Itch to Scratch

Materials

ScratchArt paper; scratching tool (toothpick, wire rake, or stylus).
   Optional: Spray fixative

Instructions

Note: There are many different colors, including neons and metallics, available in ScratchArt paper.

1. Place the paper with black side up.

2. Begin random scratching or trace a pattern onto the paper and scratch off the black waxy layer. The color will appear after the black is scratched off.

3. When finished scratching, spray a light coat of fixative, or rub your fingers across the paper. Your body oil will set the wax.

Note: While preparing this paper, work with clean hands. You don't want any body oil on the paper until you are ready to set it.

You may feel you don't want to scratch off all the black, but the best results often come from removing almost all the black waxy top coat. Experiment!

Fun and Assorted Stamping Tips from the Pros

Many very talented rubberstamp artists have generously shared some secrets to better stamping.

■ Label all your scissors and rotary cutter blades. Stick to using one pair for papers and a separate one for materials. This helps keep blades sharper longer. Rotary blades last longer and work better if you keep them clean and oiled. Sewing machine oil works very well.

■ While stamping, keep a moist sponge nearby. When you're done with a stamp, put it on the sponge. This will not only help clean the stamp, but will keep the ink moist until you're ready to stamp it again (in the same stamping session).

■ Don't throw away those clear film canisters. You can use them to store beads, embossing powder, or glitter.

■ When you purchase a new pad, purchase the re-inker at the same time—especially if it's a color you will use frequently.

■ Keep your embossing powders and glitters in sandwich containers. Trying to funnel the excess back into those tiny jars is a major challenge.

■ Place foil under cardstock to help speed up the embossing process. The foil will reflect the heat back to the cardstock.

■ Trace cardboard or paper templates on acetate to create a longer-lasting, ink-resistant template.

■ To remove excess embossing powder from your card before heating, lightly touch the offending areas with a fine, damp paintbrush. You will get better results if you lightly push toward the image, because static electricity in the plastic powder will attract the granules toward each other.

■ Store your ink pads upside down and lying flat to keep the ink at the top of the pad and in an even layer.

■ To clean metallic pigment inks off rubber, try inking your stamp with clear embossing ink before applying the metallic ink. The embossing ink should create a thin protective barrier between rubber and ink.

■ Ink your stamp with an all-over, light touch to pick up a nice amount of ink. Inking with too much pressure will cause an excess of ink on the rubber surface, which can lead to ink blotches. If you pick up too much ink, blot some of it off with a paper towel.

- If you are having trouble getting your embossing powder to stick while using a heat tool, try heating the card from underneath. The heat will melt the powder enough to make it stick, and keeps it from blowing off when you resume heating from above.

- If you use markers on your rubberstamp, drink something warm (like tea, coffee, or cocoa) while you stamp. It will keep your breath nice and moist for breathing on your stamps.

- Avoid stamping on porous papers such as construction paper or lightweight typing paper. Most inks will bleed or feather into the surrounding paper fibers.

- When using clear acetate (overhead transparency sheets), be sure to choose one that is marked for laser printer or copy machine so it will withstand the heat needed for embossing.

- Use freezer paper for gift bags or gift wrap. Stamp and decorate the paper side, not the wax-coated side.

- Add material to cards by ironing it on with fusible webbing, which can be found in most craft stores and all fabric stores. Fusible webbing works great to glue down all edges smoothly. Use a layer of white tissue paper to keep from scorching your cards.

- Never store your stamps in direct sunlight or near a heat source.

- Never touch your stamps with oily or greasy hands.

- Never use alcohol on your stamps. The solvent will dry out the rubber and seriously reduce the life span of your stamps.

- Never run your stamps under the faucet to clean them. The water will penetrate the wood and weaken the adhesive between the wood, cushion, and rubber, causing the stamp to fall apart.

- Place your card on a potholder to protect your table surface when applying the heat to emboss. Alternatively, you can use the lid of an old shoebox and place your card in the lid. This way, the powder will not fly outside the lid when you apply heat.

- Use tape to remove fuzz and glitter from stamps before inking.

- Always clean your stamps after use, and when changing ink color. Spray some water on a paper towel and blot until the stamp is clean. Some alternatives to paper towels for cleaning stamps include baby wipes, kitchen dish towels, or a moist sponge.

- Use an old toothbrush to clean the stubborn spots on your stamps.

- Use dryer sheets to wipe down surfaces to get all the static off before embossing them. This helps reduce unwanted flakes.

- Always apply heat to embossing powder in circular motion.

- When flocking, allow the glue to dry for several hours for the best result.

- Layer different colors and types of paper to give a card some extra dimension, and to allow you to use smaller stamps as a focus.

- Always start with the lightest color first, and finish up with the darkest colors, when using markers on your stamps.

- Add a very nice touch to a special card with three-dimensional elements, such as raffia, charms, beads, and ribbon. Don't be afraid to experiment!

- Use dryer sheets for layering instead of mulberry paper. Try tinting them by adding color with a brayer.

- Try mixing a little of your embossing powders together with perhaps some glitter or tiny confetti to create special effects.

- Use tiny stamps for stamping on address labels printed from your home computer.

- Fill an un-inked pad with food coloring for stamping on cookies! They make great birthday and holiday treats!

- Incorporate stickers into your projects. They are lots of fun to use, and can add a three-dimensional effect.

- If you are going on a long plane ride or car trip, but don't want to bring your stamps with you, create some stamped cards beforehand. Then just take your color pens or markers along so you can color the images during your trip. This will limit the supplies you need to take with you yet allow you to be productive as you travel.

- Join swaps! Your stamping will improve by leaps and bounds. And you'll have the fun of seeing the artwork of others.

- Save your paper scraps!! They could come in handy for later projects.

chapter 6

Your Crafts Vision

▼▼▼

LET'S FACE IT: RUBBERSTAMPING as an art and craft, is not a cheap proposition. I'm often asked why rubberstamps are so expensive compared to other art and craft materials. The answer is simple: The basic ingredients of a rubberstamp are rubber and wood. Neither is cheap in today's economy. However, if properly cared for, a rubberstamp can last a lifetime.

And speaking of money, if I had a nickel for every person who told me that he or she wished they had the freedom to work from their home and wished they were talented enough to sell crafts, I would have enough capital to start a hundred small cottage-industry businesses. Everyone has creativity within him or her just waiting to emerge. The difference between wishing, dreaming, or wanting to do something and doing it is simply sitting down and mapping out a plan. A simple business plan is a blueprint of your goals and the game plan you'll follow to accomplish your goals. Even if you choose only to supplement your hobby or to sell rubberstamp art part-time, a written plan will give you confidence to pursue your dreams.

Creativity may seem spontaneous; however, the true nature of creativity is such that an individual can *learn* to be creative. When others have stopped asking why and how and who and when, the creative person still continues to be curious and ask questions. You may not even realize what you're doing when you create a design with rubberstamps, but you are using a definite thought process to balance colors and harmonize design. You can use this same process to create a blueprint for success that will help you profit from your talent.

Putting your dreams into writing may seem to take the "fun" out of using your creativity and skills—and it can be intimidating—but a business plan is a tool that will help you in all areas of your life. Planning ahead is a habit worth acquiring.

Before you move on to the second part of this book, take time to think about your dreams and goals. Think about your talents and skills. List the assets and liabilities you bring to the table. Write down your dreams, goals, and plans for selling your rubberstamp creations. Figure out what questions you need to ask. Specify the time you have available to pursue your dream. Make lists of short-term goals and long-term goals. Break the lists down into smaller, more achievable steps. It's a starting point, and a wonderful documentation of your dreams. I still have my original 5-year plan. When I'm feeling stressed or worried about meeting new goals, I often take a moment to flip through my old business journals. I can hardly believe how far I've come since my first crafting project.

▼▼▼▼▼▼▼▼▼▼▼▼▼▼▼▼▼▼▼▼▼▼▼▼▼

Did you know???

Writing up a business plan is the most successful and proven way to meet goals.

▲▲▲▲▲▲▲▲▲▲▲▲▲▲▲▲▲▲▲▲▲▲▲▲▲

Because it can be overwhelming to sit down and chart your business course, many people put it off or don't do it at all. Following is an attempt to make it less intimidating. I've created a list that breaks down what you need to consider into small, more digestible components.

To Thine Own Self Be True

You are the most important asset of your business goals. Take some time to consider your feelings about starting a business.

1. List five reasons you like to rubberstamp.

2. List at least five skills, talents, and assets you can contribute to this hobby as an artist.

3. List any weaknesses, liabilities, or obstacles you'll have to overcome if you decide to sell your creations.

4. Determine, by asking yourself, if you have the motivation and determination to work on your own. Do you have the time-management skills to schedule your workday and your personal life?

5. Determine whether or not your family will support your efforts. Will your friends?

6. Decide if you want to make only one-of-a-kinds, or will you make multiples.

7. List what rubberstamping techniques are most interesting or challenging to you.

8. List your main goal in rubberstamping as an artistic stamper, and as a home business owner.

9. List any obstacles you see that might prevent you from reaching your goals.

10. List any ways you can come up with to overcome these obstacles. Is there someone who has the knowledge or skill you need? Is there information available that can educate you? Is there another direction you can turn and still meet your dream or goal?

Getting Started

When you really consider starting your own business, it is important to know how to measure your business's success. The best way to do that is to visualize a clear picture of what success is to you, then create goals for yourself to obtain that success.

1. What is your number 1 goal? Can it be measured? Is there a finish line or way to know when you've accomplished this goal?

2. Do you plan to support your hobby? Earn extra household income with part-time efforts? Earn extra leisure spending money with part-time efforts? Or do you want to work at rubberstamp art full-time?

3. How will you define success? By creative achievement? By your financial bottom line? By the freedom of working for yourself? By the growth of your market? By the reaction of your family and friends?

4. How much time can you realistically dedicate to your endeavor?

5. What other responsibilities do you have? Rank them in order of priority to you. Rank in order of priority to your family and friends. How do the rankings compare? How do you feel about the comparison?

Day to Day, Year to Year

It's important to know what geographical areas are potentially successful to sell your crafts. Know what to expect in your local area, then give yourself realistic short-term and long-term objectives based on the information.

1. What do you wish to accomplish during a day, a week, a month, and a year of rubberstamping?

2. Do you have room within your home to dedicate space to your work?

3. Does your local area support the arts and crafts? Will there be enough business opportunities to let you earn the income you desire? Will you have to market outside your own area? Do you want to do that?

4. What does your city, county, or state require from you in paperwork or licenses to start a business? Do you understand all the city, county, and state regulations and laws? Do you need to consult with an attorney? (See chapter 11 for help in answering these questions.)

To Market and Sell Your Rubberstamp Creations

There are so many small considerations that add up to the big picture. Merchandising, marketing, promoting, and advertising play a major role in success. Pinpoint your strengths and weaknesses— thrive on your strengths and improve the weak areas.

1. What makes your rubberstamp designs unique? What are the selling points?

2. How must your work be displayed? Do your items need explanation or do they sell on their own merits?

3. Will you need to package your work? Is the work fragile or does it need special handling?

4. If you had to come up with a business name for your endeavor, what would you call your business? Does the name

limit you? Is the name self-explanatory? Will a customer remember you by your business name?

5. Is there a market for your style of rubberstamp art and craft? Are people showing an interest in what you make?

6. What selling markets are available in your local area? Craft co-op? Craft mall? Art or craft gallery? Annual art and craft shows?

7. Do you want to sell directly to the consumer?

8. Do you want to mail order your work? Do you have space to handle the packaging and shipping supplies needed? How will you cover the costs of handling and shipping?

9. Do you want to sell on the World Wide Web? Create or maintain a Web site for sales? Be a part of a large Web site?

Handy Hint

Stay true to your own creative vision, rather than try to copy the characteristics and personality of other artists. Developing your own style will keep you focused. Don't imitate, originate!

Teaching and Demonstrating

Sometimes the best way to realize what you know—and even learn new things—is to teach others. This may seem far-fetched when you first start out, but if you stick to your hobby, teaching or demonstration could be a very achievable goal.

1. Do you want to teach others how to do your craft?

2. Are there places you can teach? Out of your home? At a retail craft store? Local art museum?

3. Do you want to sell your design (written instructions) to a magazine? Or maybe write a book?

4. How will you keep current on trends, colors, textures, motifs, techniques, lifestyles, and your consumer?

Business Is Business

The most dreaded aspect of turning a hobby into a business is that it may end up turning what you enjoy into a boring job! Careful planning and evaluation ease you into the business world, letting you continue to find joy in your creativity.

1. List at least five skills, talents, and assets you can bring to this endeavor as a businessperson.

2. Do you want to be a sole proprietor? Form a partnership? Incorporate?

3. Do you have starting capital? Can you create a company budget?

4. Do you have a system of accounting?

5. Do you want employees? Hire your family or friends?

6. Do you want to work from your home?

Profit and Bottom Line

Don't feel like a failure if you can't do everything alone. Figure out what business tasks you can handle and what is better left to the experts.

1. What business records do you need to keep? How will you organize them?

2. How will you price your rubberstamp art and designs? How are similar items priced in the marketplace? How does your pricing compare?

3. Do you need to consult an accountant or CPA?

4. Do you understand the federal income tax forms required of you for the extra income? Are you willing to keep all your receipts and invoices in order, filed and understandable?

5. Do you want to set up a business checking account? Can you keep your personal and business finances separate?

Reality Check and Planning for the Future

Review your opinions, ideas, and dreams and visualize yourself in the future. Do you like what you see?

1. Where do you want to be a year from now in relation to dreams, goals, personal life, and business?

2. Where do you want to be 5 years from now?

3. Where do you want to be 10 years from now in relation to dreams, goals, personal life, and business?

4. In your heart and mind, is there nothing you want to do more than to reach your dream or goal? Can you make the necessary sacrifices? Do you have a clear vision of what you hope to accomplish? Can you keep motivated? Can you keep positive?

As you turn this page you will begin Part Two of this book. Part Two is dedicated to the business aspects of rubberstamping for profit. But never forget that part of rubberstamping, even if you decide to sell your work, should always be fun! I wrote this book because I could enjoy rubberstamping both for fun and for profit. *Profit* seems like a cold emotionless word to associate with an art or craft, but for me, selling my work is a way to continue learning and developing an art and craft genre I love.

The possibilities are endless. As you've seen, and will continue to see, throughout this book, many people just like you who have turned their hobbies into profitable businesses. You may discover

Trend Watch

At times it may seem overwhelming to keep up with trends, but staying current is an important part of having a competitive edge over other artists. Here are some timely, enjoyable ways to keep on top of consumer favorites:

- Attend trade and consumer shows

- Read the art/craft consumer and trade journals

- Watch the gift market and visit gift shops

- Read home décor magazines

- Visit art and craft shows

- Observe the displays in furniture and home accessory shops

- Keep color, fabric, ribbon, lace, yarn, and other swatches handy

- Keep a notebook and pen handy for quick notes

- Keep a filing system organized by themes like Americana, Garden, and Victorian or by crafts like paper, painting, jewelry, or dolls

- Find common themes of what appeals to you . . . these are the trends

that you love designing rubberstamp images. You may discover that hands-on design is your true passion, and you'll create one-of-a-kind collages to sell to the public through galleries. Or maybe your journey will begin by teaching others to rubberstamp or selling your rubberstamp designs to magazines.

Any time I have a new learning experience—personal or professional—I keep one thing in mind: What would I dare to accomplish if I knew I would not fail? Once I figure out what it is, I just go for it. I hope you will too. Who knows . . . someday you might even write a book on rubberstamping!

Part Two

For Profit

Profiting from Your Talent

▼▼▼▼▼▼▼▼▼▼▼▼▼▼▼▼▼▼▼▼▼▼▼▼▼▼▼▼▼▼▼▼▼▼▼▼▼▼

THE FIRST YEAR I SOLD my work, I did it as a hobby in the eyes of my family and the IRS. Before I committed myself to creating items full-time to sell, I wanted to make sure I really did enjoy the occupation. Moreover, I needed to make sure I was going to earn a profit for my efforts, or at least be compensated for my efforts in some way. The income earned that first year was listed in the category of "Extra Income" on our income tax forms. I could subtract out only supply costs, with very limited deductions. I had made a healthy profit for my efforts. I used my income from that first year to educate myself about creativity and the business principles of operating as a sole proprietorship. I could have been very happy just being involved with art and craft as a hobby—a hobby that could pay for itself. But during that first year, I discovered I wanted to make a career out of my newfound skills and talents.

When I started, I was lucky enough to have time to consider all the options of becoming a creative businessperson. But our lifestyles and our schedules seldom allow us such an extravagance today. Maybe it's time to take back our world and our time! Creativity in art and craft might help us do just that. We are so often in a hurry that we don't take time to review all the options available to

Who Is Selling Their Crafts?

I posted an interview on several art and craft Internet Newsgroups and found 12 individuals who made either part-time or full-time income in rubberstamping art and craft. Here's an overview from my research of who is selling and what they are selling. Note: Service is defined as demonstrating or teaching.

- When asked how long they had been in business as professional rubberstamp artists, I found that half of the individuals in the interview had sold their work for 1 to 2 years and the rest of the group has sold for 3 to 6 years, with the exception of one individual who has sold for more than 10 years.

- When asked how many hours each interviewee dedicated to his or her business, half of the group considered rubberstamping a source of additional income, working 10 to 20 hours a week, while a third of them considered it a part-time job, working 20 to 40 hours a week. The remaining two in the group rubberstamped as a full-time occupation and worked over 40 hours a week.

- When asked about annual incomes, it was determined that half the group made between $4,000 and $12,000 a year, while one-third made between $14,000 and $55,000 annually. Only two individuals made under $3,000 a year.

- When asked how many worked from home or off site, results showed that everyone in the group worked primarily from home.

us as creative souls. This book will help you find the knowledge to explore, spread your wings, and take off for some clear sailing. Above all else, no matter how much information you gather, read, and study, your individual road to selling your work will be just that: individual and unique. Many possibilities, opportunities, and challenges are available to you—just keep your eyes and mind open.

Artists, artisans, and craftspeople share a few common traits. We are always thinking creatively in one form or another. Our minds rarely shut off just because we are busy doing other things in our lives. We are driven to be perfect. We bore easily if we don't

- When asked how much each interviewee charged for goods or services, it was determined that the average fee for a demonstration was $20 per hour and the average fee for a class was $25. The average costs of items sold by the group was $5 to $10 for one-third of the group and $15 to $20 for one-third of the group. One person's average fee was $35, another person's was $50, another sold items for $75, and one person sold for as high as $100.

- When asked about top-selling items, the best-selling items for this group varied. The most popular items, given by one-fourth of the group, were greeting cards and/or tags. Two people claimed classes and demonstrations were their best selling items, two others said collages and framed art worked best for them. Jewelry was also a best selling item for two members. Other best-selling items were calendars, clothing or fabric, and rubberstamps.

- When asked what the group considered the best aspect of selling their crafts, five said being their own bosses or working for themselves, two said the creativity and new challenges, two said being able to work and still be home with their children, two more said having a family business, and one person said being able to work with a disability or physical challenges.

have new challenges. We believe it's normal to do five things at once, and we don't have the indulgence of downtime or quiet reflection.

You Are Your Art to Your Customer

This book is about rubberstamping for fun *and* for profit. Making a profit from your hobby will require you to become a salesperson. Few products (including art, crafts, and creativity) sell themselves without help from a salesperson. The consumer or buyer purchases items and products that he or she needs, wants, or just has to have. Stamped items can fall into all three categories, but most often the item will be a want or desire or a just-have-to-have-it! For true success, you will have to become the salesperson of your art.

I learned early in my career that consumers don't just buy a design from me and consider it the end of the sale. They are also buying a small piece of me as an artist or craftsperson. It's human nature to be curious about who made the item you are buying. It is also human nature to want those around us to be successful—when people like your personality *and* your product, they want to see you succeed. In the business world, this is called "value added" to the product or service line. When you, your skills, and your personality become one with the item being sold, you are the value added to your product.

Let me give you an idea of just how important you can be to your product in the customer's eyes. After several years of selling my work at outdoor art and craft shows, I had an opportunity to become more involved with the art and craft industry. The opportunities included television appearances, national magazine columns, and travel to industry trade shows. I jumped at the chance to try something new. However, my outdoor art and craft show schedule conflicted with some of my new responsibilities. I decided to send my husband to the art and craft shows to sell my work, while I concentrated on preparing for my new responsibilities. After the first craft show my husband came home and said, "I don't think this is going to work. Everyone wanted to know where you were and why you weren't at the show."

I asked my husband why he didn't tell the customers about my wonderful new assignments, the opportunity to appear in a PBS series and on national magazine covers. My customers loved me and I knew they would have been thrilled for me. My husband sighed and

> ### Handy Hint
> Remain flexible and open to the options that are available to you.

said, "I told them what you were doing. They said that's nice, but next time they wanted you to schedule better and make it to the show! I'm not going back alone." I learned to schedule more carefully. Our customers want to see the human face behind our work.

Sign and Date When You Create

The bottom line of selling your designs is that you are including a small part of yourself with every purchase. When I first started out, I never made a habit of signing my work. I never felt that I made anything worth signing. Please don't mistake what I considered humility for lack of self-confidence or self-respect—I felt that an "artist" deserved to sign a painting or sculpture, but my simple designs were neither heirlooms nor valuable collectibles. My designs required limited skills and were rustic and folk in character.

After selling my work for many years, I got to know many regular customers. I would do a craft show in their town 1 year and they would remember me and come find me the next year. I started getting requests to sign my pieces for my regular customers. They repeatedly told me they were collecting my work, and it meant a lot to them to have me sign the work. I'm still uncomfortable with the practice, but as a businessperson I listened to the consumer and adhered to the old adage that the customer is always right. Especially since I wanted to build a customer base.

Yet, signing your work involves more than just a business decision. Signing one's work is also a part of being an artist. It's showing your pride in your workmanship and creativity. It's a mark of time and talent. I had hesitated in part because I grew up in a household that valued humility. It was neither proper nor acceptable to brag or boast of accomplishments. It was a tough lesson to learn that self-promotion (which is needed in promoting any creative endeavor) isn't a course in arrogance, but a vital part of marketing and advertising a business. My first editor taught me this lesson with this simple statement: "You are talented and your designs bring such joy to others. Why hide this gift? Who knows better than you do what you can accomplish? Get the word out and continue to work for yourself or go home and work for someone else."

Keeping Track of Creativity

During the past 15 years, I have learned to craft and learned to sell my crafts because many people took the time to share information, knowledge, skills, tips, hints, insights, and laughs with me. The one bit of advice that has helped more than anything else is to keep a written and illustrated journal of my designs. The type of journal doesn't matter. Use index cards, a file folder, spiral notebooks, legal pads, or a hardcover writing book with blank pages. The vehicle doesn't matter as much as what you put into it.

Use the creativity journal to hold photographs of your finished projects. Keep craft recipes and experiments in the journal. Keep trend notes and observations. Sketch a design you'd like to make in the future. Creative people find inspiration in the strangest places. I can walk through a hardware store and find the best supplies. It might look like a nut or bolt to someone else, but to the creative mind it can be anything. A visit to a local mall might give you a dozen ideas for phrases or words to use on cards. During an airplane flight you might daydream about new ways to use embossing powder. A trip to the zoo might inspire you to use animals in your next series of designs. Even in our dreams, the artistic nature in us is creating.

Yet, another common bond shared by creative souls is short memories. The creative journal is the perfect response to this situation. I have a small library of my creative journals. When I feel

Success in a Creative Business

- **Make the commitment to become a business.** You may choose to start small or work only part-time, but understand that the goal of business is to grow and to make a profit.

- **Put it all in writing.** Write a business plan and keep it with your business records. Read a book on starting a business. Your plan should include short-term and long-term goals.

- **Know your talent, skill, assets, and liabilities.** The way to succeed is to show off your best assets. Stay focused and keep up with current trends.

- **Know your markets.** Investigate. Place your best work in the markets that will make your work shine.

- **Educate yourself.** Don't just learn the business of design, but the business of anything else on the consumer's or manufacturer's mind. Yet, trust your own instincts.

- **Keep an updated résumé and portfolio.** Don't assume others know who you are or what you do. A business card in your pocket could mean a job!

- **Grow in your talents and your craft.** Experiment and have fun every once in a while. Change is part of business.

- **Share your talents in your community.** Volunteer. Network within your industry.

- **Believe in yourself and your abilities.** If you don't believe in yourself, no one else will! Self-promotion is not bragging.

- **Enjoy your work.** Rest often. Daydream every day. And go for it!

uninspired and need motivation I open up one of the journals. Keep a small pocket notebook in your purse and on your nightstand for those ideas that come out of nowhere. A journal is a written and visual record of your growth, a catchall for your creative thoughts. No idea is too small or too big for your journal. I found one benefit of keeping a craft journal by accident. I never dreamed that one day I might sell a craft design for publication in a magazine or book. But the written instructions I kept over the years made it very easy to submit designs for publication without adding extra work to my schedule.

Opportunities That May Come Your Way

There are many possibilities and opportunities for profit from your skill as a rubberstamper. Will you be bored if you produce multiples of a design? Then consider selling the original design with written instructions to a publisher. I learned to expand my business by selling some of my holiday designs (Christmas, Easter, Mother's Day, Valentine's Day, and St. Patrick's Day) to publishers of magazines and craft books. It's a thrill to see your name and designs on bookstore shelves and newsstands. There is also a need for kit, tool, and product designers in the art and craft industry. Have you created a tool that helps you in your stamped work? Do you have ideas of how to put stamps and supplies into kits for children, teenagers, or maybe scouting groups?

Handy Hint

Keep a journal of your creative thoughts and ideas.

Teaching your techniques and skills provides an additional opportunity to enjoy and explore your rubberstamping. You can turn your hobby into a service by charging teaching and class fees. You may already be a talented artist with pen, pencil, and paint. If so, you can sell your illustrations, graphics, and artwork to rubberstamp or stencil manufacturers. Do you enjoy speaking to large groups of people? There are numerous trade and consumer shows across the United States and even abroad. Contacting your favorite rubberstamp manufacturer or supplier might be your ticket to travel as you demonstrate how to use rubberstamping materials.

Often a combination of these opportunities makes for a full-time occupation in rubberstamping. You may remain an "independent" artist or designer, or you may have the chance to become part of a company's team as a designer or demonstrator. Just as there are unlimited ways to create designs with your rubberstamps, there is an unlimited mix and match of prospects for profit from your abilities.

Transition from Hobbyist to Professional

As you read this book, try to learn and to keep in mind what help you need (especially in your own mind) to become a legitimate business. You must make a leap from hobbyist to professional. Figure out what you need to do to *feel* that you are in business to make money rather than someone who is just having fun with a hobby. It's an important distinction. Use your goals and business plan to measure your success. The work of a professional in a creative industry won't fit into a 25-words-or-less job description.

The occupation of a professional artist, artisan, or craftsperson may perpetually be a round peg that doesn't fit smoothly into an industry's or society's square hole. But you are creative enough to come up with your own job title for the questions that will regularly be asked: "Do you work? Why are you making so many of those cards? Do people really buy your stuff? What do you do for a living?" Your attitude toward your efforts will be the touchstone for how others react to you. If you take yourself seriously, if you approach all challenges as a professional, if you outwardly glow with confidence and determination (no one needs to know that you might really be shaking in your boots!), the rest of the world will soon follow suit. There is only one exception. Never take yourself or your business so seriously that you can't every once in a while have a good

THE VINSONS' STORY

The Vinsons—Valerie, Vanessa, and Cyndi—started their own company, Amazing Shardz! to sell a unique rubberstamping product. Amazing shardz are cool shapes of ceramic that can be stamped and embossed to create jewelry, collages, greeting cards, and more. Vanessa has provided some helpful information for those stampers who might want to sell to retail markets. She is a wonderful inspiration to stampers who might have an invention or product line in mind, and to the stamping enthusiast.

How did you get started in rubberstamping?

VANESSA: It started as a goodwill gesture when we attended a party given by Cyndi Vinson, my sister-in-law. My sister, my mother, and I went just to see what it was all about. After watching the demonstration and trying it on our own, we really didn't think it was something we would be interested in. About 3 or 4 months after the initial party, Cyndi had another party given by a different demonstrator, and from then on we were all hooked!

How did you discover your product, Amazing Shardz!?

VANESSA: This was really a fluke as well. My sister Valerie has a pottery studio in her home that she began as a part-time business. One day while unloading her kiln she discovered some of the items being fired had broken. She started making a pile of the broken or "shard-like" pieces of

laugh. Or that you forget that your work should be a positive influence on your family and community. It's tough sometimes to keep smiling when facing deadlines, preparing for a big art and craft show, or sending off a design to a new publisher when the last publisher turned you down, but in the long run that smile will give you the energy to keep trying.

pottery. One day my mother, Judie, saw the pieces and asked if she could try stamping on them. Once she tried it and found you could emboss on them with pigment ink, we all started experimenting. From there, we started showing other stampers and stamp companies the product to see if there would be interest. We began getting requests for certain die-cut shapes and sizes. At that point, Valerie, Cyndi, and I formed Amazing Shardz! and started to expand the techniques, teach classes and workshops, and sell at stamping conventions. We also linked a page to Valerie's ceramic Web site and started receiving inquiries and orders via the Internet as well.

We are continuing to expand our product line and techniques to be used on Shardz!

What is the best aspect of rubberstamping to you personally?

Vanessa: Instant gratification! That is what made me fall in love with this art form. You can start and finish a card or gift in a short period of time

(continues)

Copyrights and Angel Companies

Rubberstamps are considered works of visual art and are covered under the guidelines and policies of the U.S. Copyright Office (see general discussion of copyrights in chapter 11). Unique to the profit possibilities of rubberstamping is the fact that rubberstamp images

(continued from page 161)

and be able to WOW! the recipient that same day. It doesn't get any better than that!

VALERIE: Since the emphasis in my creative endeavors is clay, I like the fact that stamps can be impressed into wet clay or used after firing to create either two- or three-dimensional art projects. For me, it brings together two different kinds of creative media that are not typically used together to create one unique piece.

CYNDI: Anybody can do it! You start out just stamping an image, then it sparks an idea and your finished piece is usually far from just a stamped image.

How do you decide at what shows you will demonstrate or sell your product?

VANESSA: After 5 years of research, we have found that smaller conventions, relationships with stamp companies, and regional stamp stores have worked well for our type of product. Offering and conducting demonstrations, classes, and workshops for these companies and stores has also as-

---

are copyrighted by the manufacturers of the stamps, yet in most cases the manufacturer will give permission to the buyer of the copyrighted image to use the image in his or her work. Some stamp companies allow the end user a license, which may or may not contain limitations stipulated by the artist or copyright owner, to create cards and other works of art that can then be resold.

This is a generous and positive policy, because without this permission, you as the artist could under no circumstances be allowed to sell that image for commercial gain. But, almost from the very beginning, rubberstamp manufacturers recognized that many of their

sisted in sales by showing and teaching hands-on how to use the product and experiment with different techniques. The Internet is also starting to become an integral part of our business.

Any advice to others who might like to do this type of work?

VANESSA: Be prepared to put in a lot of time and creativity to get the word out about your product. By keeping it interesting and creating varied and useful types of items, sales can continue to grow. If it is too limited, it may not have a long life span. If there are too many items, people get overwhelmed. Also, make sure persons who are new to the craft do not have to go out and purchase a lot of specialized tools or equipment.

How do you handle a "difficult" customer?

VANESSA: In the event that a customer is unhappy with our product or service, our goal is to find out what has caused the situation and rectify it *immediately*, no excuses. We also strive to go the extra mile and do something extra so even if they have a bad experience with the product, they will remember that we made it right for them *and* exceeded their expectations.

See the Resources for the Vinsons' contact information.

customers would want to use copyrighted images on finished designs, projects, or items that they in turn would sell to a third party. The companies or artists that allow these licenses are known as "angel companies."

If a rubberstamp company or manufacturer is an angel company, they have a written and public policy about using their copyrighted images. There is no set or standard angel policy. Most rubberstamp companies or manufacturers request that the image be hand-stamped, with no use of any mechanical device for stamping the image. They often request that a specific number of images be

Advice from People Who Know

It's always best to get advice from those who have been there—or especially those who are *still* there! When I asked experienced rubberstampers what advice they could give to someone who wants to start selling his or her crafts, the responses were great.

"Have a budget and stick to it. The greatest hurdle for me was the record-keeping end of having a business."

"Don't be afraid to experiment. When I started I sold hand-stamped cards and 2 years later I'm selling rubberstamps."

"The Internet is my greatest source of information. I track down suppliers and compare prices. I keep up with other rubberstampers and keep learning more and more about my art."

"Schedule regular work hours and schedule time for family and home. My first year all I did was work, and it really burned me out. My art wasn't as good as it had been when I enjoyed some time off too."

stamped. This number of images varies; on average, from 10 to 50 images are allowed per copyrighted stamp. Following are some examples of angel policies.

Rubber Poet

Rubber Poet Official Angel Policy for those craftspeople desiring to use our stamps: Pigs and Poets encourage the creative use of our designs for *hand-crafted* projects. As long as the items for sale use our *hand-stamped* designs and are not mechanically or electronically reproduced, it's OK by us.

EccenTricks

Sale of copyrighted EccenTricks designs as rubber stamps grants a limited right to reproduce the design for private or personal use and may not be mechanically reproduced by any party other than EccenTricks for the purposes of commercial profit or promotion. With regard to individual hand-crafted and hand-stamped items to be sold by the purchaser of the rubber stamp, the following limitations apply: Designs must be reproduced by hand stamping only and may not be mechanically reproduced (i.e. photocopy of any kind), enlarged or reduced and applied to the medium. Copyrighted designs by EccenTricks may not be altered in any manner, except by those techniques commonly used in the craft of hand stamping, i.e. masking or overlaying portions in the overall design. Any other alteration will be considered an infringement of copyright. Other than all the stuff above, knock yourself out and have a good time!

Keyhole Designs

COPYRIGHT POLICY: In addition to stamping out Guilt-Free CorresponDance Art, please feel free to use Keyhole rubber art stamps as tools to create your own hand-crafted artwork for sale. Please do not reproduce Keyhole designs electronically, mechanically, or in rubber, nor mount and resell them as finished stamps.

A La Art Stamp Crafters

Angel Policy: Write for permission to use stamp images for resale purposes, send sample of card also. We do allow people who are not mass producing their work to use our stamps. First we ask to see a sample of their work. Then we ask to have our name printed on the back with yours. We have to do that because most of our images are also copywritten by the artist also. We pay our artist a royalty fee, so that is why we could not allow the images to be produced in large quantities (25 or more).

A Stamp in the Hand

Angel Policy: 1. No mechanical reproduction in the making of the items. 2. Whatever design or scene is created should be limited to no more than 50 of that particular design or scene, so as to preclude the impression of mass-production.

All Night Media

Angel Policy: We are often asked whether it is OK to use All Night Media stamps to create cards, stationery, and other hand-stamped products which will be sold. Our current policy is to allow such usage as long as the designs are reproduced only by hand-stamping and it is not for a significant commercial venture. We do reserve the right to approve or disapprove such usage on a case by case basis and to change our policy at any time without notice. If you wish to use our stamps to create products to be sold within these guidelines, please send us a written request stating what products you intend to create and how you intend to sell them. You may contact us by e-mail, snail mail, or fax, but be sure to state your full name, business name if any, address, and telephone number. Please note that this policy applies only to stamps which bear the copyright notice "© All Night Media, Inc." We are not the copyright holder on Disney Classics, Pooh, Laurel Burch, Mary Engelbreit, Sanrio, Curious George, and The Wubbulous World of Dr. Seuss, among others. These stamps have a different copyright notice on them, and we cannot give you permission to use these designs. The individual companies holding these copyrights all have policies prohibiting any commercial use of their art except under the terms of a licensing agreement, so you should not use their images on products which will be sold.

> ## Handy Hint
>
> Make sure you request permission from the manufacturer if you want to use an existing rubberstamp image in a piece that you plan to sell.

It's easy to see that angel policies vary. You'll need to be familiar with the angel policies of each rubberstamp company or manufacturer that you use in any design that you sell. You can call the company or manufacturer or visit wonderful rubberstamping Web sites that list and update angel companies with reliable frequency (see Resources for Web sites and addresses).

Some images are not the property of the rubberstamp manufacturer; rather the manufacturer pays a licensing fee to use the image.

Licensed images that quickly come to mind are Mickey Mouse, Winnie the Pooh, Daffy Duck, the Coke or Pepsi logo, university or professional sports team logos, and many other corporate or creative trademarks and logos. The rubberstamp manufacturer cannot give you permission to use any image that the rubberstamp company itself is licensing. If you want to use such an image, you'll need to license the image directly from the party who owns the image. For most small business owners, this just isn't cost-effective. Do not mess around with licensed images unless you hold a contract to use the licensed image. Most licensers take misuse or abuse of their images very seriously and will not hesitate to sue for profits lost and seize any property that was used to stamp the image. If you decide you want to manufacture or even license out your own work, your first step is to seek advice from a lawyer with a background in such matters.

> ## Did you know???
>
> Rubberstamps are considered art and are protected by copyright.

Now You're in Business!

Don't panic yet! Take a deep breath and congratulate yourself on this wonderful new task before you! You've made a tremendous choice to turn a hobby into an occupation. And you aren't standing out in the cold all alone. You are in very good company!

The following chapters will answer your questions about the day-to-day business responsibilities you'll face as a professional with a business to run. You'll find business how-to's that will guide and help you make your dreams and goals a reality. You'll learn how to price and market your rubberstamp designs, items, and services. Enjoy the excitement and challenge of the learning that waits for you in the chapters ahead!

chapter 8

Pricing Your Rubberstamping

▼▼

THERE REALLY SHOULD BE some kind of law that protects craftspeople and artists from having to price their own work. Each of us is asked to put a dollar value on something we created with our hearts and hands. This task is often the absolute worst responsibility many professionals face. I took numerous business courses throughout my college days while earning a Bachelor of Science degree in Advertising, and I can't recall any instructor or teacher teaching how to price finished pieces of work or how to determine what to charge for a service. I learned the old-fashioned way: Just fake it, and once you hit upon a price that works . . . go for it. That isn't as practical or easy as it may seem.

The Three Factors of Pricing

The constant in any pricing formula is the cost of goods, supplies, and materials used to make a design. It's easy to overlook the small or even minuscule supplies that are incorporated into a finished product; yet those small bits and pieces can add up quickly and make a difference in whether you just break even or make a profit.

Pricing Tips

■ Mark all your prices in pencil. Then, if you decide to lower or raise a price, you can erase the current price and pencil in the new one.

■ Watch your customers. Do they seem thrilled with an item until they see the price? This is a good indicator that you may have priced too high compared to the competition.

■ Visit gift shops and stationery stores frequently to get a reality check on the current competitors' prices.

■ Keep your booth or exhibit balanced with a range of priced items. Stock some low- and some high-ticket items to give customers many choices and a chance to find items in their own price budget.

You'll need to test your own markets and do research to find out how similar items or services are priced. Unlike a retailer, who is given a "suggested retail price" by the manufacturer and can lower or increase this suggested price, you are not so fortunate. You've got to come up with that price! This chapter will take you through, step-by-step, using detailed examples to help you learn pricing techniques. Let's take a look at how much one standard greeting card costs to make. I chose the greeting card example because of its simplicity.

Three key factors are used to create a pricing formula for your work:

1. Cost of materials

2. Cost of labor

3. Cost of overhead

Cost of Materials

The first step in pricing your work is to very carefully list all the components of your design. I recommend making this list as you are putting the design together. Take time to note even the smallest amounts of glue, embossing powder, scraps of handmade paper, paint, notion, or drops of scent. Revise the list several times as you are making the item several times. From these notes, you can create a complete list of components and the cost of each component. Break down the total cost of an item (like a jar of embossing powder) into smaller units to find out exactly how much a finished design costs you to make.

Cost of Materials for One Greeting Card

The card or cardstock paper: $0.10
The stamps: $0.11 ($0.045, $0.05, and $0.055*)
Ink and pad: $0.05 ($5**)
Embossing powder: $0.25
Heat Tool: n/a
Total: $0.55

Cost of Labor

At this point we have only the cost of supplies needed to make a greeting card. We need to add in a labor cost before calculating a retail price for the card. The labor cost is what you will pay yourself for your efforts and time. Most artists, crafters, and artisans grossly underestimate the time involved in making a finished design. I highly

*Three different stamps were used, so I've given a percentage of 1% rather than the total cost for all three stamps. This is the standard percentage I apply to supplies or materials that have a long life.

**The whole amount for the inkpad is $5, but I'm using the standard 1% formula again, since the ink and pad have a long life too.

recommend that you time yourself several times and average the results before deciding how much time you put into a finished item.

Many professionals who sell their work don't create one item at a time from start to finish, but rather make several components in one sitting and then complete several finished items at the next sitting. This process is called "assembly line work" and in some cases "mass production" of an item. I laugh at the term *mass production* when applied to creative businesses. I always think of huge machines pumping out identical parts and pieces in quick succession. I've yet to meet an artist or craftsperson who works like a machine, but mass production is an industry-accepted term. As you experiment, you'll find a way of working that is efficient and comfortable for you.

A labor rate can be assessed in two ways. The first is by the hour, the other per piece. I will explain to you the hourly method, and once you feel you've mastered your craft, you can charge per piece if you choose. You set a rate that you feel is fair and reasonable. Most of us would be tickled to earn $25, $50, or $100 per hour for our efforts, but a reality check will tell you that at those rates your new business venture can't afford your services! Consider the national minimum wage as a starting point for your own labor rate. In this example we'll use the current federal minimum wage rate for hourly workers, $5.15 (remember, this price may vary depending on your location or raises in the federal minimum wage rate— this is just an example for demonstrational purposes). As your skills and talents grow, your labor rate per hour can be increased to reflect your efficiency and acumen.

Let's take a look at the cost of labor involved in creating a greeting card:

Cost of Labor for One Greeting Card

Gathering supplies to work area: 5 minutes
Stamping image and embossing image: 5 minutes
Total time spent in labor of one card: 10 minutes

Total time spent creating one card: 20 minutes
Price charged per hour: $5.15
Price charged per card: $1.72

Overhead Costs

The final consideration in a pricing formula is "overhead." It's a catchall category for anything outside of the cost of materials and labor. You are using electricity as you craft, you occupy space within your home for business rather than personal needs, and most crafts sold need some type of packaging, including price tags and receipts for the purchaser of the item. You may have supplies that don't directly become part of the item you are selling but are needed to make the item. For a Christmas wreath, those could be a glue gun, pick-making machine, or glue pot. Overhead includes supplies that are reused but wear out in less than a year, like rubberstamps, brushes, stencils, molds, and patterns plus equipment. Overhead also includes depreciable items like laminating machines, a computer or office or studio equipment, cameras, phone, travel, shipping and postage, show fees, display costs, packaging, insurance, and other deductibles used directly to make your finished product. Overhead is most often expressed as a percentage rate of the total of labor and cost of goods. This amount can vary, but when you add all your overhead costs, they should never be less than 10% and never exceed 35% of the total of your labor and cost of goods. A range of 10% to 35% is good overhead, but the standard overhead is 25%, which is what we will use in this pricing example. If your overhead percentage is more than 35%, you'll need to take a serious look at your expenses because the IRS may question your expenses and deductions.

Overhead Costs for One Greeting Card

Cost of materials: $0.55
Cost of labor: $1.72

Total of all overhead costs: $0.57 (25% of cost of materials + labor)

A Few More Things to Consider

When pricing your work you need to have a well-rounded knowledge of the going rate for similar items in the marketplace. For example, if you create cards for the Christmas holiday, you should visit florist shops, gift shows, Christmas stores, and any other retail establishments that sell Christmas cards. If you decide to stamp on shirts, you should gather catalogs and magazine advertisements for comparable shirts. Understanding the pricing of your competitors will give you an idea of what your consumer will find as he or she shops for such an item. In general, you want your pricing to fall in the mid-range of your competitors' selling prices for similar items. If you underprice, you are paying your customers to purchase your work. Underpricing also devalues the item in the customer's eyes. If you overprice, you will be sitting on inventory or have a low turnover rate that can cause cash-flow problems.

The Market and Economy

When pricing any item or design, you must also consider the economy of the area in which you'll be selling. You probably can't sell big-ticket items in a community that is suffering economically. Low-end designs might not sell in communities that are prospering. Also think about the economic climate and diversity of the area in which you are selling. I live in an area that is deeply affected by the space industry. When times are good people spend their money freely, but when rumors start flying about budget cuts, budgets are watched carefully. At the same time, I could travel across the state, where my customers are not as dependent on one industry, and sell at almost twice the asking price in my home community. Eventually, I decided not to sell my work within my own community; it was not cost-effective. In business, tough decisions can't be ignored.

I know that my newest designs will attract attention from loyal customers, so I may charge a higher retail price because of the higher demand for an item. Predicting demand is a combination of trusting your gut instincts and throwing caution to the wind. Can you keep up with the demand? Can you keep the item in stock? Review or read about the economic theory of supply and demand, which can be found in a basic high school or college economics book. There is no sure-fire formula, but there is a need to trust your own judgment. If the market will bear a higher price than you've calculated with a pricing formula, go for it!

> **Handy Hint**
>
> Be prepared to make tough decisions about where you'll sell your work.

Product Turnover and Competitive Pricing

Consider the turnover of your products. If you decide to sell at craft shows, home shows, or bazaars, do you want to pack up and take product home after each show? Do you want items to sit week after week at a craft mall, gathering dust? Every time the items are packed and unpacked there is a risk of damage and loss of product quality. Consider pricing your items to move.

In addition to getting a feel for how similar items are priced, you need to consider how much competition for customers there is in your area. How many other artists or craftspeople are selling the same type of motifs, media, techniques, styles, or forms? Investigate and keep a running total of other artists or craftspeople who are working in wood, painting, doll making, florals, or candles. Is your work unique? Is your craft a standout, or can you put your work next to someone else's and not see any differences? In this case, your only real difference may be in the price tag. Can you still make a profit and keep competitive?

In random testing conducted by the retail buying industry, consumers would pick an item priced at $5.95 over one priced at $6.00, and even preferred the price of $5.99 over the same item priced just 1 penny more at $6.00. It may seem deceptive or silly, but consider the lost sales caused by what amounts to 1 penny or 5 cents.

Granted, consumers are savvy and react negatively to being patronized, but when I priced my own work at $0.25, $0.50, and $0.75 increments instead of the next dollar amount, my multiple sales (customers purchasing more than one of an item) increased.

Did you know???

Consumer buying studies show that customers are more likely to buy items whose prices end in 5 or 9.

You can always test the waters with prices. Don't hesitate to go with the flow, but don't underprice your work either. The sad truth is that if a customer gets used to a price, the customer will kick and scream when that price goes up. Funny, no buyer has ever had a fit when I've lowered a price. Consider the three basics of setting a retail price, and you should be able to calculate a selling price that is fair to your customers. Use the following formula:

Cost of materials: ($0.55) + cost of labor ($1.72) = $2.27

Percentage of overhead costs ($0.57 ÷ $2.27): 25% (remember, this amount should be between 10% and 35%) = $0.57

Final selling price: Cost of materials ($0.55) + cost of labor ($1.72) + dollar amount of overhead costs ($0.57) = $2.84

You may choose to sell your greeting cards at $2.84 (or rounded up, $3.00) each, or give your customers a deal and sell them for $15 per box of 6.

Setting Fee Charges

This is the most subjective of all the pricing you may have to deal with. Demonstrating and teaching classes are services you will provide rather than a finished design, and you charge fees to your clients or customers. (Chapter 7 features a list of possible places

Frequent Buyer Appreciation

You may want to consider providing special pricing to loyal and repeat customers. This is a good way to show customer service and appreciation to those who continually support your business efforts. You don't have to give away the bank (as my mother used to say), but you should show your customers that you respect their budgets—and their business.

- Offer one free card (or other item) with every 6 or 12 purchased.

- Give a 5% or 10% discount on orders that total over $25, $50, or $100 dollars.

- Create a frequent buyer card out of your business card. Use a decorative paper punch and punch the card every time the customer makes a purchase. With every 5, 10, or 15 purchases, give the customer a free gift or discount off his or her next purchase.

- Have a drawing for a cute basket of your work at every show or exhibit. Ask your customers to fill out a form, and draw names at the end of the show. The winner receives the basket. This also gives you a mail list for future shows!

where you can set up demonstrations and hold classes.) Determining a fee for your services isn't as cut-and-dried as the pricing formula for a finished design. Labor or your time, rather than cost of goods, is the key factor to consider when setting a fee schedule for demonstrating. Teaching will include a slight consideration of the cost of goods if you supply the classes with materials, but for the most part teaching fees are based on your labor or time.

Demonstrating

In most cases, if you are working with a manufacturer or distributor, the company pays a standard fee to demonstrators or teachers. These fees range from an hourly wage to a daily wage. On average, you can expect a manufacturer or distributor to pay $10 to $25 per hour. You'll need to be clear about what the fee includes. If travel is expected of you, it's wise to make sure you can submit a travel expense report to your employer to cover mileage, meals, and lodging if applicable.

When I first became involved with the arts and crafts industry and began to attend trade shows, I would watch the demonstrators at each booth and say to myself, "That looks easy enough. I bet I could do that job." With that rather cocky attitude I applied to the Hobby Industry Association's (HIA) Certified Professional Demonstrator (CPD) program. All I had to do to become a CPD was read HIA's Body of Knowledge for demonstrators and be evaluated by several members of the industry while demonstrating. Piece of cake . . . or so I thought.

I demonstrated for Aleene's Division of Artist because I knew the company's product lines like the back of my hand. I demonstrated for 3 days from 8:00 A.M. to 5:00 P.M. I helped set up the exhibit booth and I helped tear down the exhibit. It was the hardest work I'd ever done in my entire life! No one told me my feet could hurt so badly! I passed my review with flying colors to become a CPD; however, I rarely take demonstrating jobs that require more than a few hours. I'm glad I got the training—it helped me understand how to work with crowds, how to show off a product, and how to sell a product. I was paid $75 daily, which worked out to about $8 an hour, more than double the minimum wage at the time, but to this day I've never worked so hard for money. However, the learning experience, meeting so many industry leaders, and the fun of teaching retailers how to use products made the experience priceless. I also learned that I am not cut out to be a demonstrator full-time.

This is a process you almost certainly go through if you want to succeed in a creative business. Often you will take on jobs or create designs that you might not get top dollar for, or might not be your dream situation, but that open doors for you that can lead to greater experience and larger profits. The decisions to take on these projects are made on instinct, on gut feelings, and can't be made with formulas. Not every choice will work out positively, but over time such decisions can be invaluable to your career.

Teaching and Classes

Teaching would be a dream if you could just walk into a classroom, teach a class, and walk out to collect a paycheck. But talk to any teacher of any subject, and you'll find that only in a daydream is teaching that easy. Teaching is not a job for everyone. A great deal of preparation time goes into a smooth-running class presentation. (Chapter 9 outlines the details of preparing and presenting a class to students.) It's also important that you enjoy working with the public. Be confident in your people skills before even attempting to teach a class. You might find it helpful to attend several art or craft classes and learn firsthand what you like and dislike about experienced teachers. The golden rule is that as a teacher you are there to help your students build skills, not do the work for them.

> **Handy Hint**
>
> Make sure that each student in your class takes home at least one finished design.

Remember that in most cases you will be teaching adults. Adults don't have to go "back to school"; they decide to spend their valuable time attending a leisure activity class. It's best not to lecture such students, but to make sure they have fun and enjoy the skills you are teaching them.

How much you charge for a class will depend on the length of the class. Most art and craft classes last from 1 to 3 hours. Any longer than that and students get restless and need breaks. The national averages for class fees vary widely due to regional economies, population, and standard of living. Also take into account your ability and expertise in the subject you'll be teaching. The bigger your body of work, the more you'll be able to charge for your instruction. In general, look for class fees of $10 and under (per student) for an hour class, and $25 per student for a class of 2 to 3 hours. I've found that by teaching hour-long classes, I make more income in the long run.

If you are going to kit or provide all or some of the supplies and materials needed for the class, charge an additional fee for this service. Point out that all the student needs to bring is a smile when attending your class and that you are saving each student time and effort by gathering the materials needed ahead of time.

The economy of your teaching area plays a vital role in how you price a class. To get a sense of local rates, check out the class fees of local art and craft shops or other centers that have class schedules.

Fees for Work to Be Published

I wish there were an industry standard for pricing finished designs with written instructions that are sent to a publisher. It would make business much simpler, but sadly there is no such guide available for the creative industries. However, I do know that an editor works within a set budget for each issue of a magazine. The editor must use this budget not just to gather designs to publish, but also to get the magazine from the drawing board to the printer to the newsstand.

An editor must deliberate on some subjective considerations when placing a price value on creative work. Can you compare the time it takes to make a quilt to the time it takes to make a stamped greeting card? What fee do you pay for ideas and for the execution of those ideas? I once had a conversation with a publisher about a new magazine she was considering. She just couldn't understand what was difficult about taking a few rubberstamps, some ink, and some paper, and creating a card. She was appalled at the idea that some rubberstamp artists wanted more than $10 or $15 for these "simple"

Clockwise from Right:
"Sending All My Love" Greeting Card
"Christmas Trees Sparkle" Greeting Cards
"Leaping Frog" Bookmark
"Star Gazing" Greeting Cards
"Coffee Anyone?" Bookmark
"Fall Leaf" Bookmark
"Remembrance" Bookmark

"Ivy Leaves" Wooden Frame (left)
"Winter Dream" Wooden Clock Frame (right)

"Don't Forget!" Memo Cubes

Glass Plate with Matching Tile Trivet

designs. My response was that the artist has invested heavily in the rubberstamps, ink, and paper. It's not as easy as just sitting down and stamping. The artist has to stay aware of current trends, colors, textures, and balance. He or she has to practice new techniques and experiment with developing a recognizable style. There's a workspace to maintain. And the artist wants to earn a reasonable income!

Did you know???

For every perfect card made, there is a pile of not-so-perfect ones tucked away somewhere.

When selling creativity, you need to educate the potential editor or publisher about your work. Emphasize your skills and abilities. Don't get frustrated or discouraged, and never sell a design unless you are happy with the selling price. Nothing eats up creativity quicker than being angry and nothing sours a working relationship faster than unspoken resentment between two parties. Also understand that the contract you sign with a publisher is legal and binding. Be clear about what you agree to. Did you sell first rights, meaning after the initial publication of work, the work returns as your property? All rights, meaning the design becomes the property of the publisher? Are you happy with the contract? Don't sign until your very last question is answered.

Reputation is built one deal, one job at a time. What matters in the end is not how many designs you have sold to a vast array of publishers. What matters is that your work was presented with respect and that you were paid well for your abilities. A good reputation will eventually lead to offers of higher fees. Remember that all fees are negotiable. On average, a general consumer magazine editor will pay between $50 and $200 for a design. On average, a book publisher will pay a flat fee of $1,500 to $2,000 for a craft book of 20 to 30 designs with a softbound cover that will retail for $6.95 to $15.99 in an art or craft store. Other publishers may offer a royalty of $0.25 to $0.75 per book sold rather than a flat fee. Consider all your expenses of selling your designs for publication, including materials, time to write instructions, time to illustrate, and shipping the materials to a publisher. A survey of designers in the craft industry indicates that most prefer a flat fee over a royalty except when the design sold is for a tool or technique.

Handy Hint

Before signing a publication contract, be sure you understand all its terms.

What's Needed Next?

You have your pricing all figured out, and it's time to sell your work. It may seem out of order to price a finished piece before you even know where you're going to sell the work, but without knowing that you will indeed make money selling your goods, there is no need to find a market for your work. To be very honest, finding and discovering creative markets in which to sell your designs is a lot more fun than figuring and adding up all the cost of goods and labor and overhead! The hard part is over! Let's turn the page and get ready to go to market!

chapter 9

Selling Your Rubberstamping

▼▼▼

MOST INDIVIDUALS WHO SELL their handmade items do so one of two ways. The first is simply to set up a business within their home and sell directly to family and friends, and over time a business clientele builds up through word of mouth. The artisan sells a creation to a family member or friend, who in turn gives the item as a gift to another party. A savvy artisan should include at least one business card with contact information like name, address, and phone number with each item he or she sold. The gift recipient would learn how to get in touch with the artisan by reading the business card. Word of mouth is still the best form of advertising for a professional artist, craftsperson, or artisan. Nothing beats a personal testimonial or recommendation. Word of mouth is built by consistently providing a quality product and good customer service.

The second marketplace is the art and craft show. This market has many forms, from local community-planned events to church-organized bazaars to large elaborate art shows operated by professional show promoters. Often the show is outdoors and is an annual event for the community. The sales atmosphere ranges from flea-market hip to sophisticated art-gallery elegant. The original outdoor art and craft shows have a festive, carnival feel; local community service groups sell hot dogs and popcorn and local talent entertain on a stage area from morning until closing, with dancers, singers, or poetry readings. It is hometown, small-town fun. This type of craft show still exists, but on any given day there are at least a dozen art and craft shows being held somewhere in the United States. That statistic couldn't be reported prior to the 1990s.

The appeal of handmade craft or art items seems to have peaks and valleys, just like any other retail product for sale. It may be trite, but everything old is at some point in time new again. Since the mid-1980s, there has been a steady cycle of consumers wanting to purchase homemade designs. Because of this trend, hundreds and hundreds of art and craft shows have been organized as annual, biannual, quarterly, and even monthly events in some communities. It is still a very strong marketplace for anyone selling handmade or homemade items, but competition for the consumer's dollar is stiff.

This chapter takes a close look at shows and other marketing options available to you. Selecting the right marketplace for you and your designs is just as important as selecting quality supplies or determining the right price for your stamped item. Ask yourself some serious questions: How involved do you wish to be in the selling of your items? How large a geographic area do you wish to cover? And finally, how much inventory can you make to fill the needs of your marketplace selections? Keep your answers to these questions in mind as you read about the markets available to you.

Retail Art and Craft Shows

The outdoor art and craft show is probably one of the oldest markets in our industry, and it remains today one of the most popular and profitable marketplaces for those selling handmade works.

Each week and weekend, you can count on at least one local or regional show going on. The shows may be outdoors or indoors, with or without a professional show promoter. To participate in this type of show, you need to apply to the show, pay the booth or exhibit space fee, and have a display in which to showcase your work. And in most cases, you need to free up your weekends to participate, since most shows are scheduled for both Saturday and Sunday.

Craft shows are perfect selling arenas for rubberstamped items and designs. A large percentage of your income will be earned in the last quarter of the year. You guessed it . . . during the Christmas and winter holiday buying season. You can create interesting displays and build an inventory prior to the holiday. Remember that Christmas, Halloween, and Easter are the three top holidays for buyers who want to send out holiday greetings and buy gifts for family and friends. Some Christmas motif items, like Santas and angels, can be sold year-round, but the best time to sell Christmas items is during the months of September, October, and November. (Today's consumer has been trained to assume that Christmas items should be on sale or marked down in December.) Most people attending an art and craft show are there to buy items either for personal use or gift giving. Stamped wearables, home décor items, greeting cards, and framed collage are just some of the items that sell well during the third and fourth quarters of the year.

At art and craft shows you are selling retail, so rarely is a commission taken from your sales. Retail selling involves direct contact with the consumer. It's a chance to meet and learn from your customers, who can be a great source of information. Talk with them. Ask them what they are looking for, what colors appeal to them, and what they would like to see on your shelves and tables. Art and craft

Did you know???

The art and craft show was the start of the professional craft and artisan industry as we know it today.

shows are wonderful social events. After long hours of working to complete your show inventory, take time to enjoy meeting the people who buy your efforts.

The downside to shows, especially outdoor shows, can be the weather. Wind, sun, and rain can take a toll on the best of us. Shelters or canopies are a must for the outdoor marketplace. You can find canopies and other display items advertised in show guides, Web sites, and craft trade journals.

If you exhibit at a show, be sure to consider your travel needs. You're a store on wheels! Choose a display that's designed for compactness, travel ease, quick setup and breakdown. You'll need to pack a change (cash) box, folding chairs, tables, table coverings, and a good attitude. Keep security needs in mind, especially if you specialize in high-ticket items.

> **Handy Hint**
>
> At art and craft shows, learn as much as you can about the people who buy your stamped designs.

Retail shows are known to most of us as art and craft shows but can also include seasonal boutiques, church and community bazaars, indoor or outdoor markets, and any arena in which you display your own work to sell directly to the consumer. Recently many shows have moved indoors to shopping malls and convention centers. Wherever the physical location, for many of us the art and craft shows are a great marketplace.

Juried and Non-Juried Shows

Many new craft professionals ask about the difference between juried and non-juried art and craft shows. To display your work in a non-juried show, you fill out an application and send in a show fee. Acceptance into the show is based upon a first come, first served basis until all available show spaces are filled. In a non-juried show, your work may be placed beside imports referred to as "buy/sells." It is often impossible to beat, or even compete with, an imported item's low price. You may want to inquire upon application about the type of work or products that will be on display during the show.

Juried shows, on the other hand, not only require an application and space fee, but will also request slides or photos of your stamped work and the display within your booth. They may require an additional fee for "jurying," which pays for the judges' time and is non-refundable. They will usually ask for a written description of your work. The jurying process ensures quality workmanship and in some cases limits the number of crafts in a specific medium. For example, a juried show that has 100 spaces may allow 20% for decorative painting, 20% for stained glass, 20% to the needle arts, 20% to ceramics, and 20% to mixed media. The idea is to keep variety in the showplace and to spread the competition for the consumer's dollar equally.

Selling Designs Directly to Manufacturers at Licensing Shows

When you sell or license your designs, the company you sell or license to will produce the finished product and market it. The Disney characters are great examples of licensed designs. Disney licenses the characters of Mickey Mouse, Winnie the Pooh, and Bambi to rubberstamp companies who manufacture and sell the images in rubber. The rubberstamp companies pay for use of the characters and often pay a percentage of sales for each stamp sold.

Licensing shows provide another potential source of income. The largest show is held in New York City at the same time as a large gift market show. Artists and craftspeople display goods that are available for license. To get involved in this arena, you will need to prepare very carefully. Study and understand contracts and the difference between all rights and first rights. Set up a professional display. You are playing with the "big guys," and any lack of

Handy Hint

For application to juried shows, take your time writing up a concise but accurate description of your stamped work.

showmanship will be noted immediately. I highly recommend you attend several gift shows before attempting to work in the licensing arena. Or you may wish to consider hiring an agent who specializes in the arts.

This market is not for every rubberstamp artist, but for those who create original stamps it could be a very profitable arena. Once you've found a product that you love to work with and, if you say so yourself, your designs are great, you may be able to work with the manufacturer of your favorite product. You should set up a meeting at which you present your original designs or product line to the manufacturer. If all goes well, the company may buy or license your work. Follow this list of instructions to help you.

1. Select and prepare your best designs as finished samples. Workmanship counts.

2. Photograph your work. You can do this yourself—it doesn't need to be done by a professional photographer. Use plenty of light; outdoor light is best. Use a gray or light blue sheet or towel as a backdrop; smooth it out to eliminate creases in the backdrop. If your work is small, have a ruler or other measure close to the design to give it perspective. Take several shots at several angles. Have the film developed and select one or two of the best shots. Write your name and address on the back of each photo.

3. Write a brief summary of the design piece. List all materials used, basic steps, time involved, skill level, and total expense. Include your name and address in the summary. It's a good idea to "title" the design.

4. Write a cover or query letter to the manufacturer. It's best to contact the manufacturer in advance and ask for the name of the contact person for design submission. Your design will get a quicker response if it is sent to a specific person rather than to the company in general.

5. If there is interest in your design, the manufacturer will contact you and send you a contract. Read it carefully and make sure you fully understand it before signing. This is the time to ask if the manufacturer has a demonstrator's program or designer's program that you can get involved with. These programs provide product education and reasonable product requests. Many manufacturers will also pay endorsement fees when brand names are included in print. Average endorsement fees range from $25 to $250 with proof of publication.

6. Fees for designs vary from manufacturer to manufacturer, depending on how the manufacturer will use the design. Average fees range from $50 to $150.

7. If your design is rejected, don't take it personally. It might not meet the needs of the manufacturer at that time. Feel free to ask your contact if the manufacturer is looking for designs, and what type of designs they are interested in. Remember to be polite and professional.

If your design is accepted, you'll be paid either a flat once-only fee or be offered a percentage of sales. Sometimes a company will combine the two types of payment. If you take this route, the designs you present must *absolutely* be your own original work. You can't sell a design using a rubberstamp image that belongs to another company.

Finding the Shows

You'll need to take some basic steps in preparing to participate in a show. The first step is to locate the shows themselves. Trade and gift shows can be found in calendars and advertisements located in industry trade journals like *Craftrends, Country Business,* or *Gift and Stationery News.* You can learn about retail or consumer shows by

Nondisclosure Agreements

When selling your work or your designs, it is essential that you obtain the advice of a lawyer. Legal contracts will be involved, and you need to understand wholly and without question what you are agreeing to when you sign the contract.

Some professionals request that the potential client or buyer sign a nondisclosure agreement. You may draw one up yourself or with the help of an attorney. This agreement protects your original work from being used without your permission. The signers agree that anything seen or discussed will not be repeated or used without your consent. It's a toss-up as to whether you need a nondisclosure agreement. A nondisclosure can be viewed as an aggressive or distrustful start to a working arrangement. You should always copyright your work because copyright protects your work from being used without your consent. Follow your own feelings when deciding whether you need a nondisclosure agreement. (More on copyrights in chapter 11.)

networking with fellow professionals, calling your local chamber of commerce, or using periodicals referred to as show guides. The leading national show guide is *Sunshine Artist* magazine. Searching in the *Directory of Periodicals* at your local library will let you find information about the many regional show guides. Retail shows are listed on many Web sites. The Professional Crafter Web site (www.procrafter.com) lists hundreds of craft shows throughout the United States. More Web site show guides are popping up on the Web. Just enter "craft shows" or "craft show list" into any Internet search engine.

Not all shows are created the same. Take the time to find out as much as you can before investing in a show fee for a particular show. There are no guarantees that even the most successful shows won't have a bad year, but the more you find out about a show in advance, the more likely you'll find the shows that are right for you.

See sidebar, Questions to Ask Before Applying to a Show, on page 198 for a list of questions that will help you.

Selling at Shows

Once you've been accepted to a show, you need to prepare for selling at the show. This can get hectic even for the seasoned professional, but if you have never done a show, it can be downright chaos. I've developed the following list over the past 15 years. I keep a copy of this list for each show I participate in and check off each item as I pack my vehicle. Keep the list handy for when you're breaking down your booth too. You'll find you don't forget to pack important items, and you return home with everything you brought to the show!

Basic Items Needed at a Show

- All display items: tables, table covers, shelving, crates, tools needed to assemble display, chairs, and ice chest or cooler (if allowed).

- Inventory and products: priced, packaged, and ready to display.

- Guest book: This is used to build a mailing list.

- Cash box, receipt book, plenty of coins and small bills, calculator, charge card imprinter, credit card charge slips, and a state sales tax table (if applicable).

- Pens for writing checks.

- Extra price tags.

- Business cards, brochures, any signage or other paper good items.

- Special order forms (if applicable).

- A copy of your state sales tax license to post in full view of consumers (if applicable).

- If using a canopy, a separate checklist of all items necessary to set up the canopy, including all tools required for assembly.

- A handcart to carry items (if needed).

- Items to work on or demonstrate during the slow selling times at the show. Do *not* bring reading materials. Most potential customers find sales help who read books or magazines during selling hours to be rude and will not ask for help when a salesperson is busy reading.

- Repair kit: scissors, glue, tape, and small quantities of any supply needed to make small repairs at the show.

- Snacks and beverages, plus weather gear if outside: visor, hat, change of clothing, sunscreen, and comfortable shoes.

- Also bring to each show a good attitude, positive thinking, energy, enthusiastic sales presentation, and a smile. You should leave small children, books, TV, radio, and pets at home. But keep in mind that it's important to schedule relief times for yourself during the show by asking for help from friends and family. Be willing to pay the relief team for their efforts in an hourly wage, commission of sales, or by trade of product for time. If all else fails ask your closest neighbor to exchange a break time with you.

Tips for Success

Participating in a show can bring you new markets and customers. The art and craft show has been popular since the very beginning of our industry and will always remain a mainstay. Try to make the most of these wonderful opportunities!

Prepare ample inventory in advance of each show. Don't stay up half the night before a show trying to get more inventory prepared; it is never worth the lost sleep. You're better off feeling rested and refreshed at show time. Arrive early and be prepared to unload your inventory and supplies quickly. Parking is often limited at shows; in most situations you will unload and reload near the exhibit area and then have to remove your vehicle in a short time period. Avoid loud music or strong scents within your booth.

The art and craft show is the perfect place to become a showman. It's an opportunity to share your love of your art and craft with others. Pay attention to the body language of browsers. If a potential buyer is with a friend, you may need to sell to the friend just as much as to the interested browser. Place your art or craft in the buyer's hand. Let them touch it and take control over it. Ask questions. Smile and interact with everyone in your booth, and be aware of your own body language. Make eye contact, lean closer; talk about your craft with pride and enthusiasm. Share what you love about your stamped items with your customers. If you make an item that can be worn, wear it. If the item does something special, demonstrate it. Better yet, sit down and rubberstamp for your audience!

The show business of art and craft keeps the craft professional in touch with the buyer. Enjoy your time with your customers. Be courteous not only to your customers, but also to your fellow exhibitors. Take every opportunity to network with your peers. Trust me, you will meet every kind of temperament and personality while selling at a show. Keep in mind when struggling with a difficult customer or nearby exhibitor that the situation is only temporary.

> ## Handy Hint
>
> Keep up to date with the IRS rules on travel and business deductions. Record your mileage and expenses for each show.

Many art and craft professionals feel they aren't good salespeople. If you feel you aren't cut out to sell your own work, hire someone to do it for you. The extra cost of hiring someone who enjoys selling may be worth the peace of mind you gain by not doing the selling yourself.

If you are prepared, well rested, and enthusiastic about "doing" a show, the results should be positive and profitable. Everyone has a loser show every once in a while. Bad weather, poor advertising, and regional economics sometimes directly affect sales and could reflect in poor or off sales. Don't let one poor show spoil your attitude toward shows in general. Chalk it up to a learning experience and move on!

Within a short period of time after the show, prepare a written evaluation of the show. Be sure to track total sales, total inventory count before and after, weather, traffic in the booth, and ease of setting up. This information will be valuable when you're scheduling future shows.

Home Shows

A home show is like a Tupperware or Mary Kay home party for art and crafts. Art and craft professionals can organize a home show or home party in two different ways:

- The first method is to use the home show as the main avenue for selling your stamped items. To do so successfully, you'll need to book new home shows continually in various individuals' homes to bring in income.

- The second use of the home show is as an additional source of income, with the show held in the artist's or craftsperson's own home on an annual, biannual, or quarterly basis.

As a main source of income, this market must be consistently promoted and your sales area must expand for growth. The professional artisan will often hire others to book, prepare, and sell at the home shows. The additional sales help is paid a straight fee or given a commission based on total sales. As additional income, an annual or quarterly home show is very easy to handle without additional sales help. In either case, contact the city or county where the home show will be held to make sure that there are no city or county statutes prohibiting the exchange of money for business reasons within a private home. Every state, city, and county varies on this topic. Most municipalities consider an annual or quarterly home show as similar to a garage or estate sale. Most states require that sales tax be collected. The city or county may be concerned about the additional traffic flow of the invited guests. Make sure you plan ahead for parking, and notify your neighbors when the event will take place. (More detailed information about zoning and state sales tax is provided in chapter 11.)

You will have to consider location, date, hours, inventory, invitations, and advertising. Prepare the area much like you would for an open house: Remove all personal property from the rooms in which you will display the items for sale, set up an area for bagging purchased supplies and for money exchange. Transform the rooms in the house into a selling showroom. When an item is purchased, replace it immediately. This marketplace really allows you to display your work since your potential buyer can use it. Take every opportunity to show guests how your work will brighten and cheer up their lives and homes. Consider inviting other professionals from non-competing media to join you. This will broaden the craft appeal, bring in others to share expenses, and expand your guest list.

Christmas boutiques are the most popular and successful home shows. Play Christmas music, light scented candles, decorate a tree with lights, serve punch and cookies, and hire a baby-sitter for the kids so Mom or Dad can browse without distractions. Invite the customer to bring a shopping list and stay a while. Offer gift wrapping and handmade gift tags. Have an area of lower priced items so children can purchase gifts for Mom and Dad. Offer a free ornament or a percentage off one item if your buyer brings a new guest for your mailing list. Personalize items on site. Teach a simple rubberstamping project, or have another small craft that guests can make. Your show can be a fun and enjoyable celebration of crafting, so get creative and show off. If you hold the show at the end of your fiscal year, you get the added bonus of reducing your inventory just in time for the tax preparation that's ahead of you.

Sample Show Evaluation Form

Show Name_____

Show Sponsor_____

Date of Show_____

Show Fees_____

Location_____

Annual Event_____

Number of Shows Held to Date_____

My space number_____

Number of total exhibitors_____

Number of direct competitors_____

Sponsor's attitude_____

Exhibitors' attitudes_____

Shoppers' attitudes_____

Weather and environment_____

Sales tax_____

Total sales_____

Total expenses_____

Net profit (loss)_____

Parking for vendors was good / poor

Parking for customers was good / poor

Customer turnout was excellent / good / fair /
  below average / poor

Buyers vs. browsers

Customers were men / women /children / teenagers /
  seniors / other

Publicity was good / fair / poor

Food available was good / poor

Space provided was good / fair / poor

Would a different space have increased buyer traffic?_____

Is there a better way I can set up the booth to increase buyer
  traffic?_____

Comments_____

_____

_____

_____

_____

Craft Malls

Craft malls dot the country. These retail stores sell handcrafted items much like any gift shop. By exhibiting in a mall, you have your own mini-store within the structure of a larger storefront. Your display space can vary in size from a single shelf to larger open floor space. Most malls ask you to sign a contract agreeing that you will occupy a set amount of space for a set period of time. A contract of 6 months or a year is normal. You are not required to spend any time in the mall other than the time you spend stocking your space or changing your display. The vendor is responsible for setting the selling prices of items and keeping the display stocked. The mall management is responsible for the actual selling, collecting of sales tax, and providing you with a detailed sales report.

Questions to Ask Before Applying to a Show

- What is the show fee or cost of space?

- How does the show fee compare to that of other shows?

- What is the cost of travel to the location of the show?

- What are the show's dates and hours?

- Is this an annual or a first-time event?

- Is it a group-, community-, or promoter-organized event?

- Whom should I contact to request a show application?

- What is the deadline for submitting an application?

- Are slides or photos required for entry?

- What categories of work are allowed? Are specific media not allowed?

- What's the total number of exhibitors or booths at the show?

- Is there a refund policy for cancellations or do they offer rain dates?

- Will the exhibits be indoors or outdoors?

- Are there any specific display requirements?

- What is the booth space size, in exact measurements?

- Are electrical outlets available? Will there be a separate charge for electricity?

- What was last year's show attendance?

- How is the show promoted and advertised?

The first large-scale craft mall was Coomer's Craft Mall, which opened its first store just outside of Fort Worth, Texas. Rufus Coomer, a retired IBM executive, founded Coomer's Craft Mall in 1988 to help his crafting friends sell their wares. Within 10 years,

Coomer's grew from one man's simple dream to a company with 30 craft mall locations in nine states; it serves as a retail outlet for more than 25,000 professional artisans and crafters. Imagine starting a new industry just to help some friends sell crafts! Rufus Coomer, who is still active as chairman of the company, did just that when he opened the doors of Coomer's.

Coomer's Craft Mall quickly took the lead in providing new customers to the professional crafter and artisan. "Our tenth anniversary was as much a comment on the growing acceptance and success of craft malls as a retail concept as it is about the success our company has enjoyed as the originator of this segment of the industry," said a Coomer's representative. "We continue to promote the benefits of craft malls to craftspeople. We have an understanding of the historical perspective of the industry with an exciting look at the future of this industry."

Part of that future involves new technology such as bar coding and Internet dealer sales programs that make it easier for the professional to manage their retail sites and operate their businesses. "Our purpose in introducing state-of-the-art technology into what is generally considered to be a low-tech, hands-on artistic industry is to help artisans and crafters minimize the time they spend on retail operations, such as inventory and sales, giving them more time to concentrate on what they know and love best: creating their crafts. Coomer's was built one crafter at a time. Many of our initial crafters are still with us in their original locations, while others have expanded into more markets as we opened new stores."

The original Coomer's Craft Mall was a 2,500-square-foot retail store in the town of Azle, Texas. The store had an opening day gross of $4,500. Today, the company has more than 400,000 square feet of retail space under roof in nine states, and an estimated 1.5 million buying customers a year visit the 30 retail stores. Coomer's shared its success with its professional crafters every step of the way. Rufus Coomer showed that helping promote our friends and American

Locating a Craft Mall

There are hundreds of craft malls throughout the United States and Canada. I know that not everyone uses the Internet on a regular basis, but this is the quickest way to find a craft mall in the location you are interested in. If you need a starting point to find a craft mall near you, just check out the list on the Professional Crafter Web site (see Resources). This site has a current list of craft malls organized by state.

You can also use the keywords "Craft Mall" in most search engines and find listings of craft malls all over the United States. I discovered thousand of sites with information on craft mall locations.

If you do not have access to the Web on a regular basis, there are several public Internet sites available. Call your local school system and find out if there is a way for you to use their computer system. Check out your local library. Most libraries now offer computers with Web access.

A few other craft mall resources include your local Yellow Pages, chamber of commerce, *Sunshine Artist* magazine, and word of mouth recommendations from other artists and crafters.

handicrafts is a winning idea and a profitable idea indeed! Rufus will be the first to tell you that the reason that Coomer's thrived and grew is that the people who "run our stores and the crafters who fill our shelves are the finest and most dedicated people" in the world.

Phillip Coomer, Rufus's son, served as the Coomer's Craft Mall president for many years before starting his own craft malls, called American Craft Malls, which added six more craft malls to a growing number dotting the United States. Phillip added a new element to his malls. Instead of building a stand-alone building or opening up shop in a strip mall shopping area, Phillip opened his malls in well-established shopping malls that had large department chain stores as anchors. This brought handmade art and crafts into the mainstream of American shopping where they thrived in this new marketplace. At the same time that he opened his new craft malls, Phillip Coomer took his concept of selling handmade items to the Internet with a 24-hour craft show called CraftMark, which is discussed later in this chapter.

There is no official directory of craft malls in the United States, but many craft malls advertise in show guides and supply source magazines. Check your local Yellow Pages under "Arts and Crafts" for a craft mall near you.

The right to exhibit in a craft mall is based on a legal agreement. Before you sign on the dotted line, research the mall you want to set up shop in. I found the following wonderful list of questions and considerations at the Professional Crafter Web site (see Resources). The questions apply to any type of selling market in which you aren't selling directly to your customer, including craft malls, craft co-ops, and consignment shops. The list is provided courtesy of Phillip Coomer.

Considerations When Selecting a Craft Mall

Following are some pointers to help you select a good craft mall.

Appearance

Does the store look clean?
Are the booths straightened?
Are booths well stocked?
Is the front counter cluttered?
Does the store have eye appeal?

Sales Staff

Does the staff seem helpful?
Did they greet you as you entered the store?
Do they talk to customers?
Are they smiling?

Do they seem positive and easy to talk to?

Can you talk to the manager easily? The owner?

Customer Service

Do they know the answers to your questions?

Are you able to observe how they handle customer or crafter problems?

If they don't know the answer, will they find out for you?

Jury for Quality

Does the store accept anything, with no standards?

Do they accept imports?

Do they accept factory-made or mass-produced items?

Spaces

Do they have a complete floor plan with sizes and space names marked?

Is there more than one size booth?

Can you change booths, upsize, or even downsize without penalty?

Do customers' traffic patterns take them to your booth?

Signage

Can the store and sign be easily seen from the main road?

Can you tell it's a craft mall?

Is the sign lit at night?

Location

Is the location in a high-traffic area?

What is the demographic profile of the area around the store?

Are there plenty of cars in the parking lot?

Are there complementary businesses nearby? Antique malls
or women's stores?

Hours

Are they open 7 days a week?

Are they closed more than 4 or 5 days of the year?

Are they open during the standard retail hours of the rest
of the shopping center?

Are they open when it will be convenient for you to stock
your shelves?

Crafter Resources

Do they have a resource center?

Do they keep you informed of trends?

Crafter Development

Will they help you with display?

Will they help you with pricing?

Will they help you develop new ideas?

Legal

Do they inform you of legal requirements and/or licenses?

Will they help protect your copyrights?

Do they allow others to violate copyrights in the store?

Information

Do they produce an informative newsletter?

Are the newsletter articles interesting?

Will they tell you sales levels for the store? Sales to rent?

Do they keep you informed of store events?

Do they advise you of or show you specific advertising?

Do they constantly have promotional events going on?

Are there ads for your individual store?

Do the ads affect the area immediately around the store?

Do the ads look great? Good? Boring?

Sales

Does the store allow layaways on any item?

Will the store coordinate special orders? Or are they hands-off?

Does the store protect you from check and credit card fraud?

Do they accept major credit cards?

Can you check sales for all of the stores within the chain at your store?

Remote Service

Does the mall provide a remote service for out-of-state or out-of-city vendors?

Will the mall accept shipments of crafts?

Will your products be set up and displayed with care?

Is there an additional fee charged for the remote service?

How many remote vendors are in the mall?

Terms of the Contract

Read all contracts carefully because of the legal commitments.

Understand exactly what is expected of you as a vendor.

Understand what you expect from the mall management.

Know how long you must agree to display your goods in the contract (6 months, a year?).

Read the contract several times and ask questions.

Get an opinion from a lawyer on the contract.

Payment and Money

Do they pay frequently? Every 2 weeks? End of the month?

Is the time short from close out of that time period's sales to "check in the mail"?

Can you pick up your check? Is direct deposit available?

Can you call anytime to get a summary of your sales?

Costs

Do they pay sales taxes or do you?

Do they take a commission? If so, how much?

Is the rent above or below average?

Does a space at the front counter cost as much as one in the back of the store?

When is rent due? Can you pay at the store?

Security

How do they prevent shoplifting?

If they have an electronic system, what do tags cost?

Can the tags be concealed?

Do they check containers on the way out?

Sales and Merchandising

Does the manager or staff have a booth at the store?

Can you pick your crafter number or is one assigned to you?

Do you have to buy their tags?

Are you required to bar code?

Are you required to work at the store?

Are you allowed to decorate your booth?

The Business

Has the store been around for a long time? Will they be around tomorrow?

Who is the competition?

Do they consistently pay on time?

Do they have more than one location?

Can you get discounts?

What are the benefits of a remote program?

Do they have regular sales?

Do they have crafter gatherings regularly?

Are they a credible risk? What makes them one?

What are other crafters saying?

Have you checked for complaints against the company?

Do they compete in any way with crafters?

Craft Cooperatives

The main difference between a co-op and a craft mall is that in a co-op situation the individuals who make up the co-op have ownership of the co-op. Each vendor is expected to spend a certain amount of time working in the shop as a member of the sales staff. A craft mall is run and operated by an owner or manager in conjunction with a paid sales staff. Another difference between a craft mall and a cooperative is that a co-op is normally juried. You will submit finished samples of your work for review by a committee of co-op members. The work is judged on workmanship and originality; in most cases a competitor of a current co-op member will not be admitted to the co-op. The co-op limits the number of art or craft in different media to cut down on in-store competition. For example, if you make gift tags and the co-op already has three members selling gift tags, you may be turned down. If this happens, try switching to another item. This is a great advantage of being in a cooperative.

As a co-op member, you may have a bigger voice in the management and policies of the co-op. You must take care of your own display. Change the theme and motifs frequently to keep regular customers interested. Low-ticket items from $5 to $15 will sell most quickly and will more than likely cover rent and commission expenses. Make your own unique hang tags and keep a good supply of business cards within your display. It's an excellent idea to post a brief biography and photo of yourself within your display to identify yourself to the customers. If you have the option to work in the shop once or twice a month, take advantage of the opportunity. Working on site will help you stay in contact with your buyer, see how a business operates with a storefront, and allow you to add inventory in your display. The same set of questions (listed under "Craft Malls") used when deciding on a craft mall can be applied to a craft cooperative.

Galleries and Museums

This marketplace displays more upscale art and craft than a craft mall. This is not to say that one kind of work is better than another, but in general galleries show fine art and true craft. This is the perfect venue for high-ticket items like collage and framed work. But don't overlook that the gallery might be interested in one-of-a-kind cards. Most galleries work on a commission basis: You will pay the gallery a percentage of the sale of the item.

> **Handy Hint**
>
> The most cost-effective advertising tool is your business card. Always keep several business cards handy and don't forget to hand a business card to everyone you meet!

You'll need to set up an appointment with the gallery staff or owners who will review your work. Bring a résumé and portfolio to this presentation. (See "Résumé" and "Portfolio" sections in chapter 10.) Don't feel rejected if your work is turned down. Ask why the gallery didn't think your work fit into their environment. Be aware that galleries rarely show more than one artist in a specific technique, craft, or art.

Museums are another great source for heirloom quality work. Most museums and science centers have gift stores that sell both high- and low-ticket items.

Consignment

Consignment sales are different from those of a craft mall, co-op, or museum. In simple terms, the professional allows a retailer to display the work, and when a sale is made the professional will be paid. In most cases the retailer will add a percentage to the price of an item to make the shop's profit.

There are good reasons to go into consignment sales. First, it is better to have work on display somewhere rather than just stored in inventory. Second, consignment has no up-front investment like other markets where rent, time, or other expenditures must be made in advance. In a consignment situation, there should be no investment made. Finally, in many cases, a shop will buy your work outright if the crafts are selling well to the consumer.

This category of sales is one of the most controversial, ranging from horror stories of shops closing overnight to wonderful stories of very successful sales. Yet, the artisan or craftsperson has little if any control over the final selling price, how the work will be displayed, or how well the items will be explained or highlighted.

Before displaying your work on consignment, do your homework. Talk to other consignees within the shop. Make sure there is a contract that states what is expected of both parties, even if you must write the contract yourself. The agreement should specify that the retail shop doesn't claim ownership of the art or craft, but should be responsible for damage or theft. At all times during a consignment agreement, the professional holds all ownership rights to their property.

Once you're set up with a consignment shop, stop in the store regularly to make sure there is enough of your inventory on the shelves to make this market worth your effort. Always tag your products with your company information so that future sales will come directly to your business.

The Internet

In the current business market, the Web may be the greatest business tool the art and craft professional has. Participating in a new craft mall can be a gamble if the management team isn't business savvy. More than 50% of craft malls close their doors before celebrating their first anniversary. Our communities can get overrun with craft show after craft show that saturate and compete for the same gift dollar. Artisans and craftspeople are increasingly competing against imports that are sold so cheaply the artist is tempted to buy the imports and sell them rather than put labor into original handcrafted items. How do we stay current and compete to be able to take advantage of an ever-increasing consumer base? Check out a cyber craft show on the Web!

The first and largest craft show on the Web is CraftMark. The idea of Phillip Coomer, owner of the American Craft Malls, the site opened for business in January 1995. "I always knew the craft industry would play a big part of the World Wide Web. When I first started to create my Web sites there were no craft industry Web sites at all on the Web," said Phillip, who set up a free information service for craft professionals (www.procrafter.com) and started an Internet craft show (www.craftmark.com).

In numbers, CraftMark is twice the size of its largest competitor. Others have tried to provide online markets for professional crafters and artists, but CraftMark led the way. Most important to its success was the marketing plan that Phillip implemented, spending heavy advertising dollars to get the word out to both vendors and finished craft or gift buyers. The second reason for CraftMark's success, in my opinion, is that Phillip provided the creative, yet not high-tech artisan and craftsperson with simple guidelines for getting on the Net in a hurry. CraftMark offers services like digital photography and Web page design as part of its vending contract.

CraftMark can put a crafter online with full-color photos for only $10 per month with no setup fees. Within CraftMark's first month, the original dozen professionals online increased to hundreds of artisans showing their wares on the site. With more than 250 handcrafted businesses on CraftMark, the site boasts more than 5,000 pages or screens of handmade American crafts that visitors can browse and buy. Phillip Coomer combined the high tech of the information superhighway with the down-home appeal of items made by hand. The combination has proved successful to him and his CraftMark vendors.

Web Marketing Considerations

To sell on the Internet, you do not need to access the Internet, but the more involved you are with your selling tools, the better informed you will be. You'll need to become Internet savvy, which is not that difficult or time consuming. You should have an e-mail address for inquiries. Your business must have a computer, modem, and an online service to send and receive electronic mail.

Many artists and craftspeople have been very successful online. They use the Internet as a tool to expand a customer base, build a mailing list, and increase yearly sales. Catalogs, new product information, and newsletters can all be sent very inexpensively via electronic mail.

As with any marketplace, take time to find and view established Web sites. Each site has a unique way of presenting the work of art and craft professionals. To become part of a Web site showcase or gallery, you will have to make two investments: programming time to set up your page at the site, which is normally an hourly charge, and a rental fee per month to maintain the page. Shop around, because pricing for both programming and Web site page rent varies greatly.

You can participate in bulletin board services (areas where notes are posted, usually within an online service) and newsgroups

Selling Your Work on the Web

Phillip Coomer recommends several key tips for placing your work on the Web.

1. Be a part of a large site. It's tempting to want your own domain, but to key in to buyers you need to be a part of a larger site. It means your buyer finds you quicker and easier.

2. Be creative and change your site periodically and also add different products to sell.

3. Be ready for orders. Think out payment plans and shipping needs.

4. Check out other vendors and sites. Be different. Stand out.

5. Ask about how the site advertises. Ask about the marketing plans for the site.

6. Do your research and study the contracts. Be aware of what you are being offered in services and if each service is an additional charge or part of the monthly fee.

7. Remember you are on the World Wide Web and your customer may not be using American currency. Consider money exchanges and services fees.

8. Keywords are important for search engines. What keywords will help your customer find you? Be descriptive of your product even if you have excellent graphics. Tell your buyer exactly what they are buying with materials used and dimensions.

(notes posted from all over the world about specific topics like rubberstamping, soapmaking, and print art). There are commercial bulletin board services where products can be sold directly through the board. The most successful art and craft professional keeps an eye on the future, stays aware of new marketplaces and marketing tools, and takes risks every once in a while. The Internet is the future. Whether to network with fellow professionals or to sell your wares, keep up to date on what's happening on the Net.

Displaying Your Work

I recommend that you visit several shows before preparing your first display. Look at the different products, displays, props, and pricing. Make notes of what attracted your eye, brought you into a booth, and how you reacted to prices and salesmanship.

The average retail customer will spend an average of 1 hour at an art and craft show. If the show you are participating in has 100 exhibitors, you have approximately 6 seconds of that potential buyer's time. Use it wisely by putting together an eye-catching display of your work. The average retail customer spends less than 30 minutes shopping in a retail gift shop like a craft mall or craft co-op. You still only have about 6 seconds to grab the attention of that buyer. But this time, you aren't even there in person to help promote your craft! You need a display that is itself a top-notch sales force.

> ### Did you know???
>
> Some Web sites have up to 1,000 visitors a day, from all over the globe.

Concentrate on what you want your display to accomplish. Displays can consist of simple to elaborate shelving units, tables, props, and signs.

There are several components to an eye-catching display. The first is a general or specific theme that will pull together your body of work. The theme can be built on your art or craft. As a rubberstamper, you might want to incorporate the tools of your trade in the display, using a variety of rubberstamps, colors of ink, or a palette of handmade papers. These small touches bring continuity to your visual presentation. Many artisans use seasonal or holiday themes to create a buying mood with colored lights, garlands of evergreen or fall leaves, bright spring flowers, and other symbols of the season or holiday.

Theme continues with color. Color is eye-catching, and with the right selections the color will accent and complement your work. Don't get lazy or careless when selecting your color choices. Color should enhance, not distract from, your pieces. Experiment with color choices so that your work pops out from rather than fades into your display. Use contrasting colors for your table and shelf covers so that your items do not blend into the tables or shelves.

Props can be more than just decoration in your display; you can use a pot of flowers to "demonstrate" stamped plant sticks or a rotating rack for earrings and necklaces. If you sell stamped eyeglass cases, use sunglasses to show your customer how to use your product. Props should be used to elevate items within your display. Don't just lay items out flat on a table; give the display texture and detail. Props as simple as gift-wrapped boxes, bricks, peach crates, terra cotta pots, and plastic or ceramic risers bring your items up to the buyers' eye level.

Did you know???

Color plays a very important role not just in your display, but also in your packaging.

If you make an item that can be worn, wear it. If the item does something special, demonstrate it. If it is an item that will be placed on the wall of a customer's home, hang it! Use your imagination and invite your customers in to browse and discover your art and craft.

Signs are important to "explain" certain items within displays. Never assume that your potential customer knows what and how to use your product. Easy-to-read, concise printed signs can help the uneducated buyer. Small signs can remind your buyer that Valentine's Day, Mother's Day, Father's Day, or Secretaries Day is just a few weeks away; making the customer aware of upcoming holidays can add more sales to your day. Retail guidelines for signs recommend never to use more than 3 to 4 words per line or more than 3 lines of words on a sign.

Make sure there is enough lighting within your display, so the details and workmanship of your products can be clearly seen by your buyers. Try to avoid shadows within the exhibit. For an indoor show, you may have to invest in some spots in case your booth is located in a dark corner. Outdoors, lighting is rarely a problem except if a canopy top distorts the true colors of your work. You can use an off-white or beige canopy; these offer the least amount of distortion of light and allow natural sunlight to enhance the color of the items they protect.

Last but not least, give the buyer plenty of room to move within and around your display(s). Watch your traffic flow. When designing your booth, use a U- or L-shaped layout of tables, which is favored by most professional crafters. Most booth spaces are approximately 10 feet × 10 feet, so every available nook and cranny within your display should be used efficiently. Remember that you will have to transport, set up, and break down your display many, many times. A rule of thumb is that your display items should be only one-quarter of your available transportation space in a vehicle or when shipping.

Selling Your Designs for Publication

Before getting into the who, how, and why of selling your designs to a publisher, let me be very clear about what is considered an "original design." An original design is one you created through your own merits or skills. If you use the designs of others to build your talents when you're just getting started, you may not sell that work as your own original design. You must be very careful not to infringe on the copyrights of another individual or publisher. (See chapter 11 for additional copyright guidelines.)

I'm very adamant that art and craft professionals know the law. Litigated disputes over copyright infringements are becoming commonplace, and the only way to protect your interests and have a hope of winning in such a dispute is to be well documented and prepared.

There are several ways to document and keep records of your design work. First, take photographs of each new design you create. Clear photographs can be used to jog your own memory when writing up craft instructions and can also be used to send to an editor for consideration.

It's important to keep a journal of your work and make notes in this journal about the supplies you've used. Most craft designers and artists use journals to track their productivity and as a handy reference for future projects.

You can file for a copyright for your designs by completing and sending the necessary paperwork, with a small fee, to the Library of Congress. You own the copyright to your work the minute you create it; however, to protect your rights it's best to consult a lawyer and file the appropriate forms with the government.

Once you feel confident with your understanding of copyrights, it is time to sit down and start submitting your work.

Designing for publication takes practice, discipline, and patience. Take an honest look at your ability to communicate. Writing may not be your forte or a skill you wish to develop. A healthy self-esteem comes in handy; even the best craft designers have received rejection letters. But, if you'd like to see your name in print and get paid for the effort, follow these basic steps:

> **Did you know???**
>
> Colors can set a tone. Bright, bold colors are festive. Pastel, soft colors are comforting. Country colors with gray undertones are rustic and relaxing. Black and white is stark, but builds confidence. Red or yellow means caution, slow down and yield.

1. Find a publisher whose products match your own style or work. The easiest way is to select your favorite craft magazine. If your designs are quick or easy to do, *Quick and Easy Crafts* magazine would fit the bill, whereas a collage that took you 3 weeks wouldn't. Take a look at all the art, craft, and home décor magazines on the shelf. In the reference

area of any library you'll find a directory of magazines and periodicals that categorizes magazines by subject.

2. Write a brief letter to the editor asking for the magazine's Writer's Guidelines. Guidelines may vary even if the same publisher publishes two different magazines. The editor's name and magazine's address are usually listed near the front of the magazine. Ask for a copy of the magazine's editorial calendar. This calendar will inform you what the magazine is planning for future issues and includes deadline information. It's too late to submit a design for Mother's Day in March. It's too late to have a Thanksgiving design considered for the current year's calendar in October. Most designs are needed 6 months to a year before the publication date of the magazine.

3. Send a query letter to the editor describing your design and include a sketch or clear photo of your work.

4. Allow time for the editor to review your submission. After 4 to 6 weeks, if you haven't heard from the editor, follow up with a phone call or letter.

5. If your design is accepted, find out what your deadlines are. If instructions haven't been written, do so immediately. Ship a sample and instructions to the editor.

6. You'll sign a contract. Read it and understand it. Ask questions if you don't understand any details of the contract. Most contracts ask for all rights, but you can always negotiate a contract. Don't be intimidated by the legal language.

7. If your design is rejected, don't take it personally. It may not fit the magazine's current needs. Try a different magazine.

Teaching or Demonstrating

The last marketplace we'll discuss is teaching and demonstrating your rubberstamping skills to others. You can do this as a volunteer, or you can charge a class or demonstration fee for your efforts. Teaching others can be very rewarding. It's a great opportunity to interact with others and to help others enjoy a skill you have expertise in.

Whether you want to teach or demonstrate, provide a résumé and portfolio to each store or organization that you approach. A résumé is a brief and concise written outline of your body of work and experience. (I've provided my own résumé in chapter 10 as an example of what a résumé should include. It's only a guide, and you should compose your own unique résumé.) A portfolio is a "picture" or photo spread of your body of work. It can be as simple as a three-ring binder, or you can purchase professional portfolio cases from an office or art store. You should include designs available for purchase, designs sold, and any tearsheets you may have of published work. A tearsheet is a printed page that is "torn" from a magazine; it should include the magazine's cover, table of contents, and any pages that have your design or instructions on them. Your portfolio can include illustrations, drawings, published work, awards, personal and work references, and photos. The objective of the résumé and portfolio is to show the potential client that you are professional, motivated, prepared, and ready to take on any assignment given to you. They're a visual and written display of your body of work. Be creative and be honest in your résumé and portfolio.

Teaching will require a class plan. You will have to create a project, write up an outline for the class including step-by-step instructions, prepare a list of materials each student must bring, and plan how the class lesson will flow. How much time do you need to teach your class? Will the student leave with a finished project? It's best if you can be very well prepared ahead of time.

Selling a Book

1. Submitting an idea to a book publisher is very similar to submitting one to a magazine, but usually many designs are needed for a book. You generally need to present a concept and up to 36 designs before a publisher will contract for a book. Book publishers have Writer's Guidelines available upon request.

2. To find publishers, consult your reference librarian or the Internet. You can find contact information in several directories.

3. Keep current on popular trends, including colors, media, techniques, and motifs. Check out what's at the craft retailers and shops. A design will not sell if the supplies are not readily available to the consumer.

4. You will need to write an outline of the book to submit to a publisher. Include the theme of the book, chapter contents, and illustrations or graphics. Also include your résumé, examples of your work, and any other information that will help the publisher know you are a credible artist and author.

5. Send your book proposal and outline to the acquisitions or purchase editor at the publisher. Allow at least 4 weeks, and follow up with a phone call to the editor.

6. If accepted, you will be sent a contract. Read it carefully, and don't sign until you feel comfortable and understand the contract. Now is the time to ask the editor any questions you may have. If you want more money for the design, bring it up with the editor. If you want to grant only first rights, bring it up. (See chapter 11 for more information on the sale of rights.)

7. After signing the contract, make sure to meet your deadlines and supply everything the editor requests, like supply lists, time required to make the designs, and total cost.

8. If rejected, try another publisher, or make any changes in the proposal and outline that might give the book idea a fresh look.

Check out ahead of time where the class will be held. (See sidebar, Places to Demonstrate or Teach Your Art, on page 220 for great ideas on where to teach classes.) Is there enough space to move about safely while teaching? Does the classroom have all the equipment you need, such as running water and good lighting? How many students can you put in the room without crowding the space? What will you have to bring to the classroom, such as heat guns, embossing powders, papers or card stock, glue guns, paintbrushes, or table protection? What will the store owner or school organizer provide? Some problems can be solved; others might have to be worked around or will require adjustments to your lesson plan. Preparation is the key to teaching success.

Learn as much as you can about your students too. What is the age group? Gender? Are the students beginners, with no knowledge of even the basics of crafting? To a certain degree you can set the standard for the students you want to teach, but be prepared for anything! The final decision will be how much to charge your students for the class. You can set a flat fee, by considering the cost of preparing samples, the cost of goods used during the class, and any transportation costs you may encounter, plus your time in class. Just like when you're pricing your crafts, you'll have to keep in mind the going rate of other teachers' fees and what the regional economy can afford. Some stores and organizations charge a room fee or ask for a percentage of the class fee. Carefully record all your expenses. Make sure that your bottom line is in the black, not in the red!

The more experience you get as a teacher, the higher your class fee can become. When I started teaching, my class fee was set at around $10 per hour of teaching. I often supplied materials to be used by the students in class to make it easier for the students. I still supply materials for my classes, but my average class fee is now $20 per hour of class per student. At trade shows I often earn up to $200 for an hour class; however, the planning and preparation time for a trade show class is much more intense than for a local class at a museum.

When demonstrating, you will only show others how to stamp, emboss, or color an image; the people watching the demonstration

Places to Demonstrate or Teach Your Art

If there isn't an obvious place in your community where you can teach or demonstrate your skills, create your own teaching environment! It's not that difficult, and you'll find that word of mouth will help you keep demonstrating and teaching. Following is a list of places that might welcome your talents:

Adult education programs	Family gatherings and reunions
Art supply stores	Hardware and do-it-yourself shops
Bookstores	High schools
Children's after-school care	Home shows or home parties
Churches	Libraries
City parks	Local chapters of associations
City recreational centers	Middle schools
Civic club lunches or meetings	Museums
Community colleges	Nursing homes
Community festivals	Scouting groups
Craft retail stores	Senior centers
Craft shows	Trade schools
Cultural associations	Trade shows
Day care centers	Universities and colleges
Elementary schools	Zoos

will not actually make the item. Your presentation might not be as detailed as it would be in a class; however, the most successful demonstrators often provide handouts or flyers that list the supplies needed to create what's being demonstrated.

Most demonstrations are set up at a table, and you will be allowed to stand or sit while demonstrating. Demonstrations may last several hours, but you should allow breaks. The average fee for demonstrations ranges from an hourly rate to a day rate. The industry average is around $60 for a 4- to 5-hour day. Some professional demonstrators will earn up to $25 to $50 per hour for their expertise. Just remember that your fee usually does not include setup or breakdown time. Setup and breakdown are on your time, not the hiring company's. Professional demonstrators often receive reimbursement for any travel expenses, but be sure to discuss this before the demonstration. Never assume *anything* about what is expected of you as a demonstrator. Ask questions, and better yet, get any agreements in writing.

A Chapter Ends, But You're Just Getting Started

There are so many different markets for the art and craft professional's work today that an entire book could be written on any one of the marketplaces alone. In this chapter I have highlighted a few of the most popular and easy-to-access markets. But there are many more, including selling directly to a retailer, organizing a craft fair, presenting on TV shopping channels, using direct mail, opening up a storefront, and so much more.

An artisan I know allows her customers to make appointments to come to her house to buy her work. Normally, I only sell at outdoor shows, but people pick up my business card and often call asking for items. If I don't have a show coming up in the area, I will invite the customer over during weekend or evening hours. (I do this only when I know my husband will be home when the customer comes.) I set up a few tables in the garage and let the customers go through the boxes that store my inventory.

Part of growing a business is to keep searching for new and exciting areas to promote and sell your unique art and craft. Sometimes that means taking risks, but most areas can be researched with the help of the Small Business Administration or other business consulting firms.

I hope you feel the same excitement I do when thinking about the different markets in which you can sell your handmade and hand-stamped goods. I've watched the markets change and grow over the years, but there is always a market for quality handmade items. You may select to sell your crafts only in one place, or you may decide to use a combination of markets to reach your customers. There is no right or wrong way to sell your products. Your market selection should complement your goals.

As your business grows, your interests and goals may change too. The marketplace is flexible enough to bend and turn with your business needs. But now we have to let your customers know where to find you! Can you guess how to do it? It's my first love: advertising! The next chapter will give you a head start on getting the word out about you, your business, and your stamped art.

Marketing Your Rubberstamping

Advertising and Publicity

▼▼

I JUST LOVE WATCHING TV commercials and looking at slick magazine advertisements. I enjoy figuring out, by reading and watching ads, exactly what a company wants the consumer to "feel" about the company and its products. My interest in commercials and print ads springs from my fascination with how a company presents its image to the public. Today's business world is about image and being able to communicate with the consumer and the public.

Companies and businesses consider many things when putting together an advertising campaign or plan. They decide whether to do a hard sell or a soft sell. They select the type fonts, the text styling, and the color selections of their ads. They choose the musical score or jazzy jingle, the announcer's voice and the snappy slogan. A company's advertising plan is part of its marketing and merchandising strategy. Even though many creative businesses are small sole proprietorships, every artist and craftsperson who wishes to sell his or her goods must have a marketing and merchandising plan that includes some advertising and public relations.

Public Relations

It's free advertising! Advertising your craft business may be hard on your budget, but there are some simple and free ways to publicize your work and business.

- Visit and teach a craft to a scouting group. There are plenty of parents involved who are potential customers.

- Offer to set up a display of your work at a local school's teachers' lounge. Teachers have little time to shop the craft shows and malls. Bring your crafts to them. Small items are best for this group.

- Get involved with a fund-raiser. Network and talk about what you make.

- When exciting events happen in your business—you win a ribbon at a show, you've added a new craft mall to your list, you donate to a fund-raiser—write up a press release for the newspaper (see Press Release section later in this chapter).

Business Cards

The most basic advertising tool for your company will be your business card. There are three essential elements to this calling card. The first element is a company name. You might choose to use your personal name for your company, but I strongly recommend that you use a business or company name. The name you choose should be easy to remember, easy to spell, and clearly communicate your confident expertise to the customer. The company name will be used on all company paperwork like brochures, letterhead, Web site, and invoices.

When I started to sell my work to the public, I elected to use the business name of *By Maria*, but after less than 2 years I felt the company name didn't reflect my work, and my customers didn't remember it. Around that time I was getting a new dining room set

- Have plenty of inexpensive black-and-white or color head-and-shoulder photographs of yourself or your work to send in with press releases.

- Contact a local TV station and volunteer to go on air and talk about crafting. You might demo a simple craft or show samples of your work.

- Join a local guild, crafting group, or art association. Network and be an active member to learn about opportunities. Join national guilds, societies, and associations. Keep on top of the trends, events, and activities.

- If you are involved in a charitable activity involving crafting or if you make a really unique item, contact a craft magazine. Many consumer craft magazines have regular columns that feature crafters. Some also feature "spotlights" on individual artists. Many cover pieces have been submitted by individual artists or craftspeople. Write up your story and send it in, and send along a clear photo or slide of your work.

from the Virginia House furniture manufacturing company. I liked that company name. It sounded strong and solid. Although you might not guess it was a furniture manufacturer by the name, it was a name you could trust—easy to remember, and easy to spell. The name left a mark in your mind. Thus, *Nerius House* was born. But I didn't want to limit my possibilities (I've always thought in the big picture), so I added *& Companies* to my company name. Nerius House & Companies. Consumer recognition doubled for me in less than 6 months!

Rules and regulations for business name selection are detailed in chapter 11 of this book. For example, you can't just add *incorporated, limited, unlimited,* or other legal terms to your business name unless you take the legal steps to use such terms. Your state may require you to file a fictitious name statement to inform the community that you "do business as" or are "also know as" your business name. A fictitious name is not a trademarked name, nor does it give you sole rights to use the name.

The second element of a business card is contact information about you and your company. Information should include a contact person's name (you) and a company address for correspondence. You may elect to use your home street address or rent a P.O. box. Depending on how convenient it is to rent a P.O. box in your community, I strongly recommend you do so, even though it is an additional expense. When you use your home address, there are sometimes misunderstandings with customers who assume you're in a retail storefront. People may just stop by your home "while in the neighborhood;" this can be an inconvenience to your workday or your evenings. Many companies use P.O. boxes for privacy even though they are home-based businesses.

> **Handy Hint**
>
> Use an answering machine during the day if you don't want phone interruptions as you work.

Contact information on your business card should also include a phone number. Since you are a business, don't allow children to answer the phone during business hours of 8:00 A.M. to 5:00 P.M. Although your customers might find it charming to hear your son's or daughter's voice yelling for you, a supplier or other business associate might not be so thrilled. It's one of the downsides of being in business within your home. You must be willing to show a very polished and professional business demeanor to the rest of the world.

Other important contact information to include on your card, if applicable, are an e-mail address, a Web site address, business hours, your job title, and selling slogan or trademark.

The final ingredient to a business card is a logo. For your logo you can use clip art that is copyright-free, but if you have artistic ability, create your own logo. Just like your company name, your logo should convey a strong image of what your company is about. My original logo was a clip-art doll. Once I started making enough money to budget for a graphic artist, I hired one who'd been recommended by my printing company to create an illustration of my own doll, which was unique with wild jute hair and a simple sweet face. The logo truly reflected the free spirit and sparkle of my company. I was thrilled with the image and used it immediately on all my business papers, from business cards to letterhead to invoices. My callbacks from customers increased 200% that year.

The key elements of your business card can be used on all your company's printed and electronic materials. Use the contact information and logo on your correspondence and communications as well as on all printed materials and on your Web site. Include your e-mail address and Web site address on every piece of promotional information. Be consistent. Repetition is what makes people remember your name. Reinforce your name, the company name, and contact information whenever possible. Tag all your designs and products with your contact information. Insert a business flyer in all designs you bag, ship, or package. Take every opportunity to promote and advertise your talents, skills, products, and designs.

Other Promotional Tools

We've all heard the saying, "There's no such thing as a free lunch." Yet, there is some free promotion available to you! This section explores your options.

Press Release

The first element to explore is the press release. This simple document tells the world about your business, your talents, or any other newsworthy event that happens to your company. A press release is simple. Across the top of a sheet of paper, type up your name,

Checklist of Printed Business Credentials

To support your work in any marketplace, you'll need a few items of paperwork to help establish you as a legitimate business in the eyes of your customers, suppliers, and business community. Following is a brief checklist of such items.

- Business cards: Make your card unique to your company. Include your name, business name, address, phone number, and e-mail address or Web site if you have one. Always carry several business cards when you go out, even if it is just to the local convenience store. There is always an opportunity to tell someone new about your work and your business. Handing them a business card reinforces your message.

- Résumé: This is your advertisement, your foot in the door; it introduces you to a potential buyer. Include your name, physical and e-mail addresses, contact numbers like phone and fax, photos of yourself and your work, listing of shows and other markets you've participated in, and the mission statement of your company.

business name, address, and phone number. Just below this information, type, in all caps: "FOR IMMEDIATE RELEASE." Then write up the information. You can submit a press release to any media in your area, community, and trade. Take a good look at your local newspaper. Is there a section dedicated to business? Are there regular weekly feature articles on local businesses or activities? If you can't find such sections, then call the newspaper and ask! While you are on the phone, call any local radio or TV stations and ask the same question. You might be surprised at how eager your local media is to spotlight hometown talent! Check out the magazines you read. Subscribe to trade magazines and submit your press releases to them.

- Portfolio: Picture book of your work, accomplishments, awards, and items for sale. Photos do not need to be professionally done, just clear and showing different angles of the craft. Include measurements if photos do not show proportions.

- Letterhead: Business stationery, usually to match the business card. A must for all business and professional correspondence.

- Business checking account: There is *no* business without one. It is highly recommended that you have a Business savings account as well. Consult your accountant, lawyer, bank, or savings institution on all small business matters. Do not use a personal savings or checking account for business transactions. Never mix personal and business money. Never borrow out of the business for personal reasons unless it is a true emergency.

- State, city, or county business licenses, if applicable.

- Copy of resale or tax collection certificate. Keep a copy of the original on hand at all times when selling or making a sales presentation if your state collects sales tax.

- Copies of a supplier invoice and a customer invoice. These are required by most trade shows and are needed to apply for credit from a supplier of your raw goods.

You need to include all your contact information in your press release, so that if the person receiving it has any questions, he or she can call for confirmation. Use simple language and be brief. A concise, interesting press release will be read and used more than a complicated, novel-length release. Allow 1 to 2 weeks for the press release to be received and read. Don't be afraid to follow up a press release with a phone call to the media contact.

A press release is good, free advertising for your company. It's part of your advertising plan, but will never make a hole in your advertising budget. You never know who might be reading the newspaper or watching a TV spot. An hour spent polishing a press release could lead to new work and new customers.

Résumé

The résumé is a tool that helps prospective clients or employers become familiar with your work history, skills, talents, and abilities. You can find many wonderful books, articles, and even computer software available on the topic of preparing a work résumé. However, most résumés are designed for "the real world." There is no consideration allowed for the fact that you are seeking to give information about just how creative you are! I recommend adjusting some of the standard résumé forms to better fit the creative industries. You must still get the basic information across to the person you are handing the résumé to, but don't discount your creative abilities. I've provided a basic outline below to help you create your own résumé:

Include, in the following order:

- Résumé of [your name]

- Your full name, address, phone number, e-mail address, fax number, and any other contact information that would help the recipient reach you.

- Your current employment.

- Your brief work history. Include all paying jobs and any volunteer positions that gave you additional skills. Describe your own business activities and include anyone else in the crafts industry you have performed services such as writing, teaching, or demonstrating for.

- Your craft media. List, in alphabetical order, all the craft media you work in and the kinds of designs you specialize in. Example: Angels, beads, children's crafts, florals, greeting cards, paper embossing, seasonal crafts, stamping. Your education—especially education in areas related to the management of a crafts business or any services you may provide

Your Mission Statement

A great way to start a bio sheet or résumé is to open with a mission statement. In one or two concise, concentrated sentences, write down your goals or hopes for the business. This beginning will lead the way for the other tidbits and facts in a bio sheet.

Can you guess which companies might have the following mission statements? (I made up four of the examples, but the message gets across. One mission statement is real and is used by Nerius House & Companies.)

1. Stamping our hearts out.

2. Need art? You need Fine Art Stamps On-line.

3. Teaching the world the love of stamping, one student at a time.

4. Crafting can express the care and love of our community. And the world is our community. Let us be the first to make a difference.

5. Addicted and admit it!

A. Nerius House & Companies

B. Rubber & Art Design

C. Stamped Teachers Company

D. Stamped Obsessions

E. Heartfelt Stamp Shop, Valentine, FL

Answers:

1:E, 2:B, 3:C, 4:A, 5:D

such as art, crafts, design, advertising, marketing, business management, communications, or others.

■ Magazine publications. Formatting is important: List name of periodical first (in italics), month and year of publication, and name of article. Example: *Quick and Easy Crafts* (12/00).

■ "Tea Time Journal and Frame."

■ Book publications.

■ Awards, including any community or industry activities and awards you've received. Examples: Quoted Expert: *Craftlinks,*

Bio Sheets

Here are some fun examples of bio sheets. From quite serious to downright homey fun, each example informs customers and potential customers about the person and their company.

One: Maria Nerius

Maria Nerius established Nerius House & Companies in 1985, in the city of Palm Bay in central Florida. Her unique handmade items have been treasured by customers and have decorated homes for many a holiday ever since. As the company grew, Maria branched out into design publication and has more than 500 designs published in magazines ranging from *Good Housekeeping* to *Craftworks*. Currently, she has four national consumer and trade magazine columns, which reach over 1 million readers.

In 1996, Maria was honored as Designer of the Year by the craft industry and was given her own regular weekly TV segment on *Aleene's Creative Living*. "Many opportunities have come my way, and I enjoy the variety of work available to me. However, creating rubberstamp creations is still my first love, and that love is so strong I don't think I'll ever retire."

1998, 1999; Press Day (HIA) Participant, 1993, 1995, 1996, 1998; Featured Designer: *Aleene's Creative Living* magazine, 1997; Craft Designer of the Year, 1996.

You *must* keep a record of all your work in rubberstamping.

A résumé is a great place to display that record. In the beginning this may not take up much space, but as your career grows so will this area of your résumé. You may want to make this a separate sheet attached to your résumé. List all teaching, demonstrating, and published work.

You *should* have a cover letter, even if it is just your bio sheet.

Two: Tracia Ledford-Williams

Tracia Ledford-Williams, creator of Paintabilities, started her career as a professional crafter who created wreaths for sale. She wanted a way to quickly paint clever signs on each wreath and developed a sponge stamp method that worked beautifully. A creative spirit, Tracia wanted to share this quick and easy method with others. Thus Paintabilities was born. This stamping system can make even the novice a master artist in a few hours. Give Paintabilities a try today!

Three: Daniel Boone

Looking to take a stamping class that will help you stretch and grow as a stamp artist? Mark your calendar today for the classes taught by Daniel Boone. Sign up for Reaching the Stars and Dancing on the Moon. Daniel has been stamping for more than two decades, and his designs have been published in numerous consumer magazines, but the real treat is to experience his showmanship in the classroom. Be prepared to laugh, enjoy yourself, and be delightfully entertained by this expert. "If the students aren't smiling, then I'm not doing my job! I prepare and plan for the most educationally entertaining techniques classes available in rubberstamping," exclaims Boone. "And yes, I am a descent of the famous Daniel Boone, but I don't wear a raccoon tail hat unless my students ask me to."

You *should* use excellent quality paper for your résumé.

You *should* put a photo of yourself on the cover sheet or résumé.

You *should* update your résumé at least twice a year.

You *don't* have to have the résumé professionally printed; feel free to use your own computer to prepare your résumé.

Portfolio

A portfolio is a visual presentation of your body of work. Any type of binder notebook can be used for a portfolio, and you can choose from many different styles at art, craft, and office supply stores.

Portfolios are used during one-on-one interviews and also can be mailed or shipped to prospective clients or employees. If mailing, always include a return envelope with proper postage and a set date when your portfolio should be returned.

Portfolios can include:

Your résumé

Photos of your work

Sketches of your work

Tearsheets of your published work

Letters of recommendation

Class outlines and plans

Photo of yourself

Any other examples that will help the recipient understand your work

If you include photos of sold work, clearly note that the work has been sold or published.

Have fun and get creative with this selling tool!

Handy Hint

Make sure you ask new customers how they found you or found out about your company. This will help you put your money into advertising that is reaching your target audience.

Word-of-Mouth Advertising

Another cost-free tool is word-of-mouth advertising. Your existing customers can bring in new customers. Word of mouth is based for the most part on how good your customer service is and how your customers feel about your products. Treat your customers with respect and with a smile, and they will tell others about your company. Use customer incentives. Consider giving a 5% to 10% discount on a purchase to a loyal customer for every new customer he or she brings in. Offer a discount for every $100 purchase. You can give a customer a small ornament or other small-ticket item after 6 or 10 purchases. These small incentives work and spread goodwill between you and your customer base.

Direct Mail

Keep a mailing list of all your customers. Have a mail list sign-up sheet or guest book wherever you sell your work. If you decide to have an open house, if you know you will be doing a show in the area, or if you have added new designs to your line, drop a postcard in the mail to people on your list. Offer a small discount or special gift if the customer brings the postcard back to you. I keep a list of my customers who have spent more than $100 on a purchase. Shortly after the purchase I send out a note thanking them for their business. This small gesture has paid for itself many times over by keeping my loyal customers happy and coming back for more. A mail list can work with a Web site too! Keep track of your traffic and send out announcements to your regular visitors.

> **Handy Hint**
>
> Have at your fingertips all the tools you need to promote and grow your business: business cards, a bio sheet, a résumé, and a portfolio.

Newspapers and Magazines

Consider placing a small ad in a local newspaper to advertise a show you'll be in or to advertise your business. Put a small ad in a consumer magazine or trade magazine. Many shows and events have flyers or programs that are handed out to the attendees; these are great places to advertise.

Back Up Your Credibility

No matter what you call it—bio sheet, publicity release, bragging papers, or self-promotion brochure—everyone in the field of creative business needs to write a 100- to 300-word document describing who they are and what they do. This copy should be attached to any press releases, new customer contacts, supplier credit forms,

DANIEL'S STORY

Daniel Boone is a designer for the craft industry, but he's also a generous stamper! "The concept of doing something cheaply or inexpensively means I'm using my greatest resource (my creativity) to its fullest potential," says Daniel. When it comes to sharing what I've learned over the years, however, I'm a spendthrift. Sharing fun and creative ideas means as much to my well-being as breathing clean air.

One of the aspects of being a designer and a stamper is that Daniel has learned not always to view or use supplies as the directions dictate. "I sit down and think, *How can I use this supply or product in a new way?* It keeps me fresh. It keeps me on my toes. I will stamp an image upside down or to the side and take a look at the image. 'What if . . .' should be a part of every stamper's vocabulary!"

One of Daniel's favorite techniques is to make a stamp out of craft foam. "You can cut out a design or carve a design into the foam. You can

and any other materials that let the receiver know what your company is about. This important tool can help you open doors and get others to take notice of your efforts. It is a form of introduction. For a real bonus, include a photo of yourself and your designs on your bio sheet. Ask your local printer about how to incorporate a photo into a 1-page bio sheet. The small additional cost is well worth the price of having your customers not only recognize your company, but recognize you and your design line!

None of us want to become big-headed egotists, but to survive in a very competitive creative world we must let others know what we are doing. It is not easy to sit down and come up with a few hundred words that describe you and your business. But you are doing something that is not just for others to read; the bio sheet is just as

glue cut-out shapes of foam to a can or rolling pin and have a new stamp with little fuss or cost! You can also create great stamps with hot glue gun images!" says Daniel. "Fair warning, however, once you start letting yourself enjoy the process of 'playing' with your supplies and stamps, you may find it difficult to follow instructions or have blind faith in traditional techniques."

The real success of stamping is in the sharing, according to Daniel. "Dr. Frank Lauback was world renowned for his efforts to promote literacy with the phrase, 'Each one teach one.' I believe this works with art and craft too. I know whenever I teach others, I find myself receiving a wealth of information in return."

important to you as it is to promoting your efforts. It can help you focus and concentrate on your goals. Write your bio sheet in the third person (as if you were writing about someone whom you admired) if you find yourself struggling to find the right words. Give the bio sheet interest by not just stating the facts, but by adding the flair, creativity, and imagination of your own personality.

A Fond Adieu Until
We Stamp Again . . .

Well, my part is done in this book. Barbara Brabec explains the details and legalities of a small business in chapter 11. In the sections at the back of this book, you'll find more information that can help you in your hobby or business: glossaries of terms, lists of suppliers and Web sites, and recommended books and magazines. It's important that you continue to learn and gather knowledge about techniques, designs, and business practices. Change is a part of the art, craft, and creative world. New trends form even as you read these words. Colors, textures, themes, motifs, and styles come and go and transform over the years. However, the basics as outlined and explained in this book will never be dated.

When you find your niche, when you discover that perfect something that makes your life better and brighter and bolder, you've found what you were meant to do in this world. Artists, artisans, and craftspeople make the world more colorful with their rainbows of creativity. Whether you plan to enjoy rubberstamping as a hobby or whether you make it a part-time or full-time occupation, I wish you success and satisfaction in your talents and skills. Remember to share your skills and talents with others, so the love of rubberstamping can be passed on to the next generation.

This book became a reality thanks to my family and friends who patiently helped me collect and assemble all my information without losing my writing style or personal voice. Your family and friends will also be significant to your success. I know I don't have to remind you, but make sure you always let your loved ones know how much you value them!

Writing this book has been an absolute joy for me. I've loved rubberstamping as a hobby and as a profession for many years. I've shared that love many times and in many ways, but this book was a true labor of love, and is dedicated to all the wonderful teachers and students I've had the pleasure of meeting and knowing. But most of all, I hope this book expresses the wonderful sensation you can feel as an artist. Once you feel that rush of excitement, you'll be hooked for life.

Consider yourself warmly welcomed to the world of creative rubberstamping. We are often a silly bunch of individuals who are constantly on the lookout for a new surface to stamp, a new notion to embellish our work, or a new market in which to make our stamping profitable. I am proud to be a member of this creative society. I do hope you will feel the same!

chapter 11

A Mini-Course in Crafts-Business Basics

by Barbara Brabec

▼▼

THIS SECTION OF THE BOOK will familiarize you with important areas of legal and financial concern and enable you to ask the right questions if and when it is necessary to consult with an attorney, accountant, or other business adviser. Although the tax and legal information included here has been carefully researched by the author and is accurate to the best of her knowledge, it is not the business of either the author or publisher to render professional services in the area of business law, taxes, or accounting. Readers should therefore use their own good judgment in determining when the services of a lawyer or other professional would be appropriate to their needs.

Information presented applies specifically to businesses in the United States. However, because many U.S. and Canadian laws are similar, Canadian readers can certainly use the following information as a start-up business plan and guide to questions they need to ask their own local, provincial, or federal authorities.

Contents

1. Starting Right

In preceding chapters of this book, you learned the techniques of a particular art or craft and realized its potential for profit. You learned what kinds of products are likely to sell, how to price them, and how and where you might sell them.

Now that you've seen how much fun a crafts business can be (and how profitable it might be if you were to get serious about selling what you make!) you need to learn about some of the "nitty-gritty stuff" that goes hand in hand with even the smallest business based at home. It's easy to start selling what you make and it's satisfying when you earn enough money to make your hobby self-supporting. Many crafters go this far and no further, which is fine. But even a hobby seller must be concerned about taxes and local, state, and federal laws. And if your goal is to build a part- or full-time business at home, you must pay even greater attention to the topics discussed in this section of the book.

Everyone loves to make money . . . but actually starting a business frightens some people because they don't understand what's involved. It's easy to come up with excuses for why we don't do certain things in life; close inspection of those excuses usually boils down to fear of the unknown. We get the shivers when we step out of our comfort zone and try something we've never done before. The simple solution to this problem lies in having the right information at the right time. As someone once said, "Knowledge is the antidote to fear."

The quickest and surest way to dispel fear is to inform yourself about the topics that frighten you. With knowledge comes a sense of power, and that power enables you to move. Whether your goal is merely to earn extra income from your craft hobby or launch a genuine home-based business, reading the following information will help you get started on the right legal foot, avoid financial pitfalls, and move forward with confidence.

When you're ready to learn more about art or crafts marketing or the operation of a home-based crafts business, a visit to your library or bookstore will turn up many interesting titles. In addition to the special resources listed by this book's author, you will find my list of recommended business books, organizations, periodicals, and other helpful resources later in this chapter. This information is arranged in a checklist you can use as a plan to get your business up and running.

Before you read my Mini-Course in Crafts-Business Basics, be assured that I understand where you're coming from because I was once there myself.

For a while I sold my craft work, and this experience led me to write my first book, *Creative Cash*. Now, 20 years later, this crafts-business classic ("my baby") has reached its sixth edition. Few of those who are totally involved in a crafts business today started out with a business in mind. Like me, most began as hobbyists looking for something interesting to do in their spare time, and one thing naturally led to another. I never imagined those many years ago

Social Security Taxes

When your crafts-business earnings are more than $400 (net), you must file a Self-Employment Tax form (Schedule SE) and pay into your personal Social Security account. This could be quite beneficial for individuals who have some previous work experience but have been out of the workplace for a while. Your re-entry into the business world as a self-employed worker, and the additional contributions to your Social Security account, could result in increased benefits on retirement.

Because so many senior citizens are starting home-based businesses these days, it should be noted that there is a limit on the amount seniors age 62 to 65 can earn before losing Social Security benefits. This dollar limit increases every year, however, and once you are past the age of 65, you can earn any amount of income and still receive full benefits. Contact your nearest Social Security office for details.

when I got serious about my craft hobby that I was putting myself on the road to a full-time career as a crafts writer, publisher, author, and speaker. Because I and thousands of others have progressed from hobbyists to professionals, I won't be at all surprised if someday you, too, have a similar adventure.

2. Taxes and Record Keeping

"Ambition in America is still rewarded . . . with high taxes," the comics quip. Don't you long for the good old days when Uncle Sam lived within his income and without most of yours?

Seriously, taxes are one of the first things you must be concerned about as a new business owner, no matter how small your endeavor. This section offers a brief overview of your tax responsibilities as a sole proprietor.

Is Your Activity a "Hobby" or a "Business"?

Whether you are selling what you make only to get the cost of your supplies back or actually trying to build a profitable business, you need to understand the legal difference between a profitable hobby and a business, and how each is related to your annual tax return.

The IRS defines a hobby as "an activity engaged in primarily for pleasure, not for profit." Making a profit from a hobby does not automatically place you "in business" in the eyes of the Internal Revenue Service, but the activity will be *presumed* to have been engaged in for profit if it results in a profit in at least 3 out of 5 years. Or, to put it another way, a "hobby business" automatically becomes a "real business" in the eyes of the IRS at the point where you can state that you are (1) trying to make a profit, (2) making regular business transactions, and (3) have made a profit 3 out of 5 years.

As you know, all income must be reported on your annual tax return. How it's reported, however, has everything to do with the amount of taxes you must pay on this income. If hobby income is less than $400, it must be entered on the 1040 tax form, with taxes payable accordingly. If the amount is greater than this, you must file a Schedule C form with your 1040 tax form. This is to your advantage, however, because taxes are due only on your *net profit.* Because you can deduct expenses up to the amount of your hobby income, there may be little or no tax at all on your hobby income.

Self-Employment Taxes

Whereas a hobby cannot show a loss on a Schedule C form, a business can. Business owners must pay not only state and federal income taxes on their profits, but self-employment taxes as well. (See sidebar, Social Security Taxes, page 245.) Because self-employed people pay Social Security taxes at twice the level of regular, salaried workers, you should strive to lower your annual gross profit figure on the Schedule C form through every legal means possible. One way to do this is through careful record keeping of all expenses related to the operation of your business. To quote IRS publications, expenses are deductible if they are "ordinary, necessary, and somehow connected with the operation and potential profit of your business." In addition to being able to deduct all expenses related to the making and selling of their products, business owners can also depreciate the cost of tools and equipment, deduct the overhead costs of operating a home-based office or studio (called the Home Office Deduction), and hire their spouse or children.

> ***Avoid this pitfall:*** Many new businesses that end up with a nice net profit on their first year's Schedule C tax form find themselves in financial trouble when tax time rolls around because they did not make estimated quarterly tax payments throughout the year. Aside from the penalties for underpayment of taxes, it's

a terrible blow to suddenly realize that you've spent all your business profits and now have no money left for taxes. Be sure to discuss this matter with a tax adviser or accountant when you begin your business.

Given the complexity of our tax laws and the fact that they are changing all the time, a detailed discussion of all the tax deductions currently available to small-business owners cannot be included in a book of this nature. Learning, however, is as easy as reading a book such as *Small Time Operator* by Bernard Kamoroff (my favorite tax and accounting guide), visiting the IRS Web site, or consulting your regular tax adviser.

You can also get answers to specific tax questions 24 hours a day by calling the National Association of Enrolled Agents (NAEA). Enrolled agents (EAs) are licensed by the Treasury Department to represent taxpayers before the IRS. Their rates for doing tax returns are often less than those you would pay for an accountant or CPA.

Keeping Tax Records

Once you're in business, you must keep accurate records of all income and expenses, but the IRS does not require any special kind of bookkeeping system. Its primary concern is that you use a system that clearly and accurately shows true income and expenses. For the sole proprietor, a simple system consisting of a checkbook, a cash receipts journal, a cash disbursements ledger, and a petty cash fund is quite adequate. Post expenses and income regularly to avoid year-end pile-up and panic.

If you plan to keep manual records, check your local office supply store or catalogs for the *Dome* series of record-keeping books, or use the handy ledger sheets and worksheets included in *Small Time Operator*. (This classic tax and accounting guide by CPA Bernard Kamoroff includes details on how to keep good records and prepare financial reports.) If you have a computer, there are a number of accounting software programs available, such as Intuit's Quicken, MYOB (Mind Your Own Business) Accounting, and Intuit's

An important concept to remember is that even the smallest business is entitled to deduct expenses related to its business, and the same tax-saving strategies used by "the big guys" can be used by small-business owners. Your business may be small now or still in the dreaming stage, but it could be larger next year and surprisingly profitable a few years from now. Therefore it is in your best interest to always prepare for growth, profit, and taxes by learning all you can about the tax laws and deductions applicable to your business. (See also sidebar, Keeping Tax Records.)

Sales Tax Is Serious Business

If you live in a state that has a sales tax (all but five states do), and sell products directly to consumers, you are required by law to register with your state's Department of Revenue (Sales Tax division) for a resale tax number. The fee for this in most states ranges from $5 to $25, with some states requiring a bond or deposit of up to $150.

QuickBooks, the latter of which is one of the most popular and best bookkeeping systems for small businesses. The great advantage of computerized accounting is that financial statements can be created at the press of a key after accounting entries have been made.

Regardless of which system you use, always get a receipt for everything and file receipts in a monthly envelope. If you don't want to establish a petty cash fund, spindle all of your cash receipts, tally them at month's end, and reimburse your personal outlay of cash with a check written on your business account. On your checkbook stub, document the individual purchases covered by this check.

At year's end, bundle your monthly tax receipt envelopes and file them for future reference, if needed. Because the IRS can audit a return for up to 3 years after a tax return has been filed, all accounting and tax records should be kept at least this long, but 6 years is better. Personally, I believe you should keep all your tax returns, journals, and ledgers throughout the life of your business.

Depending on where you live, this tax number may also be called a Retailer's Occupation Tax Registration Number, resale license, or use tax permit. Also, depending on where you live, the place you must call to obtain this number will have different names. In California, for example, you would contact the State Board of Equalization; in Texas, it's called the State Comptroller's Office. Within your state's revenue department, the tax division may have a name such as sales and use tax division or department of taxation and finance. Generally speaking, if you check your telephone book under "Government," and look for whatever listing comes closest to "Revenue," you can find the right office.

If your state has no sales tax, you will still need a reseller's permit or tax exemption certificate to buy supplies and materials at wholesale prices from manufacturers, wholesalers, or distributors. Note that this tax number is only for supplies and materials used to make your products, not for things purchased at the retail level or for general office supplies.

Once registered with the state, you will begin to collect and remit sales and use tax (monthly, quarterly, or annually, as determined by your state) on all *taxable sales*. This does not mean *all* of your gross income. Different states tax different things. Some states put a sales tax on certain services, but generally you will never have to pay sales tax on income from articles sold to magazines, on teaching or consulting fees, or subscription income (if you happen to publish a newsletter). In addition, sales taxes are not applicable to:

- Items sold on consignment through a charitable organization, shop, or other retail outlet, including craft malls and rent-a-space shops (because the party who sells directly to the consumer is the one who must collect and pay sales tax).

- Products you wholesale to others who will be reselling them to consumers. (Be sure to get their tax-exemption ID number for your own files, however, in case you are ever questioned as to why you did not collect taxes on those sales.)

As you sell throughout the year, your record-keeping system must be set up so you can tell which income is taxable and which is tax-exempt for reporting on your sales tax return.

Collecting Sales Tax at Craft Shows

States are getting very aggressive about collecting sales tax, and agents are showing up everywhere these days, especially at the larger craft fairs, festivals, and small-business conferences. As I was writing this chapter, a posting on the Internet stated that in New Jersey the sales tax department is routinely contacting show promoters about a month before the show date to get the names and addresses of exhibitors. It is expected that other states will soon be following suit. For this reason, you should always take your resale or tax collection certificate with you to shows.

Although you must always collect sales tax at a show when you sell in a state that has a sales tax, how and when the tax is paid to the state can vary. When selling at shows in other states, you may find that the show promoter has obtained an umbrella sales tax certificate, in which case vendors would be asked to give management a check for sales tax at the end of the show for turning over to a tax agent. Or you may have to obtain a temporary sales tax certificate for a show, as advised by the show promoter. Some sellers who regularly do shows in two or three states say it's easier to get a tax ID number from each state and file an annual return instead of doing taxes on a show-by-show basis. (See sidebar, Including Tax in the Retail Price, page 252.)

Collecting Sales Tax at a Holiday Boutique

If you're involved in a holiday boutique where several sellers are offering goods to the public, each individual seller will be responsible for collecting and remitting his or her own sales tax. (This means someone has to keep very good records during the sale so each seller receives a record of the sale and the amount of tax on that sale.) A reader who regularly has home boutiques told me that in her community she must also post a sign at her "cash station" stating that sales tax is being collected on all sales, just as craft fair sellers must do in some states. Again, it's important that you get complete details from your own state about its sales tax policies.

> *Avoid this pitfall:* Individuals who are selling "just for the fun of it" may think they don't have to collect sales taxes, but this is not true. As an official in my state's Department of Revenue told me, "Everyone who sells anything to consumers must collect sales tax. If you hold yourself out as a seller of merchandise, then you're subject to tax, even if you sell only a couple of times a year." The financial penalties for violating this state law can be severe. In Illinois, for example, lawbreakers are subject to a penalty of 20% over and above any normal tax obligation, and could receive for each offense (meaning each return not filed)

Including Tax in the Retail Price

Is it okay to incorporate the amount of sales tax into the retail price of items being sold directly to consumers? I don't know for sure because each state's sales tax law is different.

Crafters like to use round-figure prices at fairs because this encourages cash sales and eliminates the need for taking coins to make change. Some crafters tell their customers that sales tax has been included in their rounded-off prices, but you should not do this until you check with your state. In some states, this is illegal; in others, you may find that you are required to inform your customers, by means of a sign, that sales tax has been included in your price. You may also have to print this information on customer receipts as well.

If you make such a statement and collect taxes on cash sales, be sure to report those cash sales as taxable income and remit the tax money to the state accordingly. Failure

from 1 to 6 months in prison and a fine of $5,000. As you can see, the collection of sales tax is serious business.

Collecting Tax on Internet Sales

Anything you sell that is taxable in your state is also taxable on the Internet. This is simply another method of selling, like craft fairs or mail-order sales. You don't have to break out Internet sales separately; simply include them in your total taxable sales.

3. The Legal Forms of Business

Every business must take one of four legal forms:

Sole Proprietorship
Partnership
LLC (Limited Liability Company)
Corporation

to do this would be a violation of the law, and it's easy to get caught these days when sales tax agents are showing up at craft fairs across the country.

Even if rounding off the price and including the tax within that figure turns out to be legal in your state, it will definitely complicate your bookkeeping. For example, if you normally sell an item for $5 or some other round figure, you must have a firm retail price on which to calculate sales tax to begin with. Adding tax to a round figure makes it uneven. Then you must either raise or lower the price, and if you lower it, what you're really doing is paying the sales tax for your customer out of your profits. This is no way to do business.

I suggest that you set your retail prices based on the pricing formulas given in this book, calculate the sales tax accordingly, and give your customers change if they pay in cash. You will be perceived as a professional when you operate this way, whereas crafters who insist always on "cash only" sales are sending signals to buyers that they don't intend to report this income to tax authorities.

As a hobby seller, you automatically become a sole proprietor when you start selling what you make. Although most professional crafters remain sole proprietors throughout the life of their business, some do form craft partnerships or corporations when their business begins to generate serious money, or if it happens to involve other members of their family. You don't need a lawyer to start a sole proprietorship, but it would be folly to enter into a partnership, LLC, or corporation, without legal guidance. Here is a brief look at the main advantages and disadvantages of each type of legal business structure.

Sole Proprietorship

No legal formalities are involved in starting or ending a sole proprietorship. You're your own boss here, and the business starts when you say it does and ends automatically when you stop running it. As discussed earlier, income is reported annually on a Schedule C form and taxed at the personal level. The sole proprietor is fully liable for all business debts and actions. In the event of a lawsuit, personal assets are not protected.

Partnership

There are two kinds of partnerships: general and limited.

A *general partnership* is easy to start, with no federal requirements involved. Income is taxed at the personal level and the partnership ends as soon as either partner withdraws from the business. Liability is unlimited. The most financially dangerous thing about a partnership is that the debts incurred by one partner must be assumed by all other partners. Before signing a partnership agreement, make sure the tax obligations of your partner are current.

In a *limited partnership,* the business is run by general partners and financed by silent (limited) partners who have no liability beyond an investment of money in the business. This kind of partnership is more complicated to establish, has special tax withholding regulations, and requires the filing of a legal contract with the state.

> *Avoid this pitfall:* Partnerships between friends often end the friendship when disagreements over business policies occur. Don't form a partnership with anyone without planning in advance how the partnership will eventually be dissolved, and spell out all the details in a written agreement. What will happen if either partner dies, wants out of the business, or wants to buy out the other partner? Also ask your attorney about the advisability of having partnership insurance, to protect against the complications that would arise if one of the partners becomes ill, incapacitated, or dies. For additional perspective on the pros and cons of partnerships, read the book *The Perils of Partners.*

The Limited Legal Protection of a Corporation

Business novices often think that by incorporating their business they can protect their personal assets in the event of a lawsuit. This is true if you have employees who do something wrong and cause your business to be sued. As the business owner, however, if you personally do something wrong and are sued as a result, you might in some cases be held legally responsible, and the "corporation door" will offer no legal protection for your personal assets.

Or, as CPA Bernard Kamoroff explains in *Small Time Operator,* "A corporation will not shield you from personal liability that you normally should be responsible for, such as not having car insurance or acting with gross negligence. If you plan to incorporate solely or primarily with the intention of limiting your legal liability, I suggest you find out first exactly how limited the liability really is for your particular venture. Hire a knowledgeable lawyer to give you a written opinion." (See section 7, Insurance Tips.)

LLC (Limited Liability Company)

This legal form of business reportedly combines the best attributes of other small-business forms while offering a better tax advantage than a limited partnership. It also affords personal liability protection similar to that of a corporation. To date, few craft businesses appear to be using this business form.

Corporation

A corporation is the most complicated and expensive legal form of business and not recommended for any business whose earnings are less than $25,000 a year. If and when your business reaches this point, you should study some books on this topic to fully understand the pros and cons of a corporation. Also consult an accountant or attorney for guidance on the type of corporation you should select—a "C" (general corporation) or an "S" (subchapter S corporation). One book that offers good perspective on this topic is *INC Yourself—How to Profit by Setting Up Your Own Corporation.*

The main disadvantage of incorporation for the small-business owner is that profits are taxed twice: first as corporate income and again when they are distributed to the owner-shareholders as dividends. For this reason, many small businesses elect to incorporate as subchapter S corporations, which allows profits to be taxed at owners' regular individual rates. (See sidebar, The Limited Legal Protection of a Corporation, on page 255.)

4. Local and State Laws and Regulations

This section will acquaint you with laws and regulations that affect the average art or crafts business based at home. If you've unknowingly broken one of these laws, don't panic. It may not be as bad as you think. It is often possible to get back on the straight and narrow merely by filling out a required form or by paying a small fee of some kind. What's important is that you take steps now to comply with the laws that pertain to your particular business. Often, the fear of being caught when you're breaking a law is much worse than doing whatever needs to be done to set the matter straight. In the end, it's usually what you don't know that is most likely to cause legal or financial problems, so never hesitate to ask questions about things you don't understand.

Even when you think you know the answers, it can pay to "act dumb." It is said that Napoleon used to attend meetings and pretend to know nothing about a topic, asking many probing questions. By feigning ignorance, he was able to draw valuable information and insight out of everyone around him. This strategy is often used by today's small-business owners, too.

Business Name Registration

If you're a sole proprietor doing business under any name other than your own full name, you are required by law to register it on both the local and state level. In this case, you are said to be using an "assumed," "fictitious," or "trade" name. Registration enables authorities to connect an assumed name to an individual who can be held responsible for the actions of a business. If you're doing business under your own name, such as Kay Jones, you don't have to register your business name on either the local or state level. If your name is part of a longer name, however (for example, Kay Jones Designs), you should check to see if your county or state requires registration.

Local Registration

To register your name, contact your city or county clerk, who will explain what you need to do to officially register your business on

Picking a Good Business Name

If you haven't done it already, think up a great name for your new business. You want something that will be memorable—catchy, but not too cute. Many crafters select a simple name that is attached to their first name, such as "Mary's Quilts" or "Tom's Woodcrafts." This is fine for a hobby business, but if your goal is to build a full-time business at home, you may wish to choose a more professional-sounding name that omits your personal name. If a name sounds like a hobby business, you may have difficulty getting wholesale suppliers to take you seriously. A more professional name may also enable you to get higher prices for your products. For example, the above names might be changed to "Quilted Treasures" or "Wooden Wonders."

Don't print business cards or stationery until you find out if someone else is already using the name you've chosen. To find out if the name has already been registered, you

the local level. At the same time, ask if you need any special municipal or county licenses or permits to operate within the law. (See the next section, Licenses and Permits.) This office can also tell you how and where to write to register your name at the state level. If you've been operating under an assumed name for a while and are worried because you didn't register the name earlier, just register it now, as if the business were new.

Registration involves filling out a simple form and paying a small fee, usually around $10 to $25. At the time you register, you will get details about a classified ad you must run in a general-circulation newspaper in your county. This will notify the public at large that you are now operating a business under an assumed name. (If you don't want your neighbors to know what you're doing, simply run the ad in a newspaper somewhere else in the county.) After publication of this ad, you will receive a Fictitious Name Statement that you must send to the county clerk, who in turn will file it with your registration form to make your business completely legit-

▼▼▼

can perform a trademark search through a search company or hire an attorney who specializes in trademark law to conduct the search for you. And if you are planning to eventually set up a Web site, you might want to do a search to see if that domain name is still available on the Internet. Go to www.networksolutions.com to do this search. Business names have to be registered on the Internet, too, and they can be "parked" for a fee until you're ready to design your Web site.

It's great if your business name and Web site name can be the same, but this is not always possible. A crafter told me recently she had to come up with 25 names before she found a domain name that hadn't already been taken. (Web entrepreneurs are grabbing every good name they can find. Imagine my surprise when I did a search and found that two different individuals had set up Web sites using the titles of my two best-known books, *Creative Cash* and *Homemade Money*.)

▲▲▲

imate. This name statement or certificate may also be referred to as your DBA ("doing business as") form. In some areas, you cannot open a business checking account if you don't have this form to show your bank.

> *Avoid this pitfall:* Failure to register your business name may result in your losing it—after you've spent a considerable amount of money on business cards, stationery, advertising, and so on. If someone sees your name, likes it, and finds on checking that it hasn't been registered, they can simply register the name and force you to stop using it.

State Registration

Once you've registered locally, contact your secretary of state to register your business name with the state. This will prevent its use by a corporate entity. At the same time, find out if you must obtain any kind of state license. Generally, home-based crafts businesses will not need a license from the state, but there are always exceptions. An artist who built an open-to-the-public art studio on his property reported that the fine in his state for operating this kind of business without a license was $50 a day. In short, it always pays to ask questions to make sure you're operating legally and safely.

Federal Registration

The only way to protect a name on the federal level is with a trademark, discussed in section 9.

Licenses and Permits

A "license" is a certificate granted by a municipal or county agency that gives you permission to engage in a business occupation. A "permit" is similar, except that it is granted by local authorities. Until recently, few crafts businesses had to have a license or permit of any kind, but a growing number of communities now have new laws on their books that require home-based business owners to obtain a "home occupation permit." Annual fees for such permits may range from $15 to $200 a year. For details about the law in your particular community or county, call your city or county clerk (depending on whether you live within or outside city limits).

Use of Personal Phone for Business

Although every business writer stresses the importance of having a business telephone number, craftspeople generally ignore this advice and do business on their home telephone. Although it's okay to use a home phone to make outgoing business calls, you cannot advertise a home telephone number as your business phone number without being in violation of local telephone regulations. That means you cannot legally put your home telephone number on a business card or business stationery or advertise it on your Web site.

That said, let me also state that most craftspeople totally ignore this law and do it anyway. (I don't know what the penalty for breaking this law is in your state; you'll have to call your telephone company for that information and decide if this is something you want to do.) Some phone companies might give you a slap on the wrist and tell you to stop, while others might start charging you business line telephone rates if they discover you are advertising your personal phone number.

The primary reason to have a separate phone line for your business is that it enables you to freely advertise your telephone number to solicit new business and invite credit card sales, custom order inquiries, and the like. Further, you can deduct 100% of the costs of a business telephone line on your Schedule C tax form, while deductions for the business use of a home phone are severely limited. (Discuss this with your accountant.)

If you plan to connect to the Internet or install a fax machine, you will definitely need a second line to handle the load, but most crafters simply add an additional personal line instead of a business line. Once on the Internet, you may have even less need for a business phone than before because you can simply invite contact from buyers by advertising your e-mail address. (Always include your e-mail and Internet addresses on your business cards and stationery.)

If your primary selling methods are going to be consignment shops, craft fairs, or craft malls, a business phone number would be necessary only if you are inviting orders by phone. If you present a holiday boutique or open house once or twice a year, there should be no problem with putting your home phone number on promotional flyers because you are, in fact, inviting people to your home and not your business (similar to running a classified ad for a garage sale).

If and when you decide a separate line for your business is necessary, you may find it is not as costly as you think. Telephone companies today are very aware of the number of people who are working at home, and they have come up with a variety of affordable packages and second-line options, any one of which might be perfect for your crafts-business needs. Give your telephone company a call and see what's available.

Zoning Regulations

Before you start any kind of home-based business, check your home's zoning regulations. You can find a copy at your library or at city hall. Find out what zone you're in and then read the information under "Home Occupations." Be sure to read the fine print and note the penalty for violating a zoning ordinance. In most cases, someone who is caught violating zoning laws will be asked to cease and desist and a penalty is incurred only if this order is ignored. In other cases, however, willful violation could incur a hefty fine.

Zoning laws differ from one community to another, with some of them being terribly outdated (actually written back in horse-and-buggy days). In some communities, zoning officials simply "look the other way" where zoning violations are concerned because it's easier to do this than change the law. In other places, however, zoning regulations have recently been revised in light of the growing number of individuals working at home, and these changes have not always been to the benefit of home-based workers or self-employed individuals. Often there are restrictions as to (1) the amount of space in one's home a business may occupy (impossible to enforce, in my opinion), (2) the number of people (customers, students) who can come to your home each day, (3) the use of non-family employees, and so on. If you find you cannot advertise your home as a place of business, this problem can be easily solved by renting a P.O. box or using a commercial mailbox service as your business address.

Although I'm not suggesting that you violate your zoning law, I will tell you that many individuals who have found zoning to be a problem do ignore this law, particularly when they have a quiet business that is unlikely to create problems in their community.

Zoning officials don't go around checking for people who are violating the law; rather, they tend to act on complaints they have received about a certain activity that is creating problems for others. Thus, the best way to avoid zoning problems is to keep a low profile by not broadcasting your home-based business to neighbors. More important, never annoy them with activities that emit fumes or odors, create parking problems, or make noise of any kind.

Although neighbors may grudgingly put up with a noisy hobby activity (such as sawing in the garage), they are not likely to tolerate the same noise or disturbance if they know it's related to a home-based business. Likewise, they won't mind if you have a garage sale every year, but if people are coming to your home every year to buy from your home shop, open house, home parties, or holiday boutiques, you could be asking for trouble if the zoning laws don't favor this kind of activity.

> **Avoid this pitfall:** If you're planning to hold a holiday boutique or home party, check with zoning officials first. (If they don't know what a holiday boutique is, tell them it's a temporary sales event, like a garage sale.) Generally, the main concerns will be that you do not post illegal signs, tie up traffic, or otherwise annoy your neighbors. In some areas, however, zoning regulations strictly prohibit (1) traffic into one's home for any commercial reason; (2) the exchange of money in a home for business reasons; or (3) the transfer of merchandise within the home (affecting party plan sellers, in particular). Some sellers have found the solution to all three of these problems as simple as letting people place orders for merchandise that will be delivered later, with payment collected at time of delivery.

5. General Business and Financial Information

This section offers introductory guidelines on essential business basics for beginners. Once your business is up and running, however, you need to read other crafts-business books to get detailed information on the following topics and many others related to the successful growth and development of a home-based art or crafts business.

Making a Simple Business Plan

As baseball star Yogi Berra once said, "If you don't know where you are going, you might not get there." That's why you need a plan.

Like a road map, a business plan helps you get from here to there. It doesn't have to be fancy, but it does have to be in written form. A good business plan will save you time and money while helping you stay focused and on track to meet your goals. The kind of business plan a craftsperson makes will naturally be less complicated than the business plan of a major manufacturing company, but the elements are basically the same and should include:

- *History*—how and why you started your business
- *Business description*—what you do, what products you make, why they are special
- *Management information*—your business background or experience and the legal form your business will take
- *Manufacturing and production*—how and where products will be produced and who will make them; how and where supplies and materials will be obtained, and their estimated costs; labor costs (yours or other helpers); and overhead costs involved in the making of products
- *Financial plan*—estimated sales and expense figures for 1 year
- *Market research findings*—a description of your market (fairs, shops, mail order, Internet, and so on), your customers, and your competition
- *Marketing plan*—how you are going to sell your products and the anticipated cost of your marketing (commissions, advertising, craft fair displays, and so on)

If this all seems a bit much for a small crafts business, start managing your time by using a daily calendar/planner and start a

Get a Safety Deposit Box

The longer you are in business, the more important it will be to safeguard your most valuable business records. When you work at home, there is always the possibility of fire or damage from some natural disaster, be it a tornado, earthquake, hurricane, or flood. You will worry less if you keep your most valuable business papers, records, computer disks, and so forth off-premises, along with other items that would be difficult or impossible to replace. Some particulars I have always kept in my business safety deposit box include master software disks and computer back-up disks; original copies of my designs and patterns, business contracts, copyrights, insurance policies, and a photographic record of all items insured on our homeowner's policy. Remember: Insurance is worthless if you cannot prove what you owned in the first place.

notebook you can fill with your creative and marketing ideas, plans, and business goals. In it, write a simple mission statement that answers the following questions:

- What is my primary mission or goal in starting a business?
- What is my financial goal for this year?
- What am I going to do to get the sales I need this year to meet my financial goal?

The most important thing is that you start putting your dreams, goals, and business plans on paper so you can review them regularly. It's always easier to see where you're going if you know where you've been.

When You Need an Attorney

Many business beginners think they have to hire a lawyer the minute they start a business, but that would be a terrible waste of money if you're just starting a simple art or crafts business at home, operating as a sole proprietor. Sure, a lawyer will be delighted to hold your hand and give you the same advice I'm giving you here (while charging you $150 an hour or more for his or her time). With this book in hand, you can easily take care of all the "legal details" of a small-business start-up. The day may come, however, when you do need legal counsel, such as when you:

Form a Partnership or Corporation

As stated earlier, an attorney's guidance is necessary in the formation of a partnership. Although many people have incorporated without a lawyer using a good how-to book on the topic, I wouldn't recommend doing this because there are so many details involved, not to mention different types of corporate entities.

Defend an Infringement of a Copyright or Trademark

You don't need an attorney to get a simple copyright, but if someone infringes on one of your copyrights, you will probably need legal help to stop the infringer from profiting from your creativity. You can file your own trademark application (if you are exceedingly careful about following instructions), but it would be difficult to protect your trademark without legal help if someone tries to steal it. In both cases, you would need an attorney who specializes in copyright, patent, and trademark law. (If you ever need a good attorney who understands the plight of artists and crafters, contact me by e-mail at barbara@crafter.com and I'll refer you to the attorney who has been helpful to me in protecting my common-law trademark to *Homemade Money*, my home-business classic. The sixth edition of this book includes the details of my trademark infringement story.)

Negotiate a Contract

Many craft hobbyists of my acquaintance have gone on to write books and sell their original designs to manufacturers, suddenly finding themselves with a contract in hand that contains a lot of confusing legal jargon. When hiring an attorney to check any kind of contract, make sure he or she has experience in the particular field involved. For example, a lawyer specializing in real estate isn't going to know a thing about the inner workings of a book publishing company and how the omission or inclusion of a particular clause or phrase might impact the author's royalties or make it difficult to get publishing rights back when the book goes out of print. Although I have no experience in the licensing industry, I presume the same thing holds true here. What I do know for sure is that the problem with most contracts is not so much what's *in* them, as what *isn't*. Thus you need to be sure the attorney you hire for specialized contract work has done this kind of work for other clients.

Hire Independent Contractors

If you ever grow your business to the point where you need to hire workers and are wondering whether you have to hire employees or can use independent contractors instead, I suggest you seek counsel from an attorney who specializes in labor law. This topic is very complex and beyond the scope of this beginner's guide, but I do want you to know that the IRS has been on a campaign for the past several years to abolish independent contractors altogether. Many small businesses have suffered great financial loss in back taxes and penalties because they followed the advice of an accountant or regular attorney who didn't fully understand the technicalities of this matter.

If and when you do need a lawyer for general business purposes, ask friends for a reference, and check with your bank, too, because it will probably know most of the attorneys with private practices in your area. Note that membership in some small-business organizations will also give you access to affordable prepaid legal services. If you ever need serious legal help but have no funds to pay for it, contact the Volunteer Lawyers for the Arts.

Why You Need a Business Checking Account

Many business beginners use their personal checking account to conduct the transactions of their business, *but you must not do this* because the IRS does not allow commingling of business and personal income. If you are operating as a business, reporting income on a Schedule C form and taking deductions accordingly, the lack of a separate checking account for your business would surely result in an IRS ruling that your endeavor was a hobby and not a business. That, in turn, would cost you all the deductions previously taken on earlier tax returns and you'd end up with a very large tax bill. Don't you agree that the cost of a separate checking account is a small price to pay to protect all your tax deductions?

You do not necessarily need one of the more expensive business checking accounts; you just need a *separate account* through which you run all business income and expenditures. Your business name does not have to be on these checks so long as only your name (not your spouse's) is listed as account holder. You can save money on your checking account by first calling several banks and savings and loan institutions and comparing the charges they set for imprinted checks, deposits, checks written, bounced checks, and other services. Before you open your account, be sure to ask if the bank can set you up to take credit cards (merchant account) at some point in the future.

> *Avoid this pitfall:* Some banks charge extra for each out-of-state check that is deposited, an expense that is prohibitively expensive for active mail-order businesses. For that reason, I have always maintained a business checking account in a savings and loan association, which has no service charges of any kind (except for bad checks). S&L's also pay interest on the amount in a checking account, whereas a bank may not. The main disadvantage of doing your business checking through an S&L is that they do not offer credit card services or give business loans. At the

point where I found I needed the latter two services for my publishing business, I had to open a second account with a local bank.

Accepting Credit Cards

Most of us today take credit cards for granted and expect to be able to use them for most everything we buy. It's nice to be able to offer credit card services to your craft fair customers, but it is costly and thus not recommended for beginning craft sellers. If you get into selling at craft fairs on a regular basis, however, at some point you may find you are losing sales because you don't have "merchant status" (the ability to accept credit cards as payment).

Some craftspeople have reported a considerable jump in sales once they started taking credit cards. That's because some people who buy with plastic may buy two or three items instead of one, or may be willing to pay a higher price for something if they can charge it. Thus, the higher your prices, the more likely you are to lose sales if you can't accept credit cards. As one jewelry maker told me, "I always seem to get the customers who have run out of cash and left their checkbook at home. But even when they have a check, I feel uncomfortable taking a check for $100 or more."

This section discusses the various routes you can travel to get merchant status. You will have to do considerable research to find out which method is best for you. All will be costly, and you must have sufficient sales, or the expectation of increased sales, to consider taking credit cards in the first place. Understand, too, that taking credit cards in person (called face-to-face transactions where you have the card in front of you) is different from accepting credit cards by phone, by mail, or through a Web site (called non–face-to-face transactions). Each method of selling is treated differently by bankcard providers.

> ***Avoid this pitfall:*** If you are relatively new at selling, and uncertain about whether you will be taking credit cards for a long time, do not sign a leasing arrangement for credit card processing equipment. Instead, leave yourself an escape route by opting for a rental agreement you can get out of with a month's notice, such as that offered by some banks and organizations discussed below.

Merchant Status from Your Bank

When you're ready to accept credit cards, start with the bank where you have your business checking account. Where you bank, and where you live, has everything to do with whether you can get merchant status from your bank. Home-business owners in small towns often have less trouble than do those in large cities. One crafter told me Bank of America gave her merchant status with no problem, but some banks simply refuse to deal with anyone who doesn't operate out of a storefront. Most banks now insist that credit card sales be transmitted electronically, but a few still offer manual printers and allow merchants to send in their sales slips by mail. You will be given details about this at the time you apply for merchant status. All banks will require proof that you have a going business and will want to see your financial statements.

Merchant Status through a Crafts Organization

If you are refused by your bank because your business is home based or just too new, getting bankcard services through a crafts or home-business organization is the next best way to go. Because such organizations have a large membership, they have some negotiating power with the credit card companies and often get special deals for their members. As a member of such an organization, the chances are about 95% that you will automatically be accepted into its bankcard program, even if you are a brand-new business owner.

One organization I can recommend to beginning sellers is the National Craft Association. Managing Director Barbara Arena tells me that 60% of all new NCA members now take the

MasterCard/VISA services offered by her organization. "Crafters who are unsure about whether they want to take credit cards over a long period of time have the option of renting equipment," says Barbara. "This enables them to get out of the program with a month's notice. NCA members can operate on a software basis through their personal computer (taking their laptop computer to shows and calling in sales on their cell phone) or use a swipe machine. Under NCA's program, crafters can also accept credit card sales on their Internet site."

For more information from NCA and other organizations offering merchant services, see Craft and Home-Business Organizations on page 314.

Merchant Status from Credit Card Companies

If you've been in business for a while, you may find you can get merchant status directly from American Express or Novus Services, Inc., the umbrella company that handles the Discover, Bravo, and Private Issue credit cards. American Express says that in some cases it can grant merchant status immediately on receipt of some key information given on the phone. As for Novus, many crafters have told me how easy it was to get merchant status from this company. Novus says it needs only your Social Security number and information to check your credit rating. If Novus accepts you, it can also get you set up to take VISA and MasterCard as well, if you meet the special acceptance qualifications of these two credit card companies. (Usually, they require you to be in business for at least 2 years.)

Merchant Status from an Independent
Service Organization Provider (ISO)

ISOs act as agents for banks that authorize credit cards, promoting their services by direct mail, through magazine advertising, telemarketing, and on the Internet. Most of these bankcard providers are operating under a network marketing program (one agent representing one agent representing another, and so on). They are everywhere on the Internet, sending unsolicited e-mail messages to Web site owners. In addition to offering the merchant account service itself, many are also trying to get other Web site owners to promote the same service in exchange for some kind of referral fee. I do not recommend that you get merchant status through an ISO because I've heard too many horror stories about them. If you want to explore this option on the Internet, however, use your browser's search button and type "credit cards + merchant" to get a list of such sellers.

In general, ISOs may offer a low discount rate but will sock it to you with inflated equipment costs, a high application fee, and extra fees for installation, programming, and site inspection. You will also have to sign an unbreakable 3- or 4-year lease for the electronic equipment.

> ***Avoid this pitfall:*** Some people on the Internet may offer to process your credit card sales through their individual merchant account, but this is illegal as it violates credit card company rules. And if you were to offer to do this for someone else, your account would be terminated. In short, if you do not ship the goods, you can't process the sale.

•

As you can see, you must really do your homework where bankcard services are concerned. In checking out the services offered by any of the providers noted here, ask plenty of questions. Make up a chart that lets you compare what each one charges for application and service fees, monthly charges, equipment costs, software, discount rates, and transaction fees.

Transaction fees can range from $0.20 to $0.80 per ticket, with discount rates running anywhere from 1.67 to 5%. Higher rates are usually attached to non–face-to-face credit card transactions, paper transaction systems, or a low volume of sales. Any rate higher than

5% should be a danger signal because you could be dealing with an unscrupulous seller or some kind of illegal third-party processing program.

I'm told that a good credit card processor today may cost around $800, yet some card service providers are charging two or three times that amount in their leasing arrangements. I once got a quote from a major ISO and found it would have cost me $40 a month to lease the terminal—$1,920 over a period of 4 years—or I could buy it for just $1,000. In checking with my bank, I learned I could get the same equipment and the software to run it for just $350!

In summary, if you're a nervous beginner, the safest way to break into taking credit cards is to work with a bank or organization that offers equipment on a month-by-month rental arrangement. Once you've had some experience in taking credit card payments, you can review your situation and decide whether you want to move into a leasing arrangement or buy equipment outright.

6. Minimizing the Financial Risks of Selling

This book contains a good chapter on how and where to sell your crafts, but I thought it would be helpful for you to have added perspective on the business management end of selling through various outlets, and some things you can do to protect yourself from financial loss and legal hassles.

You must accept the fact that all businesses occasionally suffer financial losses of one kind or another. That's simply the nature of business. Selling automatically carries a certain degree of risk in that we can never be absolutely sure that we're going to be paid for anything until we actually have payment in hand. Checks may bounce, wholesale buyers may refuse to pay their invoices, and consignment shops can close unexpectedly without returning merchandise to crafters. In the past few years, a surprising number of craft mall owners have stolen out of town in the middle of the night, taking with them all the money due their vendors, and sometimes the vendors' merchandise as well. (This topic is beyond the scope of this book, but if you'd like more information on it, see my *Creative Cash* book and back issues of my *Craftsbiz Chat* newsletter on the Internet at www.crafter.com/brabec.)

Now, I don't want you to feel uneasy about selling or be suspicious of every buyer who comes your way, because that would take all the fun out of selling. But I *do* want you to know that bad things sometimes happen to good craftspeople who have not done their homework (by reading this book, you are doing *your* homework). If you will follow the cautionary guidelines discussed in this section, you can avoid some common selling pitfalls and minimize your financial risk to the point where it will be negligible.

Selling to Consignment Shops

Never consign more merchandise to one shop than you can afford to lose, and do not send new items to a shop until you see that payments are being made regularly according to your written consignment agreement. It should cover the topics of:

- Insurance (see Insurance Tips, section 7)
- Pricing (make sure the shop cannot raise or lower your retail price without your permission)
- Sales commission (40% is standard; don't work with shop owners who ask for more than this. It makes more sense to wholesale products at 50% and get payment in 30 days)
- Payment dates
- Display of merchandise

■ Return of unsold merchandise (some shops have a clause stating that if unsold merchandise is not claimed within 30 to 60 days after a notice has been sent, the shop can dispose of it any way it wishes)

Above all, make sure your agreement includes the name and phone number of the shop's owner (not just the manager). If a shop fails and you decide to take legal action, you want to be sure your lawyer can track down the owner. (See sidebar, State Consignment Laws, below.)

Selling to Craft Malls

Shortly after the craft mall concept was introduced to the crafts community in 1988 by Rufus Coomer, entrepreneurs who understood the profit potential of such a business began to open malls all over the country. But there were no guidebooks and everyone was flying by the seat of his or her pants, making up operating rules along the way. Many mall owners, inexperienced in retailing, have

State Consignment Laws

Technically, consigned goods remain the property of the seller until they are sold. When a shop goes out of business, however, consigned merchandise may be seized by creditors in spite of what your consignment agreement may state. You may have some legal protection here, however, if you live in a state that has a consignment law designed to protect artists and craftspeople in such instances. I believe such laws exist in the states of CA, CO, CT, IL, IA, KY, MA, NH, NM, NY, OR, TX, WA, and WI. Call your secretary of state to confirm this or, if your state isn't listed here, ask whether this law is now on the books. Be sure to get full details about the kind of protection afforded by this law because some states have different definitions for what constitutes "art" or "crafts."

since gone out of business, often leaving crafters holding the bag. The risks of selling through such well-known chain stores as Coomer's or American Craft Malls are minimal, and many independently owned malls have also established excellent reputations in the industry. What you need to be especially concerned about here are new malls opened by individuals who have no track record in this industry.

I'm not telling you *not* to set up a booth in a new mall in your area—it might prove to be a terrific outlet for you—but I am cautioning you to keep a sharp eye on the mall and how it's being operated. Warning signs of a mall in trouble include:

- Less than 75% occupancy
- Little or no ongoing advertising
- Not many shoppers
- Crafters pulling out (usually a sign of too few sales)
- Poor accounting of sales
- Late payments

If a mall is in trouble, it stands to reason that the logical time for it to close is right after the biggest selling season of the year, namely Christmas. Interestingly, this is when most of the shady mall owners have stolen out of town with crafters' Christmas sales in their pockets. As stated in my *Creative Cash* book:

> If it's nearing Christmastime, and you're getting uncomfortable vibes about the financial condition of a mall you're in, it might be smart to remove the bulk of your merchandise—especially expensive items—just before it closes for the holidays. You can always restock after the first of the year if everything looks rosy.

Avoiding Bad Checks

At a craft fair or other event where you're selling directly to the public, if the buyer doesn't have cash and you don't accept credit cards, your only option is to accept a check. Few crafters have bad check problems for sales held in the home (holiday boutique, open house, party plan, and such), but bad checks at craft fairs are always possible. Here are several things you can do to avoid accepting a bad check:

- Always ask to see a driver's license and look carefully at the picture on it. Write the license number on the check.

- If the sale is for a large amount, you can ask to see a credit card for added identification, but writing down the number will do no good because you cannot legally cover a bad check with a customer's credit card. (The customer has a legal right to refuse to let you copy the number as well.)

- Look closely at the check itself. Is there a name and address printed on it? If not, ask the customer to write in this information by hand, along with his or her phone number.

- Look at the sides of the check. If at least one side is not perforated, it could be a phony check.

- Look at the check number in the upper right-hand corner. Most banks who issue personalized checks begin the numbering system with 101 when a customer reorders new checks. The Small Business Administration says to be more cautious with low sequence numbers because there seems to be a higher number of these checks that are returned.

- Check the routing number in the lower left-hand corner and note the ink. If it looks shiny, wet your finger and see if the ink rubs off. That's a sure sign of a phony check because good checks are printed with magnetic ink that does not reflect light.

Collecting on a Bad Check

No matter how careful you are, sooner or later, you will get stuck with a bad check. It may bounce for one of three reasons:

Nonsufficient funds (NSF)
Account closed
No account (evidence of fraud)

I've accepted tens of thousands of checks from mail-order buyers through the years and have rarely had a bad check I couldn't collect with a simple phone call asking the party to honor his or her obligation to me. People often move and close out accounts before all checks have cleared, or they add or subtract wrong, causing their account to be overdrawn. Typically, they are embarrassed to have caused a problem like this.

When the problem is more difficult than this, your bank can help. Check to learn its policy regarding bounced checks. Some automatically put checks through a second time. If a check bounces at this point, you may ask the bank to collect the check for you. The check needs to be substantial, however, because the bank fee may be $15 or more if they are successful in collecting the money.

If you have accepted a check for a substantial amount of money and believe there is evidence of fraud, you may wish to do one of the following:

- **Notify your district attorney's office**
- **Contact your sheriff or police department (because it is a crime to write a bad check)**
- **Try to collect through small claims court**

For more detailed information on all of these topics, see *The Crafts Business Answer Book.*

7. Insurance Tips

As soon as you start even the smallest business at home, you need to give special attention to insurance. This section offers an introductory overview of insurance concerns of primary interest to crafts-business owners.

Homeowner's or Renter's Insurance

Anything in the home being used to generate income is considered to be business-related and thus exempt from coverage on a personal policy. Thus your homeowner's or renter's insurance policy will not cover business equipment, office furniture, supplies, or inventory of finished goods unless you obtain a special rider. Such riders, called a "Business Pursuits Endorsement" by some companies, are inexpensive and offer considerable protection. Your insurance agent will be happy to give you details.

As your business grows and you have an ever-larger inventory of supplies, materials, tools, and finished merchandise, you may find it necessary to buy a special in-home business policy that offers broader protection. Such policies may be purchased directly from insurance companies or through craft and home-business organizations that offer special insurance programs to their members.

Avoid this pitfall: If you have an expensive computer system, costly tools, equipment, or office furnishings, the coverage

Insuring Your Art or Crafts Collection

The replacement cost insurance you may have on your personal household posses-sions does not extend to "fine art," which includes such things as paintings, antiques, pictures, tapestries, statuary, and other articles that cannot be replaced with new arti-cles. If you have a large collection of art, crafts, memorabilia, or collector's items, and its value is more than $1,500, you may wish to have your collection appraised so it can be protected with a separate all-risk endorsement to your homeowner's policy called a "fine arts floater."

afforded by a simple business rider to your homeowner's policy may be insufficient for your needs. Although you may have replacement-value insurance on all your personal possessions, anything used for business purposes would be exempt from such coverage. In other words, the value of everything covered by the rider would be figured on a depreciable basis instead of what it would cost to replace it. (See also sidebar, Insuring Your Art or Crafts Collection, on page 279.)

Liability Insurance

There are two kinds of liability insurance. *Product* liability insurance protects you against lawsuits by consumers who have been injured while using one of your products. *Personal* liability insurance protects you against claims made by individuals who have suffered bodily injury while on your premises (either your home or the place where you are doing business, such as in your booth at a craft fair).

Your homeowner's or renter's insurance policy will include some personal liability protection, but if someone were to suffer bodily injury while on your premises for *business* reasons, that coverage might not apply. Your need for personal liability insurance will be greater if you plan to regularly present home parties, holiday boutiques, or open house sales in your home where many people might be coming and going throughout the year. If you sell at craft fairs, you would also be liable for damages if someone were to fall and be injured in your booth or if something in your booth falls and injures another person. For this reason, some craft fair promoters now require all vendors to have personal liability insurance.

As for product liability insurance, whether you need it depends largely on the type of products you make for sale, how careful you are to make sure those products are safe, and how and where you sell them. Examples of some crafts that have caused injury to consumers and resulted in court claims in the past are stuffed toys with wire or pins that children have swallowed; items made of yarn or fiber that burned rapidly; handmade furniture that collapsed when someone put an ordinary amount of weight on it; jewelry with sharp points or other features that cut the wearer, and so on. Clearly, the best way to avoid injury to consumers is to make certain your products have no health hazards and are safe to use. (See discussion of Consumer Safety Laws in section 8.)

Few artists and craftspeople who sell on a part-time basis feel they can afford product liability insurance, but many full-time craft professionals, particularly those who sell their work wholesale, find it a necessary expense. In fact, many wholesale buyers refuse to buy from suppliers that do not carry product liability insurance.

I believe the least expensive way to obtain both personal and product liability insurance is with one of the comprehensive in-home or crafts-business policies offered by a crafts- or home-business organization. Such policies generally offer $1 million of both personal and product liability coverage. (See A "Things to Do" Checklist with Related Resources on page 308 and the Resources section for some organizations you can contact for more information. Also check with your insurance agent about the benefits of an umbrella policy for extra liability insurance.)

Insurance on Crafts Merchandise

As a seller of art or crafts merchandise, you are responsible for insuring your own products against loss. If you plan to sell at craft fairs, in craft malls, rent-a-space shops, or consignment shops, you may want to buy an insurance policy that protects your merchandise both at home or away. Note that while craft shops and malls generally have fire insurance covering the building and its fixtures, this coverage cannot be extended to merchandise offered for sale because it is not the property of the shop owner. (Exception: Shops and malls in shopping centers are mandated by law to buy fire insurance on their contents whether they own the merchandise or not.)

This kind of insurance is usually part of the home- or crafts-business insurance policies mentioned earlier.

Auto Insurance

Be sure to talk to the agent who handles your car insurance and explain that you may occasionally use your car for business purposes. Normally, a policy issued for a car that's used only for pleasure or driving to and from work may not provide complete coverage for an accident that occurs during business use of the car, particularly if the insured is to blame for the accident. For example, if you were delivering a load of crafts to a shop or on your way to a craft fair and had an accident, would your business destination and the "commercial merchandise" in your car negate your coverage in any way? Where insurance is concerned, the more questions you ask, the better you'll feel about the policies you have.

8. Important Regulations Affecting Artists and Craftspeople

Government agencies have a number of regulations that artists and craftspeople must know about. Generally, they relate to consumer safety, the labeling of certain products, and trade practices. Following are regulations of primary interest to readers of books in Prima's For Fun & Profit series. If you find a law or regulation related to your particular art or craft interest, be sure to request additional information from the government agency named there.

Consumer Safety Laws

All product sellers must pay attention to the Consumer Product Safety Act, which protects the public against unreasonable risks of injury associated with consumer products. The Consumer Product

Safety Commission (CPSC) is particularly active in the area of toys and consumer goods designed for children. All sellers of handmade products must be doubly careful about the materials they use for children's products because consumer lawsuits are common where products for children are concerned. To avoid this problem, simply comply with the consumer safety laws applicable to your specific art or craft.

Toy Safety Concerns

To meet CPSC's guidelines for safety, make sure any toys you make for sale are:

- Too large to be swallowed
- Not apt to break easily or leave jagged edges
- Free of sharp edges or points
- Not put together with easily exposed pins, wires, or nails
- Nontoxic, nonflammable, and nonpoisonous

The Use of Paints, Varnishes, and Other Finishes

Since all paint sold for household use must meet the Consumer Product Safety Act's requirement for minimum amounts of lead, these paints are deemed to be safe for use on products made for children, such as toys and furniture. Always check, however, to make sure the label bears a nontoxic notation. Specialty paints must carry a warning on the label about lead count, but "artist's paints" are curiously exempt from CPS's lead-in-paint ban and are not required to bear a warning label of any kind. Thus you should *never* use such paints on products intended for use by children unless the label specifically states they are *nontoxic* (lead-free). Acrylics and other water-based paints, of course, are nontoxic and completely safe for use on toys and other products made for children. If you plan to use a finishing coat, make sure it is nontoxic as well.

Fabric Flammability Concerns

The Flammable Fabrics Act is applicable only to those who sell products made of fabric, particularly products for children. It prohibits the movement in interstate commerce of articles of wearing apparel and fabrics that are so highly flammable as to be dangerous when worn by individuals, and for other purposes. Most fabrics comply with this act, but if you plan to sell children's clothes or toys, you may wish to take an extra step to be doubly sure the fabric you are using is safe. This is particularly important if you plan to wholesale your products. What you should do is ask your fabric supplier for a *guarantee of compliance with the Flammability Act*. This guarantee is generally passed along to the buyer by a statement on the invoice that reads "continuing guaranty under the Flammable Fabrics Act." If you do not find such a statement on your invoice, you should ask the fabric manufacturer, wholesaler, or distributor to furnish you with their "statement of compliance" with the flammability standards. The CPSC can also tell you if a particular manufacturer has filed a continuing guarantee under the flammable Fabrics Act.

Labels Required by Law

The following information applies only to crafters who use textiles, fabrics, fibers, or yarn products to make wearing apparel, decorative accessories, household furnishings, soft toys, or any product made of wool.

Different government agencies require the attachment of certain tags or labels to products sold in the consumer marketplace, whether manufactured in quantity or handmade for limited sale. You don't have to be too concerned about these laws if you sell only at local fairs, church bazaars, and home boutiques. As soon as you get out into the general consumer marketplace, however—doing large craft fairs, selling through consignment shops, craft malls, or wholesaling to shops—it would be wise to comply with all the federal labeling laws. Actually, these laws are quite easy to comply with because the required labels are readily available at inexpensive prices, and you can even make your own if you wish. Here is what the federal government wants you to tell your buyers in a tag or label:

- *What's in a product, and who has made it.* The Textile Fiber Products Identification Act (monitored both by the Bureau of Consumer Protection and the Federal Trade Commission) requires that a special label or hangtag be attached to all textile wearing apparel and household furnishings, with the exception of wall hangings. "Textiles" include products made of any fiber, yarn, or fabric, including garments and decorative accessories, quilts, pillows, placemats, stuffed toys, rugs, and so on. The tag or label must include (1) the name of the manufacturer and (2) the generic names and percentages of all fibers in the product in amounts of 5% or more, listed in order of predominance by weight.

- *How to take care of products.* Care Labeling Laws are part of the Textile Fiber Products Identification Act, details about which are available from the FTC. If you make wearing apparel or household furnishings of any kind using textiles, suede, or leather, you must attach a permanent label that explains how to take care of the item. This label must indicate whether the item is to be dry-cleaned or washed. If it is washable, you must indicate whether in hot or cold water, whether bleach may or may not be used, and the temperature at which it may be ironed.

- *Details about products made of wool.* If a product contains wool, the FTC requires additional identification under a separate law known as the Wool Products Labeling Act of 1939. FTC rules require that the labels of all wool or textile products clearly indicate when imported ingredients are used. Thus, the label for a skirt knitted in the United States from wool yarn imported from England would read, "Made in the USA from imported products" or similar wordage.

If the wool yarn was spun in the United States, a product made from that yarn would simply need a tag or label stating it was "Made in the USA" or "Crafted in USA" or some similarly clear terminology.

The Bedding and Upholstered Furniture Law

This is a peculiar state labeling law that affects sellers of items that have a concealed filling. It requires the purchase of a license, and products must have a tag that bears the manufacturer's registry number.

A Proper Copyright Notice

Although a copyright notice is not required by law, you are encouraged to put a copyright notice on every original thing you create. Adding the copyright notice does not obligate you to formally register your copyright, but it does serve to warn others that your work is legally protected and makes it difficult for anyone to claim they have "accidentally stolen" your work. (Those who actually do violate a copyright because they don't understand the law are called "innocent infringers" by the Copyright Office.)

A proper copyright notice includes three things:

1. The word *copyright,* its abbreviation, *copr.,* or the copyright symbol, ©

2. The year of first publication of the work (when it was first shown or sold to the public)

3. The name of the copyright owner. Example: © 2000 by Barbara Brabec. (When the words *All Rights Reserved* are added to the copyright notation, it means that copyright protection has been extended to include all of the Western Hemisphere.)

The copyright notice should be positioned in a place where it can easily be seen. It can be stamped, cast, engraved, painted, printed, wood-burned, or simply written by hand in permanent ink. In the case of fiber crafts, you can attach an inexpensive label with the copyright notice and your business name and logo (or any other information you wish to put on the label).

Bedding laws have long been a thorn in the side of crafters because they make no distinction between the large manufacturing company that makes mattresses and pillows, and the individual craft producer who sells only handmade items. "Concealed filling" items include not just bedding and upholstery, but handmade pillows and quilts. In some states, dolls, teddy bears, and stuffed soft sculpture items are also required to have a tag.

Fortunately, only 29 states now have this law on the books, and even if your state is one of them, the law may be arbitrarily enforced. (One exception is the state of Pennsylvania, which is reportedly sending officials to craft shows to inspect merchandise to see if it is properly labeled.) The only penalty that appears to be connected with a violation of this law in any state is removal of merchandise from store shelves or craft fair exhibits. That being the case, many crafters choose to ignore this law until they are challenged. If you learn you must comply with this law, you will be required to obtain a state license that will cost between $25 and $100, and you will have to order special "bedding stamps" that can be attached to your products. For more information on this complex topic, see *The Crafts Business Answer Book*.

FTC Rule for Mail-Order Sellers

Even the smallest home-based business needs to be familiar with Federal Trade Commission (FTC) rules and regulations. A variety of free booklets are available to business owners on topics related to advertising, mail-order marketing, and product labeling (as discussed earlier). In particular, crafters who sell by mail need to pay attention to the FTC's Thirty-Day Mail-Order Rule, which states that one must ship customer orders within 30 days of receiving payment for the order. This rule is strictly enforced, with severe financial penalties for each violation.

Unless you specifically state in your advertising literature how long delivery will take, customers will expect to receive the product within 30 days after you get their order. If you cannot meet this shipping date, you must notify the customer accordingly, enclosing a postage-paid reply card or envelope, and giving them the option to cancel the order if they wish. Now you know why so many catalog sellers state, "Allow 6 weeks for delivery." This lets them off the hook in case there are unforeseen delays in getting the order delivered.

9. Protecting Your Intellectual Property

"Intellectual property," says Attorney Stephen Elias in his book, *Patent, Copyright & Trademark,* "is a product of the human intellect that has commercial value."

This section offers a brief overview of how to protect your intellectual property through patents and trademarks, with a longer discussion of copyright law, which is of the greatest concern to individuals who sell what they make. Because it is easy to get patents, trademarks, and copyrights mixed up, let me briefly define them for you:

- A *patent* is a grant issued by the government that gives an inventor the right to exclude all others from making, using, or selling an invention within the United States and its territories and possessions.

- A *trademark* is used by a manufacturer or merchant to identify his or her goods and distinguish them from those manufactured or sold by others.

- A *copyright* protects the rights of creators of intellectual property in five main categories (described in this section).

Perspective on Patents

A patent may be granted to anyone who invents or discovers a new and useful process, machine, manufacture, or composition of matter, or any new and useful improvement thereof. Any new, original, and ornamental design for an article of manufacture can also be patented. The problem with patents is that they can cost as much as $5,000 or more to obtain, and, once you've got one, they still require periodic maintenance through the U.S. Patent and Trademark Office. To contact this office, you can use the following Web sites: www.uspto.com or www.lcweb.loc.gov.

Ironically, a patent doesn't even give one the right to sell a product. It merely excludes anyone else from making, using, or selling your invention. Many business novices who have gone to the trouble to patent a product end up wasting a lot of time and money because a patent is useless if it isn't backed with the right manufacturing, distribution, and advertising programs. As inventor Jeremy Gorman states in *Homemade Money,* "Ninety-seven percent of the U.S. patents issued never earn enough money to pay the patenting fee. They just go on a plaque on the wall or in a desk drawer to impress the grandchildren 50 years later."

What a Trademark Protects

Trademarks were established to prevent one company from trading on the good name and reputation of another. The primary function of a trademark is to indicate origin, but in some cases it also serves as a guarantee of quality.

You cannot adopt any trademark that is so similar to another that it is likely to confuse buyers, nor can you trademark generic or descriptive names in the public domain. If, however, you come up with a particular word, name, symbol, or device to identify and distinguish your products from others, you may protect that mark by trademark provided another company is not already using a similar mark. Brand names, trade names, slogans, and phrases may also qualify for trademark protection.

Many individual crafters have successfully registered their own trademarks using a how-to book on the topic, but some would say never to try this without the help of a trademark attorney. It depends on how much you love detail and how well you can follow directions. Any mistake on the application form could cause it to be rejected, and you would lose the application fee in the process. If this is something you're interested in, and you have designed a mark you want to protect, you should first do a trademark search to see if someone else is already using it. Trademark searches can be done using library directories, an online computer service (check with your library), through private trademark search firms, or directly on the Internet through the Patent and Trademark Office's online search service (see A "Things to Do" Checklist with Related Resources on page 308). All of these searches together could still be inconclusive, however, because many companies have a stash of trademarks in reserve waiting for just the right product. As I understand it, these "nonpublished" trademarks are in a special file that only an attorney or trademark search service could find for you.

Selling How-To Projects to Magazines

If you want to sell an article, poem, or how-to project to a magazine, you need not copyright the material first because copyright protection exists from the moment you create that work. Your primary consideration here is whether you will sell "all rights" or only "first rights" to the magazine.

The sale of first rights means you are giving a publication permission to print your article, poem, or how-to project once, for a specific sum of money. After publication, you then have the right to resell that material or profit from it in other ways. Although it is always desirable to sell only "first rights," some magazines do not offer this choice.

If you sell all rights, you will automatically lose ownership of the copyright to your material and you can no longer profit from that work. Professional designers often refuse to work this way because they know they can realize greater profits by publishing their own pattern packets or design leaflets and wholesaling them to shops.

Like copyrights, trademarks have their own symbol, which looks like this: ®. This symbol can be used only after the trademark has been formally registered through the U.S. Patent and Trademark Office. Business owners often use the superscript initials ™ with a mark to indicate they've claimed a logo or some other mark, but this offers no legal protection. While this does not guarantee trademark protection, it does give notice to the public that you are claiming this name as your trademark. However, after you've used a mark for some time, you do gain a certain amount of common-law protection for that mark. I have, in fact, gained common-law protection for the name of my *Homemade Money* book and successfully defended it against use by another individual in my field because this title has become so closely associated with my name in the home-business community.

Whether you ever formally register a trademark or not will have much to do with your long-range business plans, how you feel about protecting your creativity, and what it would do to your business if someone stole your mark and registered it in his or her own name. Once you've designed a trademark you feel is worth protecting, get additional information from the Patent and Trademark Office and read a book or two on the topic to decide whether this is something you wish to pursue. (See A "Things to Do" Checklist with Related Resources on page 308.)

What Copyrights Protect

As a serious student of the copyright law, I've pored through the hard-to-interpret copyright manual, read dozens of related articles and books, and discussed this subject at length with designers, writers, teachers, editors, and publishers. I must emphasize, however, that I am no expert on this topic, and the following information does not constitute legal advice. It is merely offered as a general guide to a very complex legal topic you may wish to research further on your own at some point. In a book of this nature, addressed to hobbyists and beginning crafts-business owners, a discussion of copyrights must be limited to three basic topics:

- What copyrights do and do not protect
- How to register a copyright and protect your legal rights
- How to avoid infringing on the rights of other copyright holders

One of the first things you should do now is send for the free booklets offered by the Copyright Office (see A "Things to Do" Checklist with Related Resources on page 308). Various free circulars explain copyright basics, the forms involved in registering a copyright, and how to submit a copyright application and register a

Protecting Your Copyrights

If someone ever copies one of your copyrighted works, and you have registered that work with the Copyright Office, you should defend it as far as you are financially able to do so. If you think you're dealing with an innocent infringer—another crafter, perhaps, who has probably not profited much (if at all) from your work—a strongly worded letter on your business stationery (with a copy to an attorney, if you have one) might do the trick. Simply inform the copyright infringer that you are the legal owner of the work and the only one who has the right to profit from it. Tell the infringer that he or she must immediately cease using your copyrighted work, and ask for a confirmation by return mail.

If you think you have lost some money or incurred other damages, consult with a copyright attorney before contacting the infringer to see how you can best protect your rights and recoup any financial losses you may have suffered. This is particularly important if the infringer appears to be a successful business or corporation. Although you may have no intention of ever going to court on this matter, the copyright infringer won't know that, and one letter from a competent attorney might immediately resolve the matter at very little cost to you.

copyright. They also discuss what you cannot copyright. Rather than duplicate all the free information you can get from the Copyright Office with a letter or phone call, I will only briefly touch on these topics and focus instead on addressing some of the particular copyright questions crafters have asked me in the past.

Things You Can Copyright

Some people mistakenly believe that copyright protection extends only to printed works, but that is not true. The purpose of the copyright law is to protect any creator from anyone who would use the creator's work for his or her own profit. Under current copyright law, claims are now registered in seven classes, five of which pertain to crafts:

1. *Serials* (Form SE)—periodicals, newspapers, magazines, bulletins, newsletters, annuals, journals, and proceedings of societies.
2. *Text* (Form TX)—books, directories, and other written works, including the how-to instructions for a crafts project. (You could copyright a letter to your mother if you wanted to— or your best display ad copy, or any other written words that represent income potential.)
3. *Visual Arts* (Form VA)—pictorial, graphic, or sculptural works, including fine, graphic, and applied art; photographs, charts; technical drawings; diagrams; and models. (Also included in this category are "works of artistic craftsmanship insofar as their form but not their mechanical or utilitarian aspects are concerned.")
4. *Performing Arts* (Form PA)—musical works and accompanying words, dramatic works, pantomimes, choreographic works, motion pictures, and other audiovisual works.
5. *Sound Recordings* (Form SR)—musical, spoken, or other sounds, including any audio- or videotapes you might create.

Things You Cannot Copyright

You can't copyright ideas or procedures for doing, making, or building things, but the *expression* of an idea fixed in a tangible medium may be copyrightable—such as a book explaining a new system or technique. Brand names, trade names, slogans, and phrases cannot be copyrighted, either, although they might be entitled to protection under trademark laws.

The design on a craft object can be copyrighted, but only if it can be identified separately from the object itself. Objects themselves (a decorated coffee mug, a box, a tote bag) cannot be copyrighted.

Copyright Registration Tips

First, understand that you do not have to formally copyright anything because copyright protection exists from the moment a work is created, whether you add a copyright notice or not.

So why file at all? The answer is simple: If you don't file the form and pay the fee (currently $30), you'll never be able to take anyone to court for stealing your work. Therefore, in each instance where copyright protection is considered, you need to decide how important your work is to you in terms of dollars and cents, and ask yourself whether you value it enough to pay to protect it. Would you actually be willing to pay court costs to defend your copyright, should someone steal it from you? If you never intend to go to court, there's little use in officially registering a copyright; but because it costs you nothing to add a copyright notice to your work, you are foolish not to do this. (See sidebar, Protecting Your Copyrights, on page 292.)

If you do decide to file a copyright application, contact the Copyright Office and request the appropriate forms. When you file the copyright application form (which is easy to complete), you must include with it two copies of the work. Ordinarily, two actual copies of copyrighted items must be deposited, but certain items are exempt from deposit requirements, including all three-dimensional sculptural works and any works published only as reproduced in or on jewelry, dolls, toys, games, plaques, floor coverings, textile and other fabrics, packaging materials, or any useful article. In these cases, two photographs or drawings of the item are sufficient.

Note that the Copyright Office does not compare deposit copies to determine whether works submitted for registration are similar to any material already copyrighted. It is the sender's responsibility to determine the originality of what's being copyrighted. (See discussion of "original" in the next section, under Respecting the Copyrights of Others.)

Mandatory Deposit Requirements

Although you do not have to officially register a copyright claim, it *is* mandatory to deposit two copies of all "published works" for the collections of the Library of Congress within 3 months after publication. Failure to make the deposit may subject the copyright owner to fines and other monetary liabilities, but it does not affect copyright protection. No special form is required for this mandatory deposit.

Note that the term *published works* pertains not just to the publication of printed matter, but to the public display of any item. Thus you "publish" your originally designed craftwork when you first show it at a craft fair, in a shop, on your Web site, or any other public place.

Respecting the Copyrights of Others

Just as there are several things you must do to protect your "intellectual creations," there are several things you must not do if you wish to avoid legal problems with other copyright holders.

Copyright infringement occurs whenever anyone violates the exclusive rights covered by copyright. If and when a copyright case goes to court, the copyright holder who has been infringed on must

Changing Things

Many crafters have mistakenly been led to believe that they can copy the work of others if they simply change this or that so their creation doesn't look exactly like the one they have copied. But many copyright court cases have hinged on someone taking "a substantial part" of someone else's design and claiming it as their own. If your "original creation" bears even the slightest resemblance to the product you've copied—and you are caught selling it in the commercial marketplace—there could be legal problems.

Crafters often combine the parts of two or three patterns in an attempt to come up with their own original patterns, but often this only compounds the possible copyright problems. Let's imagine you're making a doll. You might take the head from one pattern, the arms and legs from another, and the unique facial features from another. You may think you have developed an original creation (and perhaps an original pattern

prove that his or her work is the original creation and that the two works are so similar that the alleged infringer must have copied it. This is not always an easy matter, for *original* is a difficult word to define. Even the Copyright Office has trouble here, which is why so many cases that go to court end up setting precedents.

In any copyright case, there will be discussions about "substantial similarity," instances where two people actually have created the same thing simultaneously, loss of profits, or damage to one's business or reputation. If you were found guilty of copyright infringement, at the very least you would probably be ordered to pay to the original creator all profits derived from the sale of the copyrighted work to date. You would also have to agree to refund any orders you might receive for the work in the future. In some copyright cases where the original creator has experienced considerable financial loss, penalties for copyright infringement have been as high as $100,000. As you can see, this is not a matter to take lightly.

you might sell), but you haven't. Because the original designer of any of the features you've copied might recognize her work in your "original creation" or published pattern, the designer could come after you for infringing on "a substantial part" of his or her design. In this case, all you've done is multiply your possibilities for a legal confrontation with three copyright holders.

"But I can't create my own original designs and patterns!" you moan. Many who have said this in the past were mistaken. With time and practice, most crafters are able to develop products that are original in design, and I believe you can do this, too. Meanwhile, check out Dover Publications' *Pictorial Archive* series of books (see A "Things to Do" Checklist with Related Resources). Here you will find thousands of copyright-free designs and motifs you can use on your craft work or in needlework projects. And don't forget the wealth of design material in museums and old books that have fallen into the public domain. (See sidebar, What's in the Public Domain? on page 300.)

This is a complex topic beyond the scope of this book, but any book on copyright law will provide additional information if you should ever need it. What's important here is that you fully understand the importance of being careful to respect the legal rights of others. As a crafts-business owner, you could possibly infringe on someone else's designs when you (1) quote someone in an article, periodical, or book you've written; (2) photocopy copyrighted materials; or (3) share information on the Internet. Following is a brief discussion of these topics.

1. **Be careful when quoting from a published source.** If you're writing an article or book and wish to quote someone's words from any published source (book, magazine, Internet, and so on), you should always obtain written permission first. Granted, minor quotations from published sources are okay when they fall under the Copyright Office's Fair Use Doctrine, but unless you completely understand this doctrine, you should protect yourself by

obtaining permission before you quote anyone in one of your own written works. It is not necessarily the quantity of the quote, but the value of the quoted material to the copyright owner.

In particular, never *ever* use a published poem in one of your written works without written permission. To the poet, this is a "whole work," much the same as a book is a whole work to an author. Although the use of one or two lines of a poem, or a paragraph from a book, may be considered "fair use," many publishers now require written permission even for this short reproduction of a copyrighted work.

2. **Photocopying can be dangerous.** Teachers often photocopy large sections of a book (sometimes whole books) for distribution to their students, but this is a flagrant violation of the copyright law. Some publishers may grant photocopying of part of a work if it is to be used only once as a teaching aid, but written permission must always be obtained first.

   It is also a violation of the copyright law to photocopy patterns for sale or trade because such use denies the creator the profit from a copy that might have been sold.

3. **Don't share copyrighted information on the Internet.** People everywhere are lifting material from *Reader's Digest* and other copyrighted publications and "sharing" them on the Internet through e-mail messages, bulletin boards, and the like. *This is a very dangerous thing to do.* "But I didn't see a copyright notice," you might say, or "It indicated the author was anonymous." What you must remember is that *everything* gains copyright protection the moment it is created, whether a copyright notice is attached to it or not. Many "anonymous" items on the Internet are actually copyrighted poems and articles put there by someone who not only

violated the copyright law but compounded the matter by failing to give credit to the original creator.

If you were to pick up one of those "anonymous" pieces of information and put it in an article or book of your own, the original copyright owner, upon seeing his or her work in your publication, would have good grounds for a lawsuit. Remember, pleading ignorance of the law is never a good excuse.

Clearly there is no financial gain to be realized by violating the rights of a copyright holder when it means that any day you might be contacted by a lawyer and threatened with a lawsuit. As stated in my *Crafts Business Answer Book & Resource Guide:*

> The best way to avoid copyright infringement problems is to follow the "Golden Rule" proposed by a United States Supreme Court justice: "Take not from others to such an extent and in such a manner that you would be resentful if they so took from you."

Using Commercial Patterns and Designs

Beginning crafters who lack design skills commonly make products for sale using commercial patterns, designs in books, or how-to instructions for projects found in magazines. The problem here is that all of these things are published for the general consumer market and offered for *personal use* only. Because they are all protected by copyright, that means only the copyright holder has the right to profit from their use.

That said, let me ease your mind by saying that the sale of products made from copyrighted patterns, designs, and magazine how-to projects is probably not going to cause any problems *as long as sales are limited, and they yield a profit only to you, the crafter.* That means no sales through shops of any kind where a sales commission or profit is received by a third party, and absolutely no wholesaling of such products.

It's not that designers and publishers are concerned about your sale of a few craft or needlework items to friends and local buyers; what they are fighting to protect with the legality of copyrights is their right to sell their own designs or finished products in the commercial marketplace. You may find that some patterns, designs, or projects state "no mass-production." You are not mass-producing if you make a dozen handcrafted items for sale at a craft fair or holiday boutique, but you would definitely be considered a mass-producer if you made dozens, or hundreds, for sale in shops.

Consignment sales fall into a kind of gray area that requires some commonsense judgment on your part. This is neither wholesaling nor selling direct to consumers. One publisher might con-

What's in the Public Domain?

For all works created after January 1, 1978, the copyright lasts for the life of the author or creator plus 50 years after his or her death. For works created before 1978, there are different terms, which you can obtain from any book in your library on copyright law.

Once material falls into the public domain, it can never be copyrighted again. As a general rule, anything with a copyright date more than 75 years ago is probably in the public domain, but you can never be sure without doing a thorough search. Some characters in old books—such as Beatrix Potter's *Peter Rabbit*—are now protected under the trademark law as business logos. For more information on this, ask the Copyright Office to send you its circular "How to Investigate the Copyright Status of a Work."

Early American craft and needlework patterns of all kinds are in the public domain because they were created before the copyright law was a reality. Such old patterns may

sider such sales a violation of a copyright while another might not. Whenever specific guidelines for the use of a pattern, design, or how-to project are not given, the only way to know for sure if you are operating on safe legal ground is to write to the publisher and get written permission on where you can sell reproductions of the item in question.

Now let's take a closer look at the individual types of patterns, designs, and how-to projects you might consider using once you enter the crafts marketplace.

Craft, Toy, and Garment Patterns

Today, the consumer has access to thousands of sewing patterns plus toy, craft, needlework, and woodworking patterns of every kind and description found in books, magazines, and design or project leaflets. Whether you can use such patterns for commercial use

show up in books and magazines that are copyrighted, but the copyright in this case extends only to the book or magazine itself and the way in which a pattern has been presented to readers, along with the way in which the how-to-make instructions have been written. The actual patterns themselves cannot be copyrighted by anyone at this point.

Quilts offer an interesting example. If a contemporary quilt designer takes a traditional quilt pattern and does something unusual with it in terms of material or colors, this new creation would qualify for a copyright, with the protection being given to the quilt as a work of art, not to the traditional pattern itself, which is still in the public domain. Thus you could take that same traditional quilt pattern and do something else with it for publication, but you could not publish the contemporary designer's copyrighted version of that same pattern.

depends largely on who has published the pattern and owns the copyright, and what the copyright holder's policy happens to be for how buyers may use those patterns.

To avoid copyright problems when using patterns of any kind, the first thing you need to do is look for some kind of notice on the pattern packet or publication containing the pattern. In checking some patterns, I found that those sold by *Woman's Day* state specifically that reproductions of the designs may not be sold, bartered, or traded. *Good Housekeeping,* on the other hand, gives permission to use their patterns for "income-producing activities." When in doubt, ask!

Whereas the general rule for selling reproductions made from commercial patterns is "no wholesaling and no sales to shops," items made from the average garment pattern (such as an apron, vest, shirt, or simple dress) purchased in the local fabric store *may* be an exception. My research suggests that selling such items in your local consignment shop or craft mall isn't likely to be much of a problem because the sewing pattern companies aren't on the lookout for copyright violators the way individual craft designers and major corporations are. (And most people who sew end up changing those patterns and using different decorations to such a degree that pattern companies might not recognize those patterns even if they were looking for them.)

On the other hand, commercial garment patterns that have been designed by name designers should never be used without permission. In most cases, you would have to obtain a licensing agreement for the commercial use of such patterns.

> *Avoid this pitfall:* In addition to problems in using copyrighted patterns, anyone who uses fabric to make a product for the marketplace has yet another concern: designer *fabrics*. Always look at the selvage of a patterned fabric. If you see a copyright notice with a designer's name and the phrase "for individual consumption only" (or similar wordage), *do not use this fabric to make any item for*

sale without first obtaining written permission from the fabric manu-facturer. In many instances, designer fabrics can be used commercially only when a license has been obtained for this purpose.

Be especially careful about selling reproductions of toys and dolls made from commercial patterns or design books. Many are likely to be for popular copyrighted characters being sold in the commercial marketplace. In such cases, the pattern company will have a special licensing arrangement with the toy or doll manufacturer to sell the pattern, and reproductions for sale by individual crafters will be strictly prohibited.

Take a Raggedy Ann doll, for example. The fact that you've purchased a pattern to make such a doll does not give you the right to sell a finished likeness of that doll any more than your purchase of a piece of artwork gives you the right to re-create it for sale in some other form, such as notepaper or calendars. Only the original creator has such rights. You have simply purchased the *physical property* for private use.

> ***Avoid this pitfall:*** Don't *ever* make and sell *any* replica in any material of a famous copyrighted character anywhere, such as the Walt Disney or Warner Brothers characters, Snoopy, or the Sesame Street gang. It's true that a lot of crafters are doing this, but they are inviting serious legal trouble if they ever get caught. Disney is particularly aggressive in defending its copyrights.

How-To Projects in Magazines and Books

Each magazine and book publisher has its own policy about the use of its art, craft, or needlework projects. How those projects may be used depends on who owns the copyright to the published projects. In some instances, craft and needlework designers sell their original designs outright to publishers of books, leaflets, or magazines. Other designers authorize only a one-time use of their projects, which gives

Online Help

Today, one of the best ways to network and learn about business is to get on the Internet. The many online resources included in A "Things to Do" Checklist in the next section will give you a jump start and lead to many exciting discoveries.

For continuing help and advice from Barbara Brabec, be sure to visit her Web sites at www.BarbaraBrabec.com and www.ideaforest.com. Here you will find a wealth of information to help you profit from your crafts, including newsletters, feature articles, special tips, and recommended books.

them the right to republish or sell their designs to another market or license them to a manufacturer. If guidelines about selling finished products do not appear somewhere in the magazine or on the copyright page of a book, you should always write and get permission to make such items for sale. In your letter, explain how many items you would like to make, and where you plan to sell them, as that could make a big difference in the reply you receive.

In case you missed the special note on the copyright page of this book, you *can* make and sell all of the projects featured in this and any other book in Prima's FOR FUN & PROFIT series.

As a columnist for *Crafts Magazine,* I can also tell you that its readers have the right to use its patterns and projects for money-making purposes, but only to the extent that sales are limited to places where the crafter is the only one who profits from their use. That means selling directly to individuals, with no sales in shops of any kind where a third party would also realize some profit from a sale. Actually, this is a good rule-of-thumb guideline to use if you plan to sell only a few items of any project or pattern published in any magazine, book, or leaflet.

In summary, products that aren't original in design will sell, but their market is limited, and they will never be able to command the kind of prices that original-design items enjoy. Generally speaking, the more original the product line, the greater one's chances for building a profitable crafts business.

As your business grows, questions about copyrights will arise, and you will have to do a little research to get the answers you need. Your library should have several books on this topic and there is a wealth of information on the Internet. (Just use your search button and type "copyright information.") If you have a technical copyright question, remember that you can always call the Copyright Office and speak to someone who can answer it and send you additional information. Note, however, that regulations prohibit the Copyright Office from giving legal advice or opinions concerning the rights of persons in connection with cases of alleged copyright infringement.

10. To Keep Growing, Keep Learning

Everything we do, every action we take, affects our life in one way or another. Reading a book is a simple act, indeed, but trust me when I say that your reading of this particular book *could ultimately change your life.* I know this to be true because thousands of men and women have written to me over the years to tell me how their lives changed after they read one or another of my books and decided to start a crafts business. My life has changed, too, as a result of reading books by other authors.

Many years ago, the purchase of a book titled *You Can Whittle and Carve* unleashed a flood of creativity in me that has yet to cease. That simple book helped me to discover unknown craft talents, which in turn led me to start my first crafts business at home. That experience prepared me for the message I would find a decade later in the book *On Writing Well* by William Zinsser. This author changed my life by giving me the courage to try my hand at writing professionally. Dozens of books later, I had learned a lot about the art and craft of writing well and making a living in the process.

Now you know why I believe reading should be given top priority in your life. Generally speaking, the more serious you become about anything you're interested in, the more reading you will need to do. This will take time, but the benefits will be enormous. If a crafts business is your current passion, this book contains all you need to know to get started. To keep growing, read some of the wonderful books recommended in the Resources. (If you don't find the books you need in your local library, ask your librarian to obtain them for you through the inter-library loan program.) Join one or more of the organizations recommended. Subscribe to a few periodicals or magazines, and "grow your business" through networking with others who share your interests.

Motivational Tips

As you start your new business or expand a money-making hobby already begun, consider the following suggestions:

- *Start an "Achievement Log."* Day by day, our small achievements may seem insignificant, but viewed in total after several weeks or months, they give us important perspective. Reread your achievement log periodically in the future, especially on days when you feel down in the dumps. Make entries at least once a week, noting such things as new customers or accounts acquired, publicity you've gotten, a new product you've designed, the brochure or catalog you've just completed, positive feedback received from others, new friendships, and financial gains.

- *Live your dream.* The mind is a curious thing—it can be trained to think success is possible or to think that success is only for other people. Most of our fears never come true, so allowing our minds to dwell on what may or may not happen cripples us, preventing us from moving ahead, from having confidence, and from living out our dreams. Instead of "facing fear," focus on the result you want. This may automatically eliminate the fear.

- *Think positively.* As Murphy has proven time and again, what can go wrong will, and usually at the worst possible moment. It matters little whether the thing that has gone wrong was caused by circumstances beyond our control or by a mistake in judgment. What does matter is how we deal with the problem at hand. A positive attitude and the ability to remain flexible at all times are two of the most important ingredients for success in any endeavor.

- *Don't be afraid to fail.* We often learn more from failure than from success. When you make a mistake, chalk it up to experience and consider it a good lesson well learned. The more you learn, the more self-confident you will become.

- *Temper your "dreams of riches" with thoughts of reality.* Remember that "success" can also mean being in control of your own life, making new friends, or discovering a new world of possibilities.

Until now you may have lacked the courage to get your craft ideas off the ground, but now that you've seen how other people have accomplished their goals, I hope you feel more confident and adventurous and are ready to capitalize on your creativity. By following the good advice in this book, you can stop dreaming about all the things you want to do and start making plans to do them!

I'm not trying to make home-business owners out of everyone who reads this book, but my goal is definitely to give you a shove in that direction if you're teetering on the edge, wanting something more than just a profitable hobby. It's wonderful to have a satisfying hobby, and even better to have one that pays for itself; but the nicest thing of all is a real home business that lets you fully utilize your creative talents and abilities while also adding to the family income.

"The things I want to know are in books," Abraham Lincoln once said. "My best friend is the person who'll get me a book I ain't read." You now hold in your hands a book that has taught you many things you wanted to know. To make it a *life-changing book,* all you have to do is act on the information you've been given.

I wish you a joyful journey and a potful of profits!

A "Things to Do" Checklist with Related Resources

INSTRUCTIONS: Read through this entire section, noting the different things you need to do to get your crafts business "up and running." Use the checklist as a plan, checking off each task as it is completed and obtaining any recommended resources. Where indicated, note the date action was taken so you have a reminder about any follow-up action that should be taken.

Business Start-Up Checklist

☐ Call city hall or county clerk

    ☐ to register fictitious business name
    ☐ to see if you need a business license or permit
    ☐ to check on local zoning laws
    (info also available in your library)

    *Follow up:*_____

☐ Call state capitol

    ☐ secretary of state: to register your business name; ask about a license
    ☐ Department of Revenue: to apply for sales tax number

    *Follow up:*_____

☐ Call your local telephone company about

    ☐ cost of a separate phone line for business
    ☐ cost of an additional personal line for Internet access

☐ any special options for home-based businesses

*Follow up:*_____

☐ Call your insurance agent(s) to discuss

   ☐ business rider on house insurance
     (or need for separate in-home insurance policy)
   ☐ benefits of an umbrella policy for extra liability insurance
   ☐ using your car for business
     (how this may affect your insurance)

*Follow up:*_____

☐ Call several banks or S&L's in your area to

   ☐ compare cost of a business checking account
   ☐ get price of a safety deposit box for valuable business records

*Follow up:*_____

☐ Visit office and computer supply stores to check on

   ☐ manual bookkeeping systems, such as the
     Dome Simplified Monthly
   ☐ accounting software
   ☐ standard invoices and other helpful business forms

*Follow up:*_____

☐ Call National Association of Enrolled Agents at (800) 424-4339

   ☐ to get a referral to a tax professional in your area
   ☐ to get answers to any tax questions you may have (no charge)

*Follow up:*_____

☐ Contact government agencies for information relative to your business.

(See Government Agencies checklist.)

☐ Request free brochures from organizations

(See Craft and Home-Business Organizations.)

☐ Obtain sample issues or subscribe to selected publications

(See Recommended Crafts-Business Periodicals.)

☐ Obtain other information of possible help to your business

(See Other Services and Suppliers.)

☐ Get acquainted with the business information available to you in your library.

(See list of Recommended Business Books and Helpful Library Directories.)

Government Agencies

☐ Consumer Product Safety Commission (CPSC), Washington, DC 20207. (800) 638-2772. Information Services: (301) 504-0000. Web site: www.cpsc.gov. (Includes a "Talk to Us" e-mail address where you can get answers to specific questions.) If you make toys or other products for children, garments (especially children's wear), or use any kind of paint, varnish, lacquer, or shellac on your products, obtain the following free booklets:

☐ *The Consumer Product Safety Act of 1972*
☐ *The Flammable Fabrics Act*

Date Contacted:_____Information Received:_____

*Follow up:*_____

☐ Copyright Office, Register of Copyrights, Library of Congress, Washington, DC 20559. To hear recorded messages on the Copyright Office's automated message system (general information, registration procedures, copyright search info, and so on), call (202) 707-3000. You can also get the same information online at www.loc.gov/copyright.

To get free copyright forms, a complete list of all publications available, or to speak personally to someone who will answer your special questions, call (202) 797-9100. In particular, ask for:

☐ Circular R1, *The Nuts and Bolts of Copyright*
☐ Circular R2 (a list of publications available)

Date Contacted:_____Information Received:_____
*Follow up:*_____

☐ Department of Labor. If you should ever hire an employee
  or independent contractor, contact your local Labor Department, Wage & Hour Division, for guidance on what you must
  do to be completely legal. (Check your phone book under
  "U.S. Government.")

Date Contacted:_____Information Received:_____
*Follow up:*_____

☐ Federal Trade Commission (FTC), 6th Street and Pennsylvania
  Avenue, NW, Washington, DC 20580. Web site: www.ftc.gov. Request
  any of the following booklets relative to your craft or business:

  ☐ *Textile Fiber Products Identification Act*
  ☐ *Wool Products Labeling Act of 1939*
  ☐ *Care Labeling of Textile Wearing Apparel*
  ☐ *The Hand Knitting Yarn Industry* (booklet)
  ☐ *Truth-in-Advertising Rules*
  ☐ *Thirty-Day Mail-Order Rule*

Date Contacted:_____Information Received:_____
Follow up: _____

☐ Internal Revenue Service (IRS). Check the Internet at
  www.irs.gov to read the following information online or
  call your local IRS office or (800) 829-1040 to get the following booklets and other free tax information:

  ☐ *Tax Guide for Small Business—#334*
  ☐ *Business Use of Your Home—#587*
  ☐ *Tax Information for Direct Sellers*

Date Contacted:_____Information Received:_____

*Follow up:*_____

☐ Patent and Trademark Office (PTO), Washington, DC 20231.
   Web site: www.uspto.gov.

For patent and trademark information 24 hours a day, call
(800) 786-9199 (in northern Virginia, call (703) 308-9000) to hear
various messages about patents and trademarks or to order the
following booklets:

☐ *Basic Facts about Patents*
☐ *Basic Facts about Trademarks*

To search the PTO's online database of all registered trademarks,
go to www.uspto.gov/tmdb/index.html.

Date Contacted:_____Information Received:_____

*Follow up:*_____

☐ Social Security Hotline. (800) 772-1213. By calling this number,
   you can hear automated messages, order information booklets,
   or speak directly to someone who can answer specific questions.

Date Contacted:_____Information Received:_____

*Follow up:*_____

☐ U.S. Small Business Administration (SBA). (800) U-ASK-SBA.
   Call this number to hear a variety of prerecorded messages on
   starting and financing a business. Weekdays, you can speak personally to an SBA adviser to get answers to specific questions
   and request such free business publications as:

☐ *Starting Your Business* —#CO-0028
☐ *Resource Directory for Small Business Management*—#CO-0042
   (a list of low-cost publications available from the SBA)

The SBA's mission is to help people get into business and stay there. One-on-one counseling, training, and workshops are available through 950 small-business development centers across the country. Help is also available from local district offices of the SBA in the form of free business counseling and training from SCORE volunteers. The SBA office in Washington has a special Women's Business Enterprise section that provides free information on loans, tax deductions, and other financial matters. District offices offer special training programs in management, marketing, and accounting.

A wealth of business information is also available online at www.sba.gov and www.business.gov (the U.S. Business Adviser site). To learn whether there is an SBA office near you, look under U.S. Government in your telephone directory, or call the SBA's toll-free number.

Date Contacted:_____Information Received:_____

*Follow up:*_____

☐ SCORE (Service Corps of Retired Executives). (800) 634-0245. There are more than 12,400 SCORE members who volunteer their time and expertise to small-business owners. Many crafts businesses have received valuable in-depth counseling and training simply by calling the organization and asking how to connect with a SCORE volunteer in their area.

In addition, the organization offers e-mail counseling via the Internet at www.score.org. You simply enter the specific expertise required and retrieve a list of e-mail counselors who represent the best match by industry and topic. Questions can then be sent by e-mail to the counselor of your choice for response.

Date Contacted:_____Information Received:_____

*Follow up:*_____

Craft and Home-Business Organizations

In addition to the regular benefits of membership in an organization related to your art or craft (fellowship, networking, educational conferences or workshops, marketing opportunities, and so on), membership may also bring special business services, such as insurance programs, merchant card services, and discounts on supplies and materials. Each of the following organizations will send you membership information on request.

☐ The American Association of Home-Based Businesses, PO Box 10023, Rockville, MD 20849. (800) 447-9710. Web site: www.aahbb.org. This organization has chapters throughout the country. Members have access to merchant card services, discounted business products and services, prepaid legal services, and more.

Date Contacted:_____Information Received:_____

*Follow up:*_____

☐ American Crafts Council, 72 Spring Street, New York, NY 10012. (800)-724-0859. Web site: www.craftcouncil.org. Membership in this organization will give you access to a property and casualty insurance policy that will cost between $250 and $500 a year, depending on your city, state, and the value of items being insured in your art or crafts studio. The policy includes insurance for a craftsperson's work in the studio, in transit, or at a show; $1 million coverage for bodily injury and property damage in studio or away; and $1 million worth of product liability insurance. This policy is from American Phoenix Corporation; staff members will answer your specific questions when you call (800) 274-6364, ext. 337.

Date Contacted:_____Information Received:_____

*Follow up:*_____

☐ Arts & Crafts Business Solutions, 2804 Bishop Gate Drive, Raleigh, NC 27613. (800) 873-1192. This company, known in the industry as the Arts Group, offers a bankcard service specifically for and tailored to the needs of the art and crafts marketplace. Several differently priced packages are available, and complete information is available on request.

Date Contacted:_____Information Received:_____

*Follow up:*_____

☐ Home Business Institute, Inc., PO Box 301, White Plains, NY 10605-0301. (888) DIAL-HBI; Fax: (914) 946-6694. Web site: www.hbiweb.com. Membership benefits include insurance programs (medical insurance and in-home business policy that includes some liability insurance); savings on telephone services, office supplies, and merchant account enrollment; and free advertising services.

Date Contacted:_____Information Received:_____

*Follow up:*_____

☐ National Craft Association (NCA), 1945 E. Ridge Road, Suite 5178, Rochester, NY 14622-2647. (800) 715-9594. Web site: www.craftassoc.com. Members of NCA have access to a comprehensive package of services, including merchant account services; discounts on business services and products; a prepaid legal program; a check-guarantee merchant program; checks by fax, phone, or e-mail; and insurance programs. Of special interest to this book's readers is the "Crafters Business Insurance" policy (through RLI Insurance Co.) that includes coverage for business property; art/craft merchandise or inventory at home, in transit, or at a show; theft away from premises; up to $1 million in both personal and product liability insurance; loss of business income; and more. Members have the option to select the exact benefits they need. Premiums range from $150 to $300, depending on location, value of average inventory, and the risks associated with one's art or craft.

Date Contacted:_____Information Received:_____

*Follow up:*_____

Recommended Crafts-Business Periodicals

Membership in an organization generally includes a subscription to a newsletter or magazine that will be helpful to your business. Here are additional craft periodicals you should sample or subscribe to:

☐ *The Crafts Report—The Business Journal for the Crafts Industry,* Box 1992, Wilmington, DE 19899. (800) 777-7098. On the Internet at www.craftsreport.com. A monthly magazine covering all areas of crafts-business management and marketing, including special-interest columns and show listings.

☐ *Craft Supply Magazine—The Industry Journal for the Professional Crafter,* Krause Publications, Inc., 700 E. State Street, Iowa, WI 54990-0001. (800) 258-0929. Web site: www.krause.com. A monthly magazine that includes crafts-business and marketing articles and wholesale supply sources.

☐ *Home Business Report,* 2949 Ash Street, Abbotsford, BC, V2S 4G5 Canada. (604) 857-1788; Fax: (604) 854-3087. Canada's premier home-business magazine, relative to both general and craft-related businesses.

☐ *SAC Newsmonthly,* 414 Avenue B, PO Box 159, Bogalusa, LA 70429-0159. (800) TAKE-SAC; Fax: (504) 732-3744. A monthly national show guide that also includes business articles for professional crafters.

☐ *Sunshine Artist Magazine,* 2600 Temple Drive, Winter Park, FL 32789. (800) 597-2573; Fax: (407) 539-1499. Web site: www. sunshineartist.com. America's premier show and festival guide. Each monthly issue contains business and marketing articles of interest to both artists and craftspeople.

Other Services and Suppliers

Contact any of the following companies that offer information or services of interest to you.

☐ American Express. For merchant account information, call the Merchant Establishment Services Department at (800) 445-AMEX.

Date Contacted:_____Information Received:_____

*Follow up:*_____

☐ Dover Publications, 31 E. 2nd Street, Mineola, NY 11501. Your source for thousands of copyright-free designs and motifs you can use in your craftwork or needlecraft projects. Request a free catalog of books in the *Pictorial Archive* series.

Date Contacted:_____Information Received:_____

*Follow up:*_____

☐ Novus Services, Inc. For merchant account information, call (800) 347-6673.

Date Contacted:_____Information Received:_____

*Follow up:*_____

☐ Volunteer Lawyers for the Arts (VLA), 1 E. 53rd Street, New York, NY 10022. Legal hotline: (212) 319-2910. If you ever need an attorney, and cannot afford one, contact this nonprofit organization, which has chapters all over the country. In addition to providing legal aid for performing and visual artists and craftspeople (individually or in groups), the VLA also provides a range of educational services, including issuing publications concerning taxes, accounting, and insurance.

Date Contacted:_____Information Received:_____

*Follow up:*_____

☐ Widby Enterprises USA, 4321 Crestfield Road, Knoxville, TN 37921-3104. (888) 522-2458. Web site: www.widbylabel.com. Standard and custom-designed labels that meet federal labeling requirements.

Date Contacted:_____Information Received:_____

*Follow up:*_____

Recommended Business Books

When you have specific business questions not answered in this beginner's guide, check your library for the following books. Any not on library shelves can be obtained through the library's inter-library loan program.

☐ *Business and Legal Forms for Crafts* by Tad Crawford (Allworth Press)

☐ *Business Forms and Contracts (in Plain English) for Crafts People* by Leonard D. DuBoff (Interweave Press)

☐ *Crafting as a Business* by Wendy Rosen (Chilton)

☐ *The Crafts Business Answer Book & Resource Guide: Answers to Hundreds of Troublesome Questions about Starting, Marketing & Managing a Homebased Business Efficiently, Legally & Profitably* by Barbara Brabec (M. Evans & Co.)

☐ *Creative Cash: How to Profit from Your Special Artistry, Creativity, Hand Skills, and Related Know-How* by Barbara Brabec (Prima Publishing)

☐ *422 Tax Deductions for Businesses & Self-Employed Individuals* by Bernard Kamoroff (Bell Springs Publishing)

☐ *Homemade Money: How to Select, Start, Manage, Market, and Multiply the Profits of a Business at Home* by Barbara Brabec (Betterway Books)

☐ *How to Register Your Own Trademark with Forms*, 2nd ed., by Mark Warda (Sourcebooks)

☐ *INC Yourself: How to Profit by Setting Up Your Own Corporation*, by Judith H. McQuown (HarperBusiness)

☐ *Make It Profitable! How to Make Your Art, Craft, Design, Writing or Publishing Business More Efficient, More Satisfying, and More Profitable* by Barbara Brabec (M. Evans & Co.)

☐ *Patent, Copyright & Trademark: A Desk Reference to Intellectual Property Law* by Stephen Elias (Nolo Press)

☐ *The Perils of Partners* by Irwin Gray (Smith-Johnson Publisher)

☐ *Small Time Operator: How to Start Your Own Business, Keep Your Books, Pay Your Taxes & Stay Out of Trouble* by Bernard Kamoroff (Bell Springs Publishing)

☐ *Trademark: How to Name a Business & Product* by Kate McGrath and Stephen Elias (Nolo Press)

Helpful Library Directories

☐ *Books in Print* and *Guide to Forthcoming Books* (how to find out which books are still in print, and which books will soon be published)

☐ *Encyclopedia of Associations* (useful in locating an organization dedicated to your art or craft)

☐ *National Trade and Professional Associations of the U.S.* (more than 7,000 associations listed alphabetically and geographically)

☐ *The Standard Periodical Directory* (annual guide to U.S. and Canadian periodicals)

☐ *Thomas Register of American Manufacturers* (helpful when you're looking for raw material suppliers or the owners of brand names and trademarks)

☐ *Trademark Register of the U.S.* (contains every trademark currently registered with the U.S. Patent and Trademark Office)

Glossary

▼▼

Tools of the Trade

No matter what you craft, you'll need to have a tool or two to make your work easier. Stick this list in your handy, dandy toolbox! You'll easily recognize many of these items as rubberstamping tools, but others just might pop up as you begin to stamp your world! Remember, the one with the most tools . . . wins!

Abrasives: Family of smoothing tools, including sandpaper, grit paper, steel wool, sand sticks, sand blocks, taping, and cording. Abrasives can be dry or wet.

Adhesives: Substance or chemical mixture used temporarily or permanently to bond two surfaces or items.

Awl: Sharp-pointed, usually metal tool for hand-punching holes or openings.

Blending stump: Paper or soft textile stick used to blend pencil colors, chalk, pastels, or charcoal.

Bone: Hardwood tool used to score other materials.

Brayer: Tool, similar to a rolling pin, used to smooth or flatten materials.

Brush: Natural or man-made bristles gathered and clamped to transport a medium to another medium; sponge, round, flat, stencil, and more.

Burnisher: Metal or wood instrument used to smooth, shape, embellish, polish, or transfer one material to another; also referred to as an *embossing tool*.

Embossing tool: See Burnisher.

Files: Hardened steel with rows of finely spaced cutting teeth for smoothing, trimming, and sharpening.

Stylus: Metal rounded tip used to create perfect, consistent dots.

Business Terms

Accounts payable: Money you owe for goods or services received.

Accounts receivable: Money owed to your business for goods or services delivered.

Back order: Items not shipped in an order but will be sent to buyer at a later date.

Break-even: Point where business is not making or losing money; total revenue equals total expenses.

Budget: Financial plan to control spending.

COD account: Cash or check on delivery; payment is due upon receipt from a common carrier.

Common carrier: transportation service or company that will deliver supplies; example is UPS.

Consumer: end user of the product.

Cost of goods sold: Direct cost to business owner of items that will in turn be sold to consumer.

CPD: *See Abbreviations and Acronyms.*

Dealer minimum: Lowest quantity of an item or items that must be purchased, or the lowest dollar amount that must be spent, to place an order with a supplier. Also called *minimum order.*

Distributor: Middleman that purchases from craftsperson and markets and sells to retailers.

Gross price: Price of product before discounts, deductions, or allowances.

Invoice: Itemized statement from supplier or vendor stating charges owed for merchandise.

Manufacturer: Business that makes product(s) from raw materials.

Net price: Actual price paid for products or supplies after deductions, discounts, and allowances are subtracted.

Open account: Credit extended to a business for a specific billing period.

Purchase order: Record of agreement made with supplier from buyer.

Retailer: Business that sells directly to the consumer.

SKU: *See Abbreviations and Acronyms.*

Terms of sale: Conditions concerning who can purchase goods and payment of purchase.

Trade association: Organization of businesses in the same industry that works to promote common interests.

Trade publication: Printed material intended for trade-only consumption.

Trade show: Gathering of individuals and business in a common industry to display, educate, and sell products and services to other members within that industry.

Sales representative: Person who sells a product(s), usually in a specific geographic area, for a commission; company reps work for a specific manufacturer or distributor and independents rep more than one line.

Wholesaler: Business that sells to others for resale.

Computer Terms

A bit here and a byte there. You may need to learn a few new words to understand what's going on on-line. Here's a database of terms and jargon. For most of us, it's more information than we need to know, care to know, or wish to store in our memories, extended or expanded. Just input, file, and be sure to back up the information! A computer is one of the most important tools a crafter can use!

Access code: Identification number or set of characters that is required to gain entry into a computer program or system; also known as *password* or *PIN*. Individuals and companies use access codes to protect data and resources. The computer can accept the code, but it can't determine who entered the code. Keep access codes private, and change codes regularly.

Backup or backup files: Copies of data and program files. Usually the information on a hard drive or disk is stored on a separate disk. It can be critical to back up important files and data in case of computer system or human error.

BBS: *See Abbreviations and Acronyms.*

Boot: Procedure that starts up the computer; turning the power on allows the computer to boot.

CD-ROM: *See Abbreviations and Acronyms.*

Chat or chat room: Area on-line where you can communicate with others on-line; room may be public for all users to enter, private for users who know the name of the room, or pornographic.

Clobber: To write new data over the top of good data in a file; to wipe out a file.

Computer literate: Term used to describe person who knows and can proficiently use computers.

COM port: Communications channel over which data is transferred between remote computer devices. Usually a serial port used with a modem to establish channel over telephone lines.

Computer: Electronic device that can perform high-speed arithmetic and logical operations. The computer consists of the processor, memory, input/output device, disk storage, and software.

CPU: *See Abbreviations and Acronyms.*

Crash: Something went wrong; the computer system or program became inoperable due to a malfunction of equipment or software.

Cursor: Blinking or flashing on-screen indicator, usually a thin vertical line or box; identifies a location. The cursor is controlled by the arrows on the keyboard, a mouse, trackball, or joystick.

Cybernetics: Field of science that explores the similarities and differences between human beings and machines; also can refer to robots that imitate human behavior.

Database: Set of interrelated data records stored on a direct access storage device that allows multiple applications to access the data; a large collection of information on a particular subject, organized to allow search and retrieval of any one field.

Disk: Also *disc;* direct access storage device of varied storage capacities, from a single-sided floppy diskette to a high-capacity fixed disk.

E-mail: Electronic mail; information is sent via one computer to another computer by a network of computer systems. Very quick when compared to snail mail (the post office). You need the correct address of the recipient to get your mail delivered.

Emoticon: Symbols on the keyboard used to communicate emotion, like :-) to make a smiley face or :-(to make a sad or angry face; it is hard to communicate humor, anger, and other emotions over the distances, so emoticons were developed to express feelings.

FAQ: *See Abbreviations and Acronyms.*

FAX: *See Abbreviations and Acronyms.*

Flame: Nasty or mean-spirited message, often sent to newbies who ask a question that has already been answered.

Formatting: Preparing a disk so that the operating system can find the data. A disk is unusable until formatted.

Hard disk: Disk made of a rigid base and coated with magnetic material; the rigid rotating platter of a hard drive is capable of storing megabytes, or more data than a floppy disk.

Hardware: Physical parts of a computer: printer, keyboard, monitor, scanner, hard or floppy disk, power supply, memory chips, modem, math coprocessor.

Internet: Also the *Net* or the *information superhighway*; systems of computer systems are linked together around the world to share information.

Microsoft: Software company. A very big software company. Probably the biggest software company.

Modem: Modulator-Demodulator; device that converts digital data from a computer into analog data that can be transmitted over telephone lines. It can dial and answer a phone call to send or receive data. Also *FAX/modem,* which allows for fax and modem communication.

Motherboard: Main circuit board of a microcomputer. This board holds the CPU and memory.

Newbie: Individual new to the Internet or the access provider

Newsgroup: Collection of worldwide "discussion groups" on the Internet; like message boards for people with common interests or expertise, but more people participate in Newsgroups.

Operating system: First or lowest level of software that runs on the computer. This software defines the devices the system has—disks, graphics card, serial ports, parallel ports—and allows program access to the devices. It also defines how disk files are stored and named. Yes, DOS is what limits your filenames to seven characters and a three-character extension.

Search engine: Web service that finds all applicable sites to a keyword during a search.

Software: Programs, languages, or routines that control the operations of a computer. Often stored on disks or loaded into the computer's hard drive.

Surfing: As in "surf the Net," looking at files, listings, chat rooms, bulletin boards with little or no interaction. Browsing. Just looking.

SYSOP: *See Abbreviations and Acronyms.*

Techspeak: Very formal technical language of computers.

URL: *See Abbreviations and Acronyms.*

User-friendly: Term used to describe program that is easy to understand by the average person, who may not be familiar with the program.

WWW: *See Abbreviations and Acronyms.*

Abbreviations and Acronyms

SOS, what the heck do all these initials mean? FYI, here's your guide to the important acronyms you'll encounter in the art and craft industry.

ACCI: Association of Crafts & Creative Industries; trade association

AHSCA: American Home Sewing & Craft Association.

BBS: Bulletin board system; a computer that operates with a program and modem to allow other computers with modems to communicate with it. Five categories of boards can be noted: general interest, with message boards on several topics like entertainment or news; technical boards dealing with DOS, hardware, and software; specific systems for a specific computer system like IBM; special interest, with narrow subject matter like jewelry-making or quilting; and public domain programs that can be downloaded. Messages or programs can be read and/or posted.

CCD: Certified Craft Designer; honor awarded by Society of Craft Designers.

CCHA: Canadian Craft & Hobby Association.

CD-ROM: Device that uses a compact disc (CD) to store large amounts of data—800 megabytes of information, which would equal more than 200,000 printed pages.

CK: Check.

COD: Cash or check on delivery.

COGS: Cost of goods sold.

CPD: Certified Professional Demonstrator; awarded by HIA.

CPU: Central Processing Unit.

CSM: *Craft Supply Magazine*; business journal for the professional crafter.

FAQ: Frequently asked questions; listed with answers in an area on-line.

FAX: Facsimile machine; images can be sent over telephone wires. Facsimile transmission can be done from a personal computer with an internal or an external FAX board. Speed of transmission is measured in bits per second. Most FAX machines operate on 7,200 bps up to 9,600 or 14,400 bps. The image is scanned at the transmitter, reconstructed at the receiving station, and duplicated on paper.

FOB: Free on board.

HCR: Home Craft Retailer; one who purchases raw craft supplies at wholesale to resell from the home.

HIA: Hobby Industries of America or Hobby Industries Association; trade association.

ICCPSA: International Cake, Candy, & Party Association.

MATCH: Mid-Atlantic Craft & Hobby Industry Association; regional trade association.

MIAA: Miniatures Industry Association of America.

MO: Money order

NECHIA: Northeast Craft & Hobby Association; regional trade association.

NWCHA: Northwest Craft & Hobby Association; regional trade association.

PACC: Professional Association of Custom Clothiers.

PC: Professional Crafter; one who buys raw craft supplies to incorporate supplies into a finished craft item.

PCM: *Profitable Craft Merchandising*; trade journal.

PCP: Professional Craft Producer; official trade association name of a PC.

POP: Point of purchase display; showcase of product placed where consumer can see the product and buy it.

PPD: Postage paid; postage is included in price of item.

PPFA: Professional Picture Framers Association.

SASE: Self-addressed, stamped envelope.

SCD: Society of Craft Designers.

SDP: Society of Decorative Painters.

SECHA: Southeast Craft & Hobby Association; regional trade association.

SEF: Southeastern Fabric, Notions, & Craft Association.

SEYG: Southeastern Yarncrafters Guild.

SIP: Special Interest Publication; one-time publication on a specific event, theme, or subject.

SKU: Stock Keeping Unit; number assigned to specific item used to control inventory; designated by a bar code.

SYSOP: System operator, the person who operates an electronic bulletin board.

TKGA: The Knitting Guild of America.

TNNA: The National Needlework Association.

URL: Another name for a site's address or location on the Web.

WWW: World Wide Web; A collection of sites, systems, and technologies that make up the cyber-universe. Doesn't show all of the Internet, but allows for browsing. Organized to make access and finding information on Internet more user-friendly.

Resources

▼▼▼

Recommended Books

The Artist's Way by Julia Cameron (Putnam, 1992).

Crafts Market Place: Where and How to Sell Your Crafts, edited by Argie Manolis (Betterway Books, 1997).

The Designer's Common Sense Business Book by Barbara Ganim (North Light Books, 1995).

Drawing on the Artist Within Revised Edition by Betty Edwards (Simon & Schuster, 1989).

Drawing on the Right Side of the Brain Revised Edition by Betty Edwards (Simon & Schuster, 1989).

How to Open and Operate a Home-Based Craft Business by Ken Oberrecht (The Globe Pequot Press, 1994).

How to Sell What You Make: The Business of Marketing Crafts by Paul Gerhards (Stackpole Books, 1996).

Organizing for the Creative Person by Dorothy Lehmkuhl and Dolores Cotter Lamping (Crown Trade Paperbacks, 1993).

Promoting and Marketing Your Crafts by Edwin M. Field and Selma G. Field (Macmillan Publishing Company, 1993).

Selling What You Make: Profit from Your Handcrafts by James E. Seitz, Ph.D. (TAB Books, 1993).

Working from Home by Paul and Sarah Edwards (Putnam, 1994).

Recommended Magazines

Craftrends
Published by Primedia Publications
Phone: (309) 682-6626
Fax: (309) 682-7394
Web site: www.craftrends.com
General art and craft resource; trade only.

National Stampagraphic
P.O. Box 370985
Las Vegas, NV 89137-0985
Phone: (702) 396-2188

The Rubber Stamper
225 Gordon's Corner Road
P.O. Box 420
Manalapan, NJ 07726
Phone: (800) 969-7176

Rubber Stampin' Retailer & Makin' Stamps
136 West Vallette, Suite 6
Elmhurst, IL 60126
Phone: (630) 832-5200
Trade only.

Rubberstampmadness
P.O. Box 610
Corvallis, OR 97339-0610
Phone (toll free): 877-STAMPMA
Fax: (541) 752-5475

Somerset Studio
22992 Mill Creek, Suite B
Laguna Hills, CA 92653
Phone: (714) 380-7318

Stampers' Sampler
22992 Mill Creek, Suite B
Laguna Hills, CA 92653
Phone: (714) 380-7318

Stamping Arts & Crafts
Scott Publications
30595 Eight Mile

Livonia, MI 48152-1798
Phone: (248) 477-6650

Sunshine Artist
2600 Temple Drive
Winter Park, FL 32789
Phone: (407) 539-1399
Fax: (407) 539-1499
For orders: (800) 804-4607
National show and event guide.

Vamp Stamp News
P.O. Box 386
Hanover, MD 21076-0386
Phone (information line): (410) 760-3377

Recommended Web Sites

Web sites may change addresses or even disappear. Following is a list of general and specialized search engines that can help you find a relocated or new Web site that may have the information you want:

General Search Engines

AltaVista: www.altavista.com

Excite: www.excite.com

Google: www.google.com

Lycos: www.lycos.com

Mamma: www.mamma.com

The Professional Crafter: www.procrafter.com

Search.Com: search.cnet.com

Snap: www.snap.com

Yahoo: www.yahoo.com

Tips and Project Pages

www.acslink.aone.net.au/elizastamping/tips.htm

www.bydonovan.com/templates.html

collagegallery.com/ (Collage)

www.geocities.com/Heartland/Lane/1693/index.html

www.geocities.com/Heartland/Woods/7006/index.htm

www.investorsnet.com/stampeaz/ (Carving stamps)

members.aol.com/AnnaElyCM/annasplace/homeplace.html

members.aol.com/LeStampin/index.html

www.rubbertrouble.com/projects.html

www.sgmweb.net/creastamp/index.shtml

www.verinet.com/~dawe/default.htm

victorian.fortunecity.com/gauguin/365/ (Collage/Papercraft)

Business and Personal Rubberstamper Sites

www.allnightmedia.com/

www.artistamp.com/

www.bydonovan.com/

www.calligraphyhouse.com/

www.closetstamper.com/welcome.html

www.comotion.com/

www.crafterstoybox.com/

www.doodle-art.com/

www.graphistamp.com/

www.hankodesigns.com/welcome.htm

www.herrubber.com/

www.hotpotatoes.com/ (Fabric stamping)

www.iofaith.com/ (Religious stamps)

members.aol.com/keyholers/index.htm

www.procrafter.com

www.stampzia.com/

www.tamp-a-stamp.com/

members.tripod.com/~URSM/

www.wubbastampa.com/

Art and Craft Supplies Used in Rubberstamping

www.clearsnap.com/

www.fancifulsinc.com/ (Charms and more)

www.fiskars.com/ (Scissors and punches)

www.interlog.com/~washi/ (Japanese papers)

www.marcopaper.com/ (Papers, templates)

www.paper-paper.com/ (Paper, ceramic surfaces, templates, tools)

rangerink.com/ (Ink, pads, embossing powder)

www.rubber-stamp.com/ (Rubberstamp making equipment)

www.thecreativezone.com/ (Papercraft supplies and parchment craft)

www.wubbastampa.com/ (Mounting systems)

Suppliers and Product Resources

The asterisk (*) indicates that this company's supplies or materials were used in preparing, writing, or creating a design in this book. The star (★) means that this company provided valuable or vital information or knowledge for this book.

Specialty Suppliers

Adhesive Technologies
3 Merrill Industrial Drive
Hampton, NH 03842-1995
Phone: (603) 926-1616
Fax: (603) 926-1780
Sells low-temperature glue
guns and specialty glues with
Magic Melt.

Amazing Shardz!
A Division of VC Design
Valerie Vinson, Manufacturing/
Orders
Vanessa Vinson, Design
Cyndi Vinson, Design
349 West Felicita Avenue, Suite 109
Escondido, CA 92025
Phone (Valerie Vinson): (760) 743-4908
Mail, telephone, or Web site orders only—
not a storefront.
Web site: www.amazingshardz.com

American Art Clay Company
4717 West 16th Street
Indianapolis, IN 46222
Phone: (800) 374-1600
Sells polymer clay, tools, stamps,
and Genesis System

American Traditional Stencils
442 First New Hampshire
Northwood, NH 03261
Phone: (800) 448-6656
Carries stencils and brass templates.

Art Institute Glitter*★
720 North Balboa Street
Cottonwood, AZ 86326

B & B Products, Inc.*★
18700 North 107th Avenue #13,
Sun City, AZ 85373-9759
Phone (USA toll free): (888) 382-4255
Fax (USA toll free): (877) 329-3824
Fax (International): (623) 815-9095
Carries etching supplies.

Christy's Crafts*★
P.O. Box 492
Hinsdale, IL 60521
Phone: (630) 323-6505
Fax: (630) 323-8344
Carries pinpricking supplies, quilling
paper, and other tools.

Creative Beginnings
P.O. Box 1330
Morro Bay, CA 93443
Phone: (800) 367-1739
Carries charms.

Creative Paperclay Co.
79 Daily Drive, Suite 101
Camarillo, CA 93010
Phone: (805) 484-6648

Crystal Creations*★
23727 19th Avenue NE
Arlington, WA 98223
Phone: (360) 435-8327
Carries scented embossing powders.

Delta Technical Coatings*✩
2550 Pellissier Place
Whittier, CA 90601
Phone: (consumer information line):
(562) 695-7969
Web site: www.deltacrafts.com
Carries rubberstamping paints, foam
stamps, and stencils.

Dove Brush Mfg., Inc.
1849 Oakmount Avenue
Tarpon Springs, FL 34689
Phone: (727) 934-5283
Phone (toll-free): 800-334-DOVE
Carries the Dove blender pen.

Dremel*✩
4915 21st Street
P.O. Drawer 1468
Racine, WI 53406
Phone: (800) 747-6344, Ext.2

Environmental Lighting Concepts
1214 W. Cass Street
Tampa, FL 33606
Phone: (800) 842-8848
True spectrum lighting/OTT Lite

Highsmith, Inc.
W. 5527 Highway 106
Fort Atkinson, WI 53538
(800) 554-4661
Web site: www.highsmith.com

Leather Factory*✩
P.O. Box 50429
Fort Worth, TX 76105
Phone: (713) 880-8235
Web site: www.leatherfactory.com
Carries all leather goods, tips to
stamp.

Loew-Cornell*
563 Chestnut Avenue
Teaneck, NJ 07666-2490
Carries brushes and sponges.

McGill, Inc.*✩
P.O. Box 177
Marengo, IL 60152
Phone: (800) 982-9884
Carries paper punches.

Polyform Products
1901 Estes
Elk Grove Village, IL 60007
Carries polymer clay.

Ranger Ink*✩
15 Park Road
Tinton Falls, NJ 07724
Phone: (732) 389-3535
Fax: (732) 389-1102
Carries inks, inkpads, embossing
powders, embossing tools.

Silver Brush*
P.O. Box 414
92 North Main Street, 18E
Windsor, NJ 08561-0414
Phone: (609) 443-4900
Carries brushes and sponges.

Xuron Corp.
60 Industrial Park Road
Saco, ME 04072
Carries scissors.

Xyron, Inc.
14698 North 78th Way
Scottsdale, AZ 85260
Carries laminators and other
supplies.

Coloring Tools

Binney & Smith, Inc.
1100 Church Lane
P.O. Box 431
Easton, PA 18044 0431
Phone: (610) 253-6271

Koh'inoor
P.O. Box 68
100 North Street
Bloomsbury, NJ 08804
Phone: (800) 628-1910

Staedtler*
P.O. Box 2196
21900 Plummer
Chatsworth, CA 91311
Phone: (800) 776-5544

Tsukineko
15411 NE 95th Street
Redmond, WA 98052-2548
Phone: (425) 883-7733

Paper Suppliers

Cache Junction*
1717 South 450 West
Logan, UT 84321
Phone: (800) 333-3279
Carries velvet paper.

Daniel Smith, Inc.
4150 First Avenue South
P.O. Box 84268
Seattle, WA 98134-5568
Phone: (800) 426-6740

The Japanese Paper Place
887 Queen Street West
Toronto, Ontario, Canada M6J 1G5

Phone: (416) 703-0089
Fax: (416) 703-0163

Oblation Earthworks
6503 SW Luana Beach Drive
Vashon Island, WA 98070

Paper Adventures
Phone: (800) 727-0699
www.paperadventures.com

PaperDirect, Inc,
1005 E. Woodmen Road
Colorado Springs, CO 80920
Phone: (800) A-PAPERS

Paper Journey
450 Raritan Center Parkway
Edison, NJ 08837
Phone: (800) 827-2737

Paper Reflections /DMD Industries*✭
1205 ESI Drive
Springdale, AR 72764
Phone: (501) 750-8929

General Art Supplies

Craft King
P.O. Box 90637
Lakeland, FL 33804
Phone: (888) 272-3891

Dick Blick Art Materials
P.O. Box 60401
695 Route 150
Galesburg, IL 61402
Phone: (309) 343-6181
Orders: (800) 447-8192

National Artcraft
7996 Darrow Road
Twinsburg, OH 44087
Phone (toll free): (888) 937-2723

Plaid Enterprises
3225 Westech Drive
Norcross, GA 30092
Phone: (800) 392-8673

Sax
P.O. Box 510710
New Berlin, WI 53151-0710
Fax (U.S.): (800) 328-4729
Fax (Canada): (905) 356-3700

Stan Brown Arts & Crafts
13435 NE Whitaker Way
Portland, OR 97230
Phone (U.S. and Canada): (800) 547-5531

Sunshine Discount Crafts
P.O. Box 101
12335 62nd Street North
Largo, FL 33773
Phone: (800) 729-2878

Zim's
Box 57620
Salt Lake City, UT 84157
Phone: (801) 268-2505

Rubberstamp Companies and Manufacturers

Above the Mark
P.O. Box 8307
Woodland, CA 95776
Phone: (530) 666-6648

Acorn Art Stamps
1506 Tomlynn Street
Richmond, VA 23230
Phone: (888) 414-ATRS
Fax: (804) 353-5258

Addicted to Rubber Stamps
P.O. Box 69753

Seattle, WA 98168-1753
Phone: (206) 901-0072

A La Art Stamp
3110 Payne Avenue
Cleveland, OH 44110
Phone: (800) 942-7885
Fax: (800) 942-7888

All Night Media*★
454 Du Bois
San Rafael, CA 94901
Phone: (415) 459-3013
Fax: (415) 459-0606

American Art Stamp
3892 Del Amo Boulevard, Suite 701
Torrance, CA 90503
Phone: (310) 371-6593
Fax: (310) 371-5545

American Marking Systems
1015 Paulison Avenue
Clifton, NJ 07015
Phone: (201) 478-5600
Fax: (201) 478-0039

Ampersand Press
750 Lake Street
Port Townsend, WA 98368
Phone: (360) 379-5187
Fax: (360) 379-0324

Ann-ticipations
6852 Pacific Avenue, Suite 102
Stockton, CA 95207
Phone: (209) 952-5538
Fax: (209) 952-4579

The Artful Dodger Rubber Stamp Shop
3228 Laurel Road
Longview, WA 98632-5526
Phone: (360) 414-8123

Art Gecko Designs
1963 Sunburst Terrace
West Linn, OR 97068
Phone: (503) 655-5284
Fax: (503) 656-0924

The Artist Stamps
1535 North Niagara Street
Burbank, CA 91505-1653
Phone: (818) 845-6704
Fax: (818) 563-2762

Art-Stamp Express
100 Jefferson Boulevard
Big Lake, MN 55309
Phone: (800) 634-0322

Bartholomew's Ink
57 Kearsarge Mountain Road
Warner, NH 03278
Phone: (603) 456-2056

Berry Patch Designs
1 Alcott Street, Suite #1
Norway, ME 04268
Phone: (207) 743-7607

Biblical Impressions—Rubber Stamps
2311 T-75 Lane
Cederidge, CO 81413
Phone: (970) 856-7459

Claudia Rose
15 Baumgarten Road
Saugerties, NY 12477
Phone: (914) 679-9235
Fax: (914) 679-9235

ClearSnap, Inc.*✭
509 30th Avenue
Anacortes, WA 98221
Phone: (800) 448-4862
Fax: (360) 293-6699

Coffee Break Designs
Box 34281
Indianapolis, IN 46234
Phone: (317) 290-1542
Fax: (800) 229-1824

CowTown Stamps
1623 Wisconsin Avenue
New Helstein, WI 53061
Phone/Fax: (920) 898-1325

Craftsman Rubber Stamps
2650 Chuckanut Street
Eugene, OR 97408-7330
Phone: (541) 345-4226
Fax: (541) 345-4336

Craft Stamps
P.O. Box 681
Oak Lawn, IL 60454
Phone: (773) 585-6918
Fax: (773) 582-2244

Crazy Stamps
123 East 5th Street
Vanderhoof, British Columbia, Canada
V0J 3AO
Phone: (250) 567-5858
Fax: (250) 567-5899

Creative Cousins Rubber Stamps
10842 SE 208th, Suite 144
Kent, WA 98031
Phone: (360) 414-3118

Del-Rose Stamping
2698 South Sheridan Boulevard
Denver, CO 80227
Phone: (303) 975-0595
Fax: (303) 975-0595

Distinctive Impressions
209 G Street

Antioch, CA 94509
Phone: (510) 778-3110

Distinked Impressions
5606 Greendale Road
Richmond, VA 23228-5816
Phone: (804) 266-7691
Fax: (804) 266-6110

Doodle Art Rubber Stamp
Company
1447 North Van Ness
Fresno, CA 93728
Phone: (559) 233-2733
Fax: (559) 233-3525

EccenTricks
P.O. Box 1789
Pomona, CA 91769
189 South East End Avenue
Pomona, CA 91766
Phone: (909) 622-2484
Fax: (800) 548-0839

Embossing Arts
Company Inc.*
P.O. Box 439
Tangent, OR 97389
Phone: (541) 928-9898
Fax: (541) 928-9977

The Escape Artist
P.O. Box 6155
San Pedro, CA 90734-6155
Phone: (310) 831-5303
Fax: (310) 831-5303

Eureka! Stamps
4442 Breeze Place
San Antonio, TX 78259
Phone: (210) 979-8200
(800) 679-8740
Fax: (210) 979-8383

Evolving Images Rubber Stamp Designs
P.O. Box 3611
Ocala, FL 34478
Phone: (352) 867-8086

FC Bumpers & Company
24 Etta Place
Durango, CO 81301
Phone: (970) 385-7973

First Impression Rubber Stamp Arts
4803 NE Freemont
Portland, OR 97213
Phone: (503) 288-2338
Fax: (503) 282-1878

First Impressions
662 South Main Street, Suite B
Central Square, NY 13036
Phone: (315) 668-9352
Fax: (315) 668-9352

Gingerwood Enterprises
7234 South Callie Drive
West Jordon, UT 84084
Phone: (801) 565-3793

Good Impressions
P.O. Box 33
Shirley, WV 26434-0033
Phone: (800) 846-6606

G-Rated Rubberstamps
40575 California Oaks, #241
Murrieta, CA 92562
Phone: (909) 698-0109

Great Impressions
6430 103rd SW
Olympia, WA 98502
Phone: (360) 357-5908
Fax: (360) 357-2814

H.A.L.O.S.
2972 West 10460 South
South Jordon, UT 84095
Phone: (801) 254-0928
Fax: (801) 253-3112

Hampton Art Stamps*★
19 Industrial Boulevard
Medford, NY 11763
Phone: (800) 229-1019
Fax: 631 924-1669

Handstamps
Box 1118
Volcano, HI 96785
Phone: (808) 967-7383

Happy Daze Publishing
376 West 14th Street
San Pedro, CA 90731-4214
Phone: (800) 696-9679
Fax: (800) 696-9679

Heartfelt Impressions
P.O. Box 6088
Kingsport, TN 37663
Phone: (423) 239-9097
Fax: (423) 239-5999

Holly Berry House and Giftshop
2411 West Colorado Avenue
Colorado Springs, CO 80904
Phone: (719) 633-2026

Holly Berry House Originals
2223 North Weber
Colorado Springs, CO 80933-8109
Phone: (719) 636-2752
Fax: (719) 636-2765

Hot Potatoes Fabric & Wall Stamps
209 10 Avenue South
Nashville, TN 37203
Phone: (615) 255-4055

Impress Me!
382 East 520 North
American Fork, UT 84003
Phone: (801) 756-5447

Imprint Factory
P.O. Box 797
Newbury Park, CA 91319
Phone: (805) 495-6640
Fax: (805) 495-6640

Ink Blocks
1523 Sunrise Lane
Yuma, AZ 85365
Phone: (520) 726-1699
Fax: (520) 726-4799

L.A. Stampworks
P.O. Box 2329
North Hollywood, CA 91610-0329
Phone: (818) 761-8757

Las Vegas Art Stamps
3626 Pecos McLeod, Suite 7
Las Vegas, NV 89121
Phone: (702) 367-0411
Fax: (702) 367-2123

Magenta
351 Blain Street
Mont Saint-Hilaire,
Quebec, Canada
J3H 3B4
Phone: (450) 446-5253
Fax: (450) 464-6353

Maine Street Stamps
P.O. Box 14
Kingfield, ME 04947
Phone: (207) 265-2500
Fax: (207) 265-2500
Web site: www.opdag.com/stamps

Manatee Rubber Stamp Company
328 5th Avenue SW
Naples, FL 34117
Phone: (941) 352-0377

Mars Tokyo
P.O. Box 65006
Baltimore, MD 21209
Phone: (410) 358-1985

Midnight Press Rubber Stamps
& Scrapbooking Supplies
1995 Scott Road
Springfield, OR 97477
Phone: (206) 227-9954

Mill Creek Stamp Company
P.O. Box 220698
Newhall, CA 91322-0698
Phone: (661) 255-5440
Fax: (805) 255-0077

Mount Rubbermore
P.O. Box 93136
Southlake, TX 76092
Phone: (817) 491-3136
Fax: (817) 491-3133

Museum of Modern Rubber
6705 Albunda Drive
Knoxville, TN 37919
Phone: (865) 584-9991
Fax: (865) 584-9992

Neato Stuff
P.O. Box 4066
Carson City, NV 89702
Phone: (775) 883-9351
Fax: (775) 883-3253

Painted Turtle Studio
1118 Strahle
Philadelphia, PA 19111
Phone: (215) 745-5029
Fax: (215) 745-7322

The Paper Garden, Inc.
555 Bitters Road
San Antonio, TX 78216
Phone: (210) 341-0918
Fax: (210) 341-8553

Penny Black Rubber Stamps
P.O. Box 11496
Berkeley, CA 94712
Phone: (510) 849-1883
Fax: (510) 849-1887

Personal Stamp Exchange*✩
360 Sutton Place
Santa Rosa, CA 95407
Phone: (707) 763-8058
Fax: (707) 588-7476

Print Kraft
3109 Mandigo Avenue
Portage, MI 49002
Phone: (616) 649-3175

Raindrops on Roses
4808 Winterwood Drive
Raleigh, NC 27613
Phone: (919) 571-9060
(800) 245-8617
Fax: (919) 571-0670

Red Castle, Inc.
P.O. Box 398001
Edina, MN 55439-8001
Phone: (612) 820-0756
Web site: www.red-castle.com

Retro Rubber Stamps
2960 Butte Street
Hayward, CA 94541
Phone: (510) 886-0567

Rhapsody in Rubber
809 North La Reina Street
Anaheim, CA 92801
Phone: (714) 952-3856

Rise Reading Designs
P.O. Box 1033
Manhattan Beach, CA 90267-1033
Phone: (310) 318-3786

Rubber Designs
14014 Crest Hill Lane
Silver Spring, MD 20905
Phone: (301) 384-1478

Rubbermania Stamps
P.O. Box 271333
Concord, CA 94520
Phone: (510) 458-4403
Fax: (510) 458-4403

Rubber Monger
P.O. Box 435
Moorpark, CA 93020
Phone: (805) 529-0221
Fax: (805) 529-0221

The Rubber Poet
218 River Road
Rockland, UT 84763
Phone: (801) 772-3441
Fax: (801) 772-3441

Rubber Stamping across America
403 G Banana Cay Drive
South Dayton Beach, FL 32119
Phone: (904) 322-9752

Rubber Stampsations
3648 South Park Avenue
Blasdelle, NY 14219
Phone: (716) 821-0503

Rubber Stamps of America
Warner Center
P.O. Box 567
Saxtons River, VT 05154
Phone: (802) 869-2622
Fax: (802) 869-2262

Rycraft Stamps*★
4205 SW 53rd Street
Corvallis, OR 97333
Phone: (541) 753-6707
Fax: (541) 757-0367

Silver Fox Stamps
Rural Route 3 Box 1350
Lincoln, ME 04457-9516
Phone: (207) 736-4500

SonLight Expressions
125 Business Center Drive
Corona, CA 91720
Phone: (909) 278-5656
Fax: (909) 278-3008

Sparky Dog Stamp Company
2520 Pearl
Columbus, IN 47201
Phone: (812) 378-5090
Fax: (812) 372-2316

Stampacadabra
5091 North Fresno Street,
Suite 133
Fresno, CA 93710
Phone: (559) 227-7247
Fax: (559) 227-7247

Stamp Affair
P.O. Box 819
Lake Villa, IL 60046
Phone: (800) 446-5723
Fax: (847) 265-3331

Stampa Rosa★
2322 Midway Drive
Santa Rosa, CA 95405
Phone: (707) 527-8267
Fax: (707) 527-5159

Stampendous*
1240 N. Red Gum
Anaheim, CA 92806

Phone: (714) 688-0288
(800) 578-2329
Fax: (714) 688-0297

Stamper's Delight
7917 Bond Street
Lenexa, KS 66214-1557
Phone: (913) 888-0192
Fax: (913) 888-0168

Stamp Fever
1315 North Tustin Street, Unit C
Orange, CA 92667
Phone: (714) 532-6530
Fax: (714) 532-2565

Stamp Happy Rubber Stamps
P.O. Box 3472
Modesto, CA 95353
Phone: (209) 544-8621
Fax: (209) 544-8621

Stamping with Style
3939 Highlands West Drive
Fort Collins, CO 80526
Phone: (970) 282-0975
Fax: (970) 282-8691

Stamp It! Rubber Stamps
317 Laskin Road
Virginia Beach, VA 23451
Phone: (757) 425-0721
Fax: (757) 425-1439

Stamp Me Tender!
1008 East Sahara Avenue
Las Vegas, NV 89104
Phone: (702) 836-9118
Fax: (702) 648-1698

Stamp Oasis
4750 West Sahara, Suite 17
Las Vegas, NV 89102

Phone: (702) 878-6474
Fax: (702) 878-7824

Stamp Off the Old Block
3420 South Logan Avenue
Milwaukee, WI 53207-3544
Phone: (414) 481-7411

Stamps by Impression
P.O Box 641
Lewes, DE 19958
Phone: (302) 645-7191
Fax: (302) 645-7191

Stamps Happen, Inc.
419 South Acacia Avenue
Fullerton, CA 92831
Phone: (714) 879-9894
Fax: (714) 879-9896

Stampworks of Florida, Inc.
208 North Woodland Boulevard
Deland, FL 32720
Phone: (904) 736-6262
Fax: (904) 736-6572

Stars & Stamps Forever
3821 Voltaire Street
San Diego, CA 92107
Phone: (619) 224-2680

Stubby Stampers
P.O. Box 1127
Brookhaven, MS 39602
Phone: (601) 835-1835

Touche Rubber Stamps
1827 16 ½ Street NW
Rochester, MN 55901
Phone: (507) 288-2317
Fax: (507) 286-1428

U B Stamping
837 SE 3rd Place

Cape Coral, FL 33990
Phone: (941) 574-1225
Fax: (941) 574-1225

Uneeda Stamp Co.
P.O. Box 72270
Louisville, KY 40272
Phone: (502) 935-5432

Visual Image Printery
1215 North Grove Street
Anaheim, CA 92806
Phone: (714) 632-2441
Fax: (714) 632-3953

Viva Las Vegas Stamps
1008 East Sahara Avenue
Las Vegas, NV 89104
Phone: (702) 836-9118
Fax: (702) 648-1698

When the Rubber Hits the Road
P.O. Box 142
Petaluma, CA 94953-0142
Phone: (707) 766-8996

Windy City Stamps
1030 Summit Street, Suite 306

Elgin, IL 60120
Phone: (847) 888-9705
Fax: (847) 888-9705

Wood Cellar Graphics
87180 563rd Avenue
Coleridge, NE 68727
Phone: (402) 283-4725
Fax: (402) 283-4987
Web site: www.woodcellargraphics.com

The Write Impression
883 Park Avenue NE
Bainbridge Island, WA 98110
Phone: (206) 842-1527
Fax: (206) 780-0946

Yes! Pigs Can Fly
P.O. Box 218
Rockville, UT 84763
Phone: (435) 772-3441
Fax: (800) 906-POET
Web site: www.rubberpoet.com

ZimPrints, Inc.
340 Rocky Hill Way
Bolivar, TN 38008
Phone: (901) 659-2368

Trade and Consumer Associations, Societies, and Guilds

I've spent hours searching out groups and organizations that fit under the umbrella of art and craft. You will not have a need for every one of these groups, but the list is a great reference for you and your friends. The trade-only groups are noted by an asterisk (*). *Trade only* means you must qualify for membership within the craft industry trade. Trade associations promote the business of a trade.

About the Author

BILL ADAMS, THINGS TO REMEMBER

MARIA GIVEN NERIUS graduated with a degree in Advertising and worked in that field briefly before discovering her love of crafting. She sells her original folk wood dolls at craft shows in Florida and has published over 1,000 of her designs. Maria has helped establish education and information resources for the crafter in consumer magazines, on television, and on the Internet. In Maria's own words, "Crafting is the expression of care, love, and joy straight from the heart." Feel free to contact Maria Nerius at: PO Box 100205, Palm Bay, FL 32907 or by e-mail at: Mnerius@aol.com.

About the Series Editor

BARBARA BRABEC is one of the world's leading experts on how to turn an art or crafts hobby into a profitable home-based business. She regularly communicates with thousands of creative people through her Web site and *The Crafts Report*.

To Order Books

Please send me the following items:

Quantity	Title	U.S. Price	Total
_____	**Craft Sewing For Fun & Profit**	$ 19.99	$ _____
_____	**Crocheting For Fun & Profit**	$ 19.99	$ _____
_____	**Decorative Painting For Fun & Profit**	$ 19.99	$ _____
_____	**Holiday Decorations For Fun & Profit**	$ 19.99	$ _____
_____	**Knitting For Fun & Profit**	$ 19.99	$ _____
_____	**Quilting For Fun & Profit**	$ 19.99	$ _____
_____	**Soapmaking For Fun & Profit**	$ 19.99	$ _____
_____	**Woodworking For Fun & Profit**	$ 19.99	$ _____
_____	_____	$ _____	$ _____

Subtotal $ _____

7.25% Sales Tax (CA only) $ _____

7% Sales Tax (PA only) $ _____

5% Sales Tax (IN only) $ _____

7% G.S.T. Tax (Canada only) $ _____

Priority Shipping $ _____

Total Order $ _____

FREE
Ground Freight
in U.S. and Canada

Foreign and all Priority Request orders:
Call Customer Service
for price quote at 916-787-7000

By Telephone: With American Express, MC, or Visa,
call 800-632-8676 ext. 4444, Monday–Friday, 8:30–4:30
www.primapublishing.com

By E-mail: sales@primapub.com

By Mail: Just fill out the information below and send with your remittance to:
Prima Publishing ▪ P.O. Box 1260BK ▪ Rocklin, CA 95677

Name _____

Address _____

City _____ State _____ ZIP _____

MC/Visa/American Express# _____ Exp. _____

Check/money order enclosed for $ _____ Payable to Prima Publishing

Daytime telephone _____

Signature _____